CITIZEN WARRIORS

CITIZEN WARRIORS

America's National Guard
and Reserve Forces & the
Politics of National Security

STEPHEN M. DUNCAN

PRESIDIO

Copyright © 1997 by Stephen M. Duncan

Published by Presidio Press
505 B San Marin Drive, Suite 300
Novato, CA 94945-1340

Library of Congress-in-Publication Data

Duncan, Stephan M.
    Citizen warriors : America's National Guard & Reserve Forces and the politics of national security / Stephen M. Duncan.
        p.   cm.
    Includes bibliographical references and index.
    ISBN 0-89141-609-9
    1. United States—National Guard. 2. United States—Armed Forces—Reserves. 3. National security—United States. 4. Operation Desert Shield, 1990–1991. 5. Persian Gulf War, 1991. I. Title.
    UA42.D84   1997
    355.3'7'0973—dc20   96-42301
                                                      CIP

Printed in the United States of America

Contents

Acknowledgments

I acknowledge first my debt to the men and women of the Armed Forces of the United States. Since 1959 I have had the honor of serving with them in some capacity, and my admiration for their patriotism and professionalism is unlimited.

I owe particular thanks to former secretaries of defense Caspar Weinberger, Frank Carlucci, and Dick Cheney. Each brought special abilities and leadership to the Department of Defense at a time of great historical importance. Each offered me new opportunities for public service. Each contributed greatly to the improvements in the Total Force and the performance of America's citizen-warriors in the Persian Gulf War which are chronicled in these pages.

My daughters, Kelly and Paige, encouraged me in ways they will never understand. They have always been beautiful and special people. Now they are accomplished professionals engaged in their own public service. Kelly began her service with her graduation from the U.S. Naval Academy nine weeks before Operation Desert Shield began. Since then she has demonstrated the kind of junior officer leadership that contributed to the victory in Desert Storm. Paige was uprooted on her sixteenth birthday from an idyllic life in the mountains of Colorado so that her dad could assume new responsibilities at a place 1,600 miles from home. Her encouragement and tangible assistance on this book were substantial. Now she is a teacher of world history to students who will hopefully never experience another Desert Storm.

But the help and inspiration that meant most to me was that given by the person from whom this book demanded the most, my beloved wife, Luella. As the book was going to print, she went to be with God. The brilliant light that had brightened each of my days, was suddenly and unexpectedly, extinguished.

Lue always understood how important the book was to me and encouraged me to turn to it during those brief moments that were available in the middle of a hectic and fulltime law practice. Her thoughtful and wise suggestions, patience, and tireless work in helping me prepare the manuscript, made it all possible. The sacrifices she made over thirty-one years in support of my military and public service can be appreciated only by the families of our men and women in uniform who have made the same kinds of sacrifices. The love, joy, beauty and nobility of character that she brought to our family can be appreciated fully only by me. She was, and will always be, the gentle but powerful wind beneath our wings. To her this book is lovingly dedicated.

Prologue

It was the middle of a warm summer night in 1966 during a pouring rain. As the weapons officer of the U.S.S. *Carronade* (IFS-1), I was supervising the ship's company as the entire crew labored frantically to load ammunition at the weapons pier, U.S. Naval Station, Subic Bay, Philippine Islands. One of only four rocket-firing assault ships, the *Carronade* brimmed with firepower, which had already proven to be very effective for the close-in gunfire support of American soldiers and marines in South Vietnam. It was soon to be the subject of a *Time* magazine article. Operational commitments required a return to Vietnam as soon as the ammunition was loaded.

Taking a brief break, I walked to a telephone at the end of the pier and called Washington, D.C. I suspected that correspondence regarding a new duty assignment had been mailed to me, and because it often took six weeks for mail to reach a destination in the war zone, I was fairly certain that someone was impatiently waiting for a response. The navy detailer went straight to the point. The navy wanted me to report to a Naval Reserve Officers Training Corps unit at an American college or university to teach students who aspired to commissions in the navy.

My reaction was total surprise. I knew that after two seagoing assignments I was scheduled for shore duty, but I expected a much different set of orders. I was a Naval Academy graduate with a regular officer's commission, not a reserve commission. I was totally unfamiliar with the organization, the training, and even the capabilities of naval reservists. I had no experience whatsoever with the reservists of the other military services or the National Guard.

Any respite from combat duty would have been welcome. Almost two years earlier and only ten days after my wedding, I had left on my first assignment to the wartime theater of operations. An unexpected development had suddenly made a change in orders even more desirable. Shortly before I detached from my ship, navy doctors in Japan had diagnosed my wife as a victim of tuberculosis. Believing that she would require institutional care, possibly for years, I had traveled home alone while she was flown to the East Coast aboard a military medical evacuation plane loaded with casualties from Vietnam. Shortly after her arrival, a new examination revealed that she suffered only from pneumonia, which was by then under control.

On New Year's Day, 1967, we drove onto the wintry campus of Dartmouth College in Hanover, New Hampshire. Thus began my first direct association with the reserve forces of the United States, an association that would include eighteen years of subsequent service in the Naval Reserve and that would reach its zenith almost a quarter of a century later as America's "citizen soldiers, sailors, marines, and airmen" engaged in a different war. This one was called Desert Storm.

During the last months of the presidency of Ronald Reagan and the four years of the administration of President George Bush, I was privileged to serve three secretaries of defense as the assistant secretary of defense for reserve affairs. My responsibilities involved the Army National Guard, the Naval Reserve, the Air Force Reserve, the Marine Corps Reserve, the Air National Guard, and the Army Reserve (the term "Reserve" as used here is intended to include the Army and Air National Guard). I write, therefore, with more authority and personal contact with certain of the events that occurred during those years than would someone who viewed the same events from a distance.

Soon after I was appointed by President Reagan, I was asked why I had accepted appointment to a senior but difficult defense policy and management position. It was assumed that most lawyers would prefer a general counsel or other position in which they could gain exposure in an area that would be of financial benefit upon their return to the law. My answer was simple. I preferred the opportunity to work with warriors in all the uniformed services rather than to give legal advice to others who did. The challenges of the office of assistant secretary offered opportunity for both advocacy and action. I have never regretted my decision.

During my five years and three months of public service in the Department of Defense, the nation passed through some of the most significant events in its history. The Iron Curtain was lifted, the Cold War ended, and the Soviet Union and the Communist ideology on which it was founded were relegated to the historical scrapheap. As a result, a tentative new American military strategy was developed and work to change the size and shape of the armed forces began. For the first time since the nation adopted the All-Volunteer Force eighteen years earlier, almost 246,000 American reservists were ordered to active duty for a major armed conflict 8,000 miles from American shores. Other reservists volunteered for an unprecedented humanitarian operation in Somalia called Restore Hope. Yet others volunteered to serve in Operation Just Cause in Panama, Operation Provide Comfort in Iraq, the fight against illegal drug trafficking, and in other peacetime operations.

The title of this book suggests a tension between actual national security needs and the politics traditionally associated with reserve military units. That connection is intended. Whatever else may be involved, questions regarding the size, shape, and use of the reserve components of America's armed forces most assuredly involve contentious political considerations. This should not be surprising. Military manpower systems have long been considered inherently political. French Marshal Saint-Cyr captured the idea succinctly with his reported remark in 1867 that systems of military service must be treated as political institutions because of the "direct, powerful, and permanent effect they have on the dearest interests, aspirations, mores, and practices of the entire population."

To understand the modern American reservist, one must first understand the American tradition of "citizen soldier." The use of part-time military forces to supplement regular or full-time forces is at least as old as the Middle Ages. The American concept of citizen soldier, however, is somewhat unique. Part of the historic attraction to the idea rests on a general admiration of the courage and selflessness associated with military service. Another part relates to attitudes about civic obligation. William Blackstone, whose legal "Commentaries" influenced so many early American leaders, asserted that a man "put not off the citizen when he enters the camp; but it is because he is a citizen, and would wish to continue so, that he makes himself for a while a soldier."

Yet another part of our citizen soldier tradition has probably evolved from early American concern that a large standing army could be used by a tyrannical leader to curtail liberties won at such great cost in the Revolution. Some part of the attractiveness of the idea of citizen soldier may even have practical roots. Since military campaigns in the eighteenth century usually started with the spring and continued only until winter weather prevented operations, it is unlikely that many leaders of the new nation were interested in paying for a professional army on a year-round basis. Whatever the relative importance of each of these elements, it is fact that with the exception of the Civil War and the world wars, until the middle of this century the standing armed forces of the United States were comparatively small.

This tradition does not, however, fully explain the modern reservist. To appreciate today's air national guardsman, marine reservist, or any of their fellow citizen warriors, one must also understand certain aspects of the warrior culture. The distinguished British military historian John Keegan has observed that generally soldiers are not as other men. Rather, they belong to "world apart, a very ancient world, which exists in parallel with the everyday world but does not belong to it." Broad generalizations are dangerous, but perhaps it may at least be said that service in uniform in the last half of the last decade of this century attracts a special breed of American citizen and influences its adherents in unique ways. Justice Oliver Wendell Holmes, who was thrice wounded in the Civil War, reportedly said that the fact that he had been in combat forever separated him in small but vital ways from those who had not. Keegan asserts that military service casts a spell on people who engage in it, a spell that is in part "one of experience—of strange places, of unfamiliar responsibility, of excitement and even of danger."

Most senior American reservists, officer and enlisted, have experienced active service in uniform. Many have several years of active service. Many have combat experience. All are volunteers. This necessarily sets them apart from the vast majority of their fellow citizens who have never served.

Most reservists also make substantial sacrifices in their personal lives and in their civilian professional-occupational lives in order to continue their military service on a part-time basis. The extra pay is not an ultimate or defining value. Often, the financial benefits associated with reserve service are not part of their motive at all. This is especially true among senior officers and noncommissioned officers. The adventure element is important, but it alone can't explain the sacrifices made. The key is patriotic service. As they have for over two hundred years, most of America's citizen warriors yearn to place themselves in the service of the nation.

My own admiration for Americans who serve in uniform, whether active or reserve, is based on experience which, since the abolition of the draft in 1973, is shared by fewer families each year. My grandfather was a doughboy in France in World War I. My father was an army signal corpsman in World War II who helped intercept enemy radio traffic in the China and India-Burma theaters. My daughter is an Annapolis graduate who has served aboard ship and who is currently assigned to the staff of the U.S. Naval Academy. She and her husband, a submarine officer, teach leadership there.

Something can be said for the idea of leaving to future historians the task of recording the story of American reserve forces in the last three decades of the twentieth century, but I have always believed that while memories are fresh, events of consequence should be written about soon after they occur. Several of the sources I have relied upon are secondary, but much of what follows is a personalized account of the recent history of American reservists and a personal view of certain fundamental principles that should affect decisions on how they are to be used in the future. In writing the account, I have relied heavily on my personal papers from the Pentagon. The manuscript was given a security review by the Department of Defense Directorate for Freedom of Information and Security Review. The views expressed in the book are, of course, my own and do not in any way reflect the official policies or positions of the Department of Defense or the U.S. government.

In telling the story of past events, I have attempted to give a description of the major policy and operational context of each of the developments discussed. I have also tried to demonstrate the connection between relevant policy and subsequent action. While I would not presume to characterize this tale and analysis as detached,

I have attempted to suggest a principled approach to the use of reserve forces that rests upon our actual experience rather than upon theoretical musings. I leave others to judge how well I have succeeded.

In dealing with a period of time in which so many important developments affecting the nation's reserve forces have taken place, it has been necessary to be selective. I have tried, however, to be sensitive to the admonition of Will and Ariel Durant that even a writer who seeks to rise above partiality betrays his secret predilection in his choice of materials and in the nuances of his adjectives. I have also tried to focus on the major developments that have contributed to or demonstrate the current capabilities of America's modern citizen warriors. This has necessarily meant the sacrifice of any discussion of many internal debates and developments within the Department of Defense during my service there that however intensely contested did not result in significant changes in policy.

There are many standards by which the performance of American national guardsmen and reservists in recent years can fairly be measured. No evaluation meant more to me, however, than that expressed by President Bush in his March 6, 1991, address to the nation after the temporary cease-fire was reached in the Persian Gulf War. That night, the commander in chief of the armed forces declared that ". . . this victory belongs . . . to the regulars, to the reserves, to the National Guard. This victory belongs to the finest fighting force this nation has ever known in its history." So it did.

The national security waters that lay ahead are, in many ways, uncharted. The boundaries that define the post–Cold War use of America's armed forces are still being drawn. A critically important national debate is under way on the size and shape of the armed forces that are most appropriate for the protection of our security in the future. That debate necessarily includes consideration of the proper balance between career, full-time, active professional soldiers, and part-time National Guard and reserve soldiers. As the resources applied to our defense needs have been reduced in recent years, the ability of the armed forces to effectively respond to future threats to peace has, of course, been reduced accordingly. If, however, we build upon our experience in the use of Reserve forces, we will have every reason to be confident that our forces of the future, including the "citizen soldiers, sailors, marines, airmen, and coast guardsmen," who constitute our modern citizen warriors, are as capable as those to which President Bush referred in March 1991.

Stephen M. Duncan
Alexandria, Virginia
September 28, 1996

PART I

Desert Shield and Desert Storm

CHAPTER I
The Decision to Sound the Bugle

". . . even a limited call-up . . . would put to rest the doubt that Reserve forces will [ever] be used unless they volunteer."

—Author's memorandum to the secretary
of defense, August 8, 1990

"The flags of war like storm-birds fly,
The charging trumpets blow."

—John Greenleaf Whittier

In late July 1990, the month of August held great promise for senior officials of the Department of Defense. The traditional vacation period was expected to be quiet by Washington standards. Domestic attention was focused on President Bush's recent abandonment of his 1988 campaign pledge not to raise taxes. Foreign developments were encouraging. The armed forces were still basking in the afterglow of the success of Operation Just Cause in Panama. Manuel Noriega was in an American jail awaiting trial. Only five months had passed since Daniel Ortega and his Sandinista National Liberation Front were defeated in a stunning election upset in Nicaragua. Historic and encouraging change in the global security environment was under way. The Warsaw Pact had begun to disintegrate and the possibility of an armed conflict with the Soviet Union was becoming less likely by the day.

In the Pentagon, work was proceeding on several policy fronts. In his March 1990 report on the national security strategy of the United States, President Bush had noted that the change that marked the international landscape was "breathtaking in its character, dimension, and pace," and that the "familiar moorings of post-war security policy" were being loosened "by developments that were barely imagined years or even months ago."[1] On July 6, the president and other NATO leaders had pledged broad changes in NATO's political and military strategy in response to the changes. Senior civilian and military officials were scrambling energetically to obtain a handhold from which the increasingly ambiguous threats presented by the Soviet Union and in the developing world could be addressed.

After months of vigorous internal debate on the structure of forces and the mix of active and reserve units and personnel that would be most appropriate to current and projected threats, the changing military strategy, and available resources, a decision had been made. A particular force structure that had become known as the "Base Force" was now the choice of Secretary of Defense Dick Cheney and General Colin Powell, the Chairman, Joint Chiefs of Staff. The Base Force concept had been briefed to the president on July 9, but he had given no public stamp of approval to the proposal. Because of strong congressional support for a military force much richer in reserves and national guardsmen than that presented by the Base Force, arrangements were quietly being made for the president during an address in Colorado to the Aspen Institute Symposium on August 2 to announce the broad outline of his plan to restructure the armed forces. The remarks prepared for the president would call for an active, professional force twenty-five percent smaller than the existing force. In words that escaped the attention of most because of imminent and unexpected events, but which immediately sounded ominous to supporters of a military force weighted more heavily toward the reserve components, the president further declared that "in our restructured forces, reserves will be important, but in new ways. The need to be prepared for a massive, short-term mobilization has diminished. We can now adjust the size, structure, and readiness of our reserve forces. . . ."[2]

Meanwhile, the nation's citizen warriors, who were the subject of so much senior-level attention, were engaged in predictable summer activities. In between vacations and the demands of their civilian occupations, national guardsmen and reservists were attending routine weekend training drills at armories and reserve centers in cities, suburbs, and rural communities all over the nation. Others were participating in traditional two-week periods of summer field training. National guardsmen were still discussing the unanimous decision by the United States Supreme Court the previous month. The court had rejected the claims of Governors Rudy Perpich of Minnesota and Michael Dukakis of Massachusetts that governors have the authority to stop National Guard troops from participating in training missions in Central America or in other locations to which the governors are opposed.[3]

On July 17, Saddam Hussein angrily accused Kuwait and the United Arab Emirates (UAE) of conspiring with the United States to cheat on oil production quotas previously set by the Organization of Oil Exporting Countries (OPEC). At the same time, evidence began accumulating of a large military buildup by Iraq on its disputed border with Kuwait. On July 24, and in response to its request, two U.S. KC-135 aerial-refueling tankers were made available to the UAE so that it could keep patrol aircraft aloft as a precaution. A short-notice U.S. naval exercise in the Persian Gulf was also announced.

In the early morning hours of Thursday, August 2, the very day that President Bush was to deliver the address in which he would discuss the broad outline of his proposals for restructuring the armed forces, two Iraqi Republican Guard Forces Command armored divisions and a mechanized infantry division attacked across the Kuwaiti frontier. Separate assaults were made against the palace of the Kuwaiti emir and key government facilities by commando teams and a special operations force.

Few American reservists had reason to take particular note of these developments or to believe that events taking place so far away in desolate Arab countries would affect them personally. Even when the president declared on August 5 that the invasion of Kuwait "will not stand" and Secretary Dick Cheney flew to Saudi Arabia to meet with King Fahd, there was little apparent reason to be concerned. After all, the nation was at peace and the large reductions in the number of career military professionals being called for by several members of Congress had not even been decided upon, much less taken place.

Moreover, there was substantial precedent for the widespread belief that political leaders were more than reluctant to turn to reservists in time of crisis. Even junior officers who had been too young for the war in Vietnam were aware of Lyndon Johnson's rejection of the advice of then Army Chief of Staff Harold Johnson and other military leaders to call up the reserves. At the time, a range of political advisors to the president had argued that the mobilization of reservists would be tantamount to a declaration of war and would likely result in a full-scale conflict.[4]

In the mid-1970s, however, military force planners began to assign increasing responsibilities to national guardsmen and reservists pursuant to the new "Total Force Policy" of the Department of Defense. Within a few years the implementation of the new policy required defense planners to seek the most effective mix and integration of active, reserve, and National Guard military forces.[5] As the policy gained favor, it became increasingly apparent that a need existed to make Reserve units available in situations that did not attract sufficient numbers of volunteers, but that were not serious enough to warrant a formal declaration of war or national emergency and the attendant mobilization. As a result, new legislation was approved by Congress in 1976 that authorized a president to involuntarily activate members of the Selected Reserve without congressional approval, "to augment the active forces for any operational mission."[6] The legislation, commonly referred to as the "Section 673b provisions" for the section of the U.S. Code in which the authority appears, had been amended twice since that time to permit as many as 200,000 selected reservists to be activated for as long as 180 days.

It was fact, however, that since Vietnam, no American president had involuntarily activated a single reservist for an armed conflict. Volunteers had served in limited numbers in Grenada in 1983, and in Panama in 1989–90, but strong doubts about the willingness of political leaders to rely upon reserve forces continued among much of the uniformed leadership of the armed forces. In its 1990 Total Force report, for example, the navy had proudly chronicled its claimed progress in "integrating Naval Reserve and Active forces across the complete spectrum of naval warfare," but it spotlighted an issue of major concern:

> The limited availability of Selected Reserve personnel is the biggest obstacle that must be overcome in using Naval Reserve

assets to support contingencies short of mobilization. The equipment is there; it is combat-ready. The problem is being able to call up Reservists to man it.

While there are a broad range of statutory options available to involuntary recall Selected Reservists, both the domestic and international implications tied to these actions have severely restricted their use. This reluctance to initiate a Reserve call-up places the Navy in a dilemma. Congressional direction and fiscal constraints require that we place equipment and personnel assets in the Reserve component. However, in crisis situations, ready access to those assets is denied.[7]

The issue was not unfamiliar to me. It had been one of the central themes of my confirmation hearing before the Senate Armed Services Committee on October 16, 1987. Senator John Glenn had asked the following question:

> Senator Glenn:
> The navy recently deployed six minesweepers to the Persian Gulf. The minesweepers are assigned to the Naval Reserve. Now, reportedly, the Reserve members, who comprise about twenty-five percent of the crew, did not deploy with the minesweepers and were replaced, for the most part, by active duty personnel.
> Do you know the reason for this decision?
> What does the action indicate to you about the effectiveness of the Department of Defense Total Force Policy?

The senator had continued:

> Senator Glenn:
> . . . we are going to be watching this issue.
> If at the first time we have a deployment, it is a reserve ship, a reserve force, or part of it, and it is activated for a certain purpose, and we suddenly have to replace a large percentage of the crew with regulars, then I think we want to know what the reasons for this are, so we will know whether this same kind of

thing is going to apply over a much broader mobilization in the future.[8]

Similar questions had been asked by Sen. James Exxon. After I subsequently inquired into the matter with the Department of the Navy, I responded in writing to Senator Glenn that I was satisfied that the navy's actions in the Gulf had been reasonable, but I pointedly declined to take a position on whether the actions were the most appropriate that could have been taken.

Disagreement on the Armed Services Committee itself had been apparent from the questioning of Sen. John Warner, the ranking Republican member:

> Senator Warner:
> I . . . talked with the secretary of the navy yesterday. I am not sure if some of these things are public, but essentially we have been discussing the utilization of reserves in the Persian Gulf operations for some time. I am very sensitive to any involuntary call-up. Secretary Weinberger and Secretary Webb assured me that will not occur.
>
> I have a particularly vivid memory, although I volunteered at the time Korea broke out, of when I was in units where they were not all volunteers. I remember the dissention in those days. I don't want to see that return, absent a major reversal in international relations, which would necessitate involuntary call-ups.
>
> I urge you to continue that policy.[9]

One of the reasons for the perceived reluctance of civilian leaders to call up reservists was the notion at the time that such a call-up might spur a legal challenge to the action under the 1973 War Powers Act by members of Congress opposed to the particular use of military force for which reservists were needed. That act requires a president to seek congressional approval when U.S. armed forces are engaged in hostilities for more than ninety days.[10] Successive presidents have asserted that the act is an unconstitutional intrusion on their executive powers, and Congress has never tried to enforce it. No court has ruled on its constitutionality.

By June 1990 the question of whether reservists could or would be involuntarily activated for an armed conflict had become the subject of significant public debate as well as a heated internal debate. Rumors continued to circulate that as recently as the invasion of Panama only six months earlier, the U.S. Southern Command had quietly requested a limited presidential call-up of selected reservists, particularly of reserve military police and troops skilled in civil affairs and psychological operations, and that the request had not been forwarded by the Joint Chiefs of Staff to the secretary of defense. I was at the vortex of both debates.

As a consequence of legislation passed in 1988, I had begun work in January 1990 as the vice chairman of a Department of Defense study group that had been charged with the task of reviewing the "operation, effectiveness, and soundness" of the Total Force Policy. The study group included representatives of each of the military services, the Joint Chiefs of Staff, and various agencies within the office of the secretary of defense. Considerable disagreement had arisen over the question of whether the armed forces of the future should be shaped in ways that would increase reliance on national guardsmen and reservists. In response to the fact and standard assertion that no reservist had been involuntarily activated since the nation ended the draft and adopted an all-voluntary force, I was able to establish that the record was also devoid of any evidence that the Joint Chiefs had ever requested such a call-up from a president or a secretary of defense.

It was commonly known that during his tenure as Army Chief of Staff in the early 1970s, Gen. Creighton Abrams had set out to integrate the army's active and reserve components in a way that would ensure reserve participation in future conflicts.[11] As intelligence reports in 1990 indicated a greatly increased warning time of a Soviet attack in Europe, I had consistently urged the military departments to explore ways in which certain specific missions might be shifted to the less expensive reserve components of each of the military services as an efficient way of reducing the cost of the Total Force.

It was well known, however, that as defense budgets began to decline in the late 1980s, many military-force planners were opposed to such shifts in responsibility. They believed that the increased warning time permitted a smaller overall force which should be made up primarily of full-time active forces with higher states of readiness. Whatever the historical reasons for the failure to call up reserve forces, I was determined to ensure to the extent that I could, that in the future, decisions on the use of reserve forces would be based on the merits of the need at hand, and not on unreasonable fears of congressional or judicial action or the hidden agendas of faceless military force planners.

On Saturday, August 4, I worked several hours at the Pentagon trying to anticipate the problems that would most likely be encountered in the first hours of a presidential call-up of reservists. I had no official indication that a call-up was even under consideration, but there were several informal signals that suggested that the president was contemplating some use of military force. I could see no way that we could project any sizable force into the Persian Gulf without the use of reserve units that were trained in skills that would be critical to such an operation. The airlift operations alone would require air guardsmen and Air Force Reserve personnel. I was unaware that less than three hours before I arrived at the Pentagon that day, the commander in chief of the U.S. Central Command, Gen. H. Norman Schwarzkopf, had made the same point to the president in a meeting at Camp David.[12]

On Monday morning I met with one of my deputies, army Maj. Gen. Tom McHugh. Tom was responsible for helping me develop policies affecting the training of all of the reserve components. We discussed the possibility of an involuntary call-up and the training that would be needed for certain kinds of units if a call-up became necessary. The previous afternoon, as he returned to the White House from Camp David, the president had heatedly told the journalists who were waiting on the White House lawn that "this will not stand. This will not stand, this aggression against Kuwait." As Tom and I met, Secretary Cheney had just arrived in Saudi Arabia and was preparing to meet King Fahd to offer American troops for the defense of the kingdom. The future fate of large numbers of American reservists was about to be decided.

The next day, the normally intense pace of my Pentagon routine quickened. After standing in for Cheney to deliver remarks at a luncheon meeting of 640 members of Women in Defense and the

Women Officers Professional Association,[13] I met with senior members of my staff and Lt. Gen. John Conaway, the chief of the National Guard Bureau. We considered a range of matters on which we should be prepared to act promptly in the event an activation of reserve personnel became necessary.

I recognized that the first question that would be raised by those opposed to a reserve call-up would be "Will they show up if called?" Our experience to date on this question was encouraging but limited. I remembered well one of my first staff meetings as a new assistant secretary with then Secretary of Defense Caspar Weinberger on October 26, 1987, in which the preliminary results of the first ever test call-up of reservists had been discussed. The limited test had been conducted over the weekend of October 24–26, 1987, as a result of an earlier rhetorical question by the secretary to the same effect, i.e., "Will they show up if called?"

On December 22, 1987, I had briefed the news media at the Pentagon on the results of the test. While the results had been good, it had been difficult to draw many broad conclusions. The test had been a limited-notice, partial call-up only, designed to exercise and measure the notification and reporting procedures under the Section 673b authority for each of the reserve components, including the Army National Guard, Marine Corps Reserve, Air Force Reserve, Air National Guard, Army Reserve, and Naval Reserve. Instead of calling up an entire force package of 200,000 personnel, the 15,451 participants from 120 units were selected to represent nothing more than a statistically valid sample of units and individuals in the Selected Reserve. Each military service had been given wide latitude to conduct its own tests. The services had been able to contact 93.8 percent of the participants within the seventy-two-hour period of the tests.

The symbolic value of the tests was, I had hoped, much greater. Since few reservists then serving had ever been involuntarily activated, it was important that they be reminded of their obligation. I had subsequently made the point to Pentagon media representatives:

> . . . the point that we were trying to make, aside from testing to see how our system worked, was to get the message out to

the individual selected reservists, that he or she and their family and their employer have to understand that they're really only a quick telephone call away from active duty in a potentially hostile environment. And [despite the] fact that the President hasn't exercised that option, we wanted to make the point that they'd have to be ready.[14]

Even though I thought it prudent to remind guardsmen and reservists of their continuing liability to be mobilized for a conflict, I strongly suspected that contrary to the conventional wisdom and myths that then prevailed among many of those opposed to greater reliance on reserve forces, national guardsman and reservists would promptly respond to a call-up, especially if the crisis at hand involved an obviously important American security interest. While some reservists had undoubtedly been attracted to reserve service because of the financial or educational benefits, my own eighteen years of experience as a reservist had led me to the strongly held view that a desire to serve the nation, the "adventure" factor, and other elements of the military ethic, the collegiality that exists among those engaged in service under arms, the need for change from the dull routine of civilian occupations, and other similar interests were the primary motivating factors.

My experience to date as assistant secretary had confirmed my belief. Senior naval reservists were still outraged that active crews had been substituted for the regular reserve crews of the minesweepers that had been sent to the Gulf in August 1987. National guardsmen and reservists were, after all, primarily "part-time" volunteer soldiers, sailors, marines, airmen, and coastguardsmen. Having voluntarily made significant time commitments, and often financial and other personal sacrifices to serve, they were hardly likely to oppose en masse an opportunity to exercise and demonstrate the combat skills for which they had trained so arduously for years. It would, of course, be necessary for the president to clearly state the nation's objectives and to define its interests in the Gulf conflict if the American people and their citizen warriors were to see the connection between those interests and the additional sacrifices that reservists would incur in the event of a call-up.

* * *

Before the myth of reserve opposition to activation could be disproved, the other threshold myth had to be put to rest. Would the civilian leadership be willing to call the reserves? I could not speak for anyone but myself, but I had consistently urged military leaders not to speculate on either the reaction of civilian leaders to a military request for an involuntary activation of reserve forces, or on the likely political consequences of such action. I had further urged them to assume that civilian leaders would be willing to make the necessary, if difficult, decision to call upon reservists rather than to assume that they would not.

Fortunately, I had recent opportunities to drive home my views on how civilian and military leaders should react in a crisis in which a call-up of reservists might become necessary. In earlier war-gaming exercises in the Pentagon and at the Naval War College, I had emphasized that before I determined my own recommendation to the secretary of defense in a particular set of circumstances, I would first ask hard questions. I would need to satisfy myself that in exercising their military judgment that a call-up was necessary, military leaders had explored other alternatives and could establish a strong prima facie case for the call-up. In the absence of more than one crisis, it would make neither military nor political sense to involuntarily activate reservists if the skills that they had could be found in available active personnel. I would then evaluate the "costs" of the requested call-up, including our ability to demonstrate its necessity to Congress and in the court of public opinion. I had constantly emphasized that if a call-up was militarily necessary, I would not hesitate to recommend it to the secretary of defense. The president alone would have to determine whether the interests at stake in the pending crisis were worth the potential political or other costs of pulling the nation's citizen warriors away from their civilian jobs and other pursuits.

By fortuitous chance, I had also had a very recent opportunity to discuss this and several important related issues with Secretary Dick Cheney. On Monday morning, July 16, Cheney had convened a meeting of the Defense Planning and Resources Board (DPRB), the principal and formal vehicle used to focus on particular programmatic and budgetary questions and to deliberate resource allocations. In addition to Deputy Secretary of Defense Don Atwood, the under secretaries of defense for policy and acquisition, and other officials within the office of the secretary of defense, the meeting had been attended by Colin Powell, the other members of the Joint Chiefs of Staff, the secretaries of the air force and navy, and the under secretary of the army.

For much of the two-hour meeting, I had briefed the group in detail on the historical role and performance of the six reserve components in each of the nation's wars, their current capabilities and the missions currently assigned to them, the history of all major legislation that affected the reserve components, and the factors that were important to maintaining their current quality. I had also discussed the genesis and recent development of the Total Force Policy and the various legislative authorities for the call-up of reserve forces across the spectrum of potential conflict from small crises to global war.

No final decisions had been made on what budgetary action should be taken in connection with the reserve components, but the discussion that followed had been vigorous and would prove to be timely. In response to a question by Cheney, Secretary of the Air Force Don Rice had emphasized that "we cannot do any deployment without the reserve components for the airlift missions." Cheney had then asked, "Would it be fair to say that we have not called on the reserves, except on a volunteer basis, since 1968? What is the level of expectation of a call-up on the part of the guys out there?" Rice had volunteered his view that "nobody knows the answer."

After a brief discussion of the high percentage of national guardsmen and reserve personnel in the navy and air force that had prior active duty experience, Secretary Cheney had turned to Gen. Al Gray, the blunt-speaking commandant of the Marine Corps, to ask, "How long would it take the Marine Corps Reserve to get ready to deploy?" and "What is the state of the Marine Corps Reserve now?" Gray had instantly replied that the Marine Corps Reserve was in a good state of readiness, basing his conclusion on the results of no-notice readiness exercises where the response of marine reservists had been superb.

Later in the discussion, Colin Powell had acknowledged that there had been "massive improvements" in the reserve forces in recent years, but he had then asserted that as a result of the recent geopolitical changes, "times are now different" and that it was no longer necessary to have reserve units trained to deploy to Europe or anywhere else within thirty days. Little had I realized when the meeting adjourned that in less than six weeks we would be forced to test the reliability of large numbers of reservists in the most realistic laboratory of all—a major armed conflict, 8,000 miles away!

On the evening of August 6, and after a meeting in Jidda with Cheney and General Schwarzkopf, King Fahd invited U.S. forces to help him defend his kingdom against the invading forces of Iraq, which were even then proceeding through Kuwait to the Saudi border. In a national television address at nine A.M. on the morning of Wednesday, August 8, President Bush declared that "a line had been drawn in the sand." Following up his statement five days earlier that the integrity of Saudi Arabia was one of America's "vital interests," he then announced a major deployment of U.S. forces to Saudi Arabia to take up "defensive positions." The president's address was followed at one P.M. by a Pentagon press conference by Cheney and Powell.

While it was not yet clear how many ground troops would be sent to the area, it was fact that almost seventy percent of the army's combat service support, i.e., its transportation units, ammunition units, water purifying units, medical units, and the other critical parts of its logistical base, resided in the Army Reserve and the Army National Guard. Unless an unnatural—and in my opinion, very unwise— attempt was made to deploy active forces only for such a large enterprise, it was inevitable that significant numbers of national guardsmen and reservists would be required.

I did not, however, want a decision to activate reservists to be based on the slender reed of no other alternative. There were solid reasons for activating reserve forces. In an effort to focus Cheney's attention on those reasons, I drafted a personal memorandum to him on the afternoon of August 8 and had it hand-delivered.

Memorandum for the Secretary of Defense
August 8, 1990

One of the major challenges to a fully successful implementation of the Total Force Policy has been the perception that political leaders are reluctant to rely upon reserve forces. As you know from recent DPRB discussions, however, the fact is that no military department has ever recommended the use of the reserve call-up authority, and no secretary of defense has otherwise recommended the use of the authority to the president. The current conflict with Iraq presents a unique political opportunity to send a strong message of deterrence to that nation, to ensure the availability of reserve manpower needed for the execution of military options, and, as a collateral matter, to put to rest the false impressions about the perceived reluctance to use the call-up authority.

Volunteer selected reservists, primarily in the Air Reserve components, are already flying strategic airlift missions to transport troops to Europe and the Mideast. It may eventually become necessary to exercise the call-up authority to obtain necessary manpower for certain special missions. Even if it does not, there are strong political reasons for exercising the call-up authority.

First, this authority presents the president with yet another vehicle for sending a strong message to Iraq of our seriousness and determination at little or no risk. While a call-up pursuant to Section 673b is technically *not* a form of mobilization (the call-up can be used for peacetime operational missions unrelated to armed conflict), that distinction would not be recognized by Iraq. Moreover, there is a broad and strong national consensus in support of the president's actions in the Persian Gulf. It is unlikely that there would be any significant opposition to a call-up of certain selected reservists who are, after all, trained for such exigencies. Second, our recent experience in Operation Just Cause established a clear need to involuntarily call-up reservists, including many of those who had volunteered or who would otherwise volunteer. Civilian employers usually understand what is easily perceived to be a military necessity requiring an involuntary call-up of reservists, but many find it difficult to accept that their employee-reservists have *volunteered* to leave their civilian workplace in the absence of "orders." Subsequent employment pressures often drive high-quality reservists out of the force. Third, and in view of the president's declaration that our "vital interests" are involved, even a limited call-up (i.e., of a small number of selected reservists) would put to rest the doubt in certain quarters of Congress and elsewhere that reserve forces will [ever] be used unless they volunteer.[15]

At a routine morning briefing the following day in the Secretary of Defense Crisis Coordination Center, a representative of the Joint Staff announced that each of the military services was being asked to submit a list to the Joint Staff no later than eight P.M. that evening of the types and numbers of reserve units and personnel that would be needed to perform currently assigned missions for the deployment to Saudi Arabia. That sounded simple enough, but the request being made to the military services masked a major problem. The operations plan that would guide decisions on which units would perform what missions was sketchy and only partially complete. In late July, Schwarzkopf and his staff had participated for the first time in a computerized command post exercise that tested the plan, but it had not been approved by the Joint Chiefs of Staff or civilian policy makers.[16] Moreover, no time-phased deployment list (TYPFDL— commonly known in the Pentagon as a "tip-fiddle") had been prepared for the plan.[17] The TYPFDL would normally be expected to lay out the deployment sequence of particular reserve units once they were identified as essential to the execution of the operation plan.[18]

Rumors of a reserve call-up began to spread during the course of the day, while I was meeting with my staff and senior air force and army leaders on matters relating to the implementation of a call-up. Late in the day I received a telephone call from David Addington, Cheney's political assistant, who expressed concern that the rumors might gain currency with the media at a time when he did not believe that we should take any action that might be interpreted by Iraq as "aggression," as opposed to action related clearly to the defense of Saudi Arabia. I felt that such misplaced concern was nonsense. We were already committing combat troops, and rumors of a possible call-up of reservists was as likely to have a deterrent effect on Saddam Hussein as it was to make him mad. Nevertheless, I directed my staff to attempt to dampen the rumors even while we continued our preparations for just such a development.

On Friday, August 10, and over the weekend of August 11, I worked to resolve a number of questions relating to a possible call-up. Several policy and legal issues had been raised. If the president should declare a national emergency and direct a partial mobilization of reserve forces, as many as one million reservists could be activated for a period as long as one year. If, however, the president did not wish to declare a national emergency, or did not anticipate the need for so many reservists, he could simply exercise his authority under the "augmentation" provisions of Section 673b. Since it had never before been exercised, no one knew with certainty whether the maximum 180-day period of activation (actually the first of possibly two consecutive 90-day periods) would start at the moment the president authorized a call-up, or at the moment when individual reservists or their units actually received orders.

By August 14, media speculation about a possible call-up of reserve forces was rampant. At a news conference in Atlanta, where he spoke to a veterans group, Secretary Cheney noted the president's authority to call up as many as 200,000 reservists. He went on to say that "we have not made any decision yet in terms of an overall call-up. The fact is we have, over the years, built in a very heavy reliance on reserve units into our forces. For example, when you start to look at the medical personnel, you find that an awful lot of those are reservists. The way you fill that kind of need in the midst of a major deployment like this is to call upon those individuals."[19]

The next day, war fever was in the air! In the morning I had to deal with several matters relating to a large counterdrug operation commencing that day off the coast of South America. I also continued to deal with several matters relating to the likely call-up. Meanwhile, in a meeting in Cheney's office that morning, following a briefing by the military chiefs, Colin Powell had informed the president that if the buildup of U.S. troops in Saudi Arabia continued at the current pace, the president would have only a week or less to authorize an involuntary call-up of reservists.[20]

Just before noon, the president delivered remarks to Pentagon officials and employees and a large group of reporters just outside the river entrance to the Pentagon. Sitting immediately in front of the president, I was surprised at the force of his remarks. They left no doubt about his total commitment to the defense of Saudi Arabia: "Our action in the Gulf is not about religion, greed, or cultural differences. . . . What is at stake is truly vital. Our action in the Gulf is about fighting aggression—and preserving the sovereignty of nations. . . . And it is about our own national security interests and ensuring the peace and stability of the world."[21] I also had no doubt that he would authorize the first involuntary call-up of reserve forces in over two decades if he believed that it was necessary to accomplish his objective.

That afternoon I received a telephone call from Congressman G. V. "Sonny" Montgomery of Mississippi. Sonny was the scourge of many military-force planners because of his dogmatic championship of the reserve components, especially the National Guard. It would not be by accident that when the construction of the beautiful new National Guard Memorial Building—only a short walk from the Capitol—was completed and dedicated in 1991, its large conference room would be named the Montgomery Executive Council Chamber and be adorned with a large oil portrait of former National Guard major general Sonny Montgomery in uniform. There was no doubt, however, either of his patriotism or of his influence. I had always found Sonny to be straightforward. I also remembered that he was a close friend of the president's and that they had entered Congress at the same time.

Sonny called to inform me that he had just telephoned Brent Scowcroft, the president's national security advisor, to urge a call-up of reservists. His comments were particularly interesting in view of the fact that as recently as May 1, and during a colloquium hosted by our Total Force Policy Study Group, Sonny had expressed the view that presidents should be very reluctant to exercise the authority given to them by Congress in Section 673b.

Media speculation continued to be intense. The potential for a call-up had become the topic of the day. My office was barraged with calls seeking information. During an ABC News segment that evening devoted to the subject of a possible call-up, a commentator expressed a view to the effect that a call-up would be a major psychological step and would finally communicate to reservists that they had finally "made the varsity."

I was beginning to be concerned, however, that the decision-making process was not working as it should. With the military leadership of the department gearing up for likely combat, there was an increasing tendency on the Joint Staff to treat the call-up decision as a minor military operational matter rather than as a sensitive policy decision with potentially major political implications.

In an important speech to the National Press Club in November 1984, Cap Weinberger, the first of the three secretaries of defense I was privileged to serve, had addressed the critical question of "under what circumstances and by what means does a great democracy such as ours reach the painful decision that the use of the military is necessary to protect our interests or to carry out our national policy?" He had observed that when democratic nations do not have the support of the people, they are inevitably at a disadvantage in a conflict, but when they do have that support, they cannot be defeated.[22] It was clear to me that a decision by the secretary of defense of whether to recommend to the president a mobilization of the nation's citizen warriors was one that should be made for the right reasons, in compliance with the law, and only after a full consideration of all relevant factors. The professional judgment of the secretary's military advisors should, of course, be a major factor, but not the only one. Other factors that might be brought to his attention by senior civilian advisors who were politically accountable and who would have key responsibilities in securing and maintaining congressional and public support for whatever decision was made also had to be considered.

While there may have been some people in uniform who still subscribed to the opinion of the Prussian field marshal Moltke that "the politician should fall silent the moment mobilization begins and not resume his precedence until the strategist has informed the 'King,' after the total defeat of the enemy, that he has completed his task,"[23] the question at hand was whether a mobilization of reservists should begin at all. Moreover, this was not the nineteenth century, and we were not in Prussia. I believed that if civilian control of military policy meant anything, it meant ensuring that military advice on the question of calling up the nation's reserve forces—whatever that advice might be—was fully scrutinized by the secretary's senior civilian advisors. While there is obvious merit in Churchill's assertion that in war it is impossible to draw precise lines between military and non-military problems,[24] the answer to this question would clearly be based on political and other policy considerations, as well as on operational factors.[25]

I was particularly sensitive, however, to the twin imperatives of avoiding unnecessary civilian interference in the conduct of war and of ensuring the flow of unfettered military advice to the secretary of defense and the president. As a young warrior in Vietnam, I had seen the disastrous results of the usurpation by civilian defense officials of professional military matters that were inherently operational in nature, and the micromanagement of that war within the theater of operations by those same officials.

I was also aware that as a result of the Goldwater-Nichols legislation that had become law the year before I entered the government, the chairman of the Joint Chiefs of Staff occupied a much more powerful position than had his predecessors, and he had complete control of the Joint Staff.[26] This particular chairman was also no ordinary military advisor. While his critics thought Colin Powell too willing to inject himself into matters that were more political in nature than military and then to shape his advice to the political views of his civilian superiors, he had unquestionably important and unique experience as national security advisor to President Reagan. He also enjoyed a good relationship with Cheney.

It was no secret that I was very hopeful that the nation's reserve forces would be given an opportunity to perform. Only in that way could we bury the myth that the modern American reservist is less capable than his active-duty counterpart. I also considered it inevitable that the Joint Staff would recommend a reserve call-up to Powell, and that he would recommend a call-up to Cheney and the president. As a matter of historical precedent, however, and for the reasons I have already explained, I thought it important to do everything I could to ensure that the secretary was fully advised. I did not anticipate that my efforts would be temporarily frustrated by the secretary himself.

Shortly after noon on August 16, I met with Addington to discuss the status of a possible call-up, what I could do to assist the secretary in preparing appropriate memoranda to the president, and any guidance memorandum from the secretary to the service secretaries and others within the department. Addington expressed his frustrations with Cheney's developing habit of looking to Powell for the preparation of all necessary policy memoranda and recommendations relating to a call-up under Section 673b. He informed me that three assistant secretaries of defense had already struck out trying to "play a role" in some aspect of the decision-making process and that he had even had difficulty in making arrangements for the department's general counsel to see Cheney to give advice on legal issues directly related to a call-up.

I explained that I had very clear responsibilities to the secretary on matters relating to a call-up and that I was not going to be put off by his acquiescence to the Joint Staff's efforts to control the process. I pointed out that the military services and the secretaries of each of the military departments would be required to implement any reserve call-up that may be decided upon, and that some form of uniform and centralized guidance from the secretary of defense to the three military departments was essential if we were to prevent the kinds of problems that would inevitably result in the absence of clear direction. Addington agreed. He warned me, however, that given the secretary's practice of the last few days, there was a ninety-percent chance that he would reject my recommendations. I responded that a far worse result would occur if I made no recommendations at all and problems developed that could have been prevented.

After Addington had expressed his own frustration with a sarcastic comment to the effect that it was awfully difficult to see where the principle of "civilian control" was currently being applied, I told him that I would promptly meet with the assistant secretaries of each of the military departments. Those officials were responsible for the reserve components of their departments, and I wanted their help in identifying the problems we could expect if a call-up was ordered. I further told Addington that I would do all that I could to ensure uniformity of action by the individual military services in order to avoid a perception of unfairness to any particular group of reservists. He again concurred.

Later in the day Addington sent a memorandum to me informing me that Cheney had asked me to take the lead, working with the assistant secretaries of defense for public affairs and legislative affairs and the chairman of the Reserve Force Policy Board, to ensure that any units and individuals called to duty in support of Operation Desert Shield would receive the support they needed within their respective states and communities. He further informed me that Cheney had specifically asked me to ensure that the National Committee for Employer Support of the Guard and Reserve (NCESGR), an agency within my office, was ready to work with the military departments. Assistance would be needed in individual cases in which special employer conflicts, family emergencies, or other unusual hardships were complicating the ability of individual guardsmen or reservists to report to their military unit as ordered.

After completing a series of routine matters the following day, I convened an afternoon meeting of the three assistant secretaries of the departments of the army, navy, and air force, who were responsible for manpower and reserve matters within their departments. Together we explored a range of personnel issues that would immediately become important once a call-up was ordered. These included questions on how to provide support to reserve families living at a distance from military bases; how to handle the flood of anticipated questions by the civilian employers of activated reservists; how to continue effective administration of the educational benefits available under the G.I. Bill to reserve college students who were activated; how to deal with questions regarding benefits available to reservists under the old Soldiers and Sailors Civil Relief Act. I directed the executive director of NCESGR to establish a twenty-four-hour telephone operation to handle the thousands of calls that I expected from civilian employers, reserve families, college administrators, and others. I also asked him to prepare a proposed plan of action that could be immediately implemented if a call-up were authorized. Meanwhile, my staff worked on the final preparation and coordination of the documents that would be required to implement a call-up decision.

At five forty-five P.M. I went to the Washington studios of C-SPAN to participate in a live television talk show that commenced at six thirty P.M. on the subject of the role of the armed forces in the interdiction of drug traffickers. During the course of the program I was informed by the host that CNN had just reported that the president had decided to authorize a reserve call-up. No official announcement had been made, however, and I was unaware of any other formal action that had been taken by the president, who remained at his home in Kennebunkport, Maine. I also remembered that Cheney had just departed on his second trip to Saudi Arabia. Given the circumstances, I suspected that a presidential decision had been made, but I doubted that it would be formally announced until Cheney's return.

On Monday, Secretary Cheney, who was still in the Persian Gulf, instructed Deputy Secretary Don Atwood to direct the service secretaries to prepare plans for the anticipated involuntary activation of reservists. The plans were to include the specific reserve units to be called to active duty, the missions each would be assigned, and the anticipated duration of their service, "together with related justification."[27] At the same time, a draft memorandum for Cheney's signature that had been jointly prepared by my staff, the office of the assistant secretary of defense for force management and personnel, and the Joint Chiefs of Staff, was faxed to Cheney. The purpose of the memorandum was to establish uniform policy guidance to the military services on the utilization of any reserve call-up authority or any other authority that might be delegated to them. It was important to ensure that active duty personnel and reservists in one service were not treated differently from those in another branch of the armed forces unless there were clear reasons for doing so. The memorandum addressed a range of subjects, such as the duration of the call-up, the possible release of certain reservists on humanitarian grounds, the management by each service of its authority to stop the release from active duty of career personnel who were scheduled to retire, and other similar matters. After minor changes, the policy guidance was approved by Cheney.

The overall objective was clear. In the event of a formal approval of a reserve call-up by the president, the Joint Staff and the individual departments of the army, navy, and air force would work together to identify specific reserve units to be activated pursuant to the needs of Schwarzkopf. My office and the other agencies of the office of the secretary of defense would provide policy guidance to ensure uniformity and fairness to the extent that it was possible to do so and still meet the requirements of the combat commanders in the theater of operations.

The next day, intense media speculation about an imminent reserve call-up continued despite the absence of any formal announcement. The issue assumed even greater importance by the release that day of an important statement by the chairman of the Senate Armed Services Committee.

Sam Nunn was widely respected within the Pentagon. Over the course of several years of service on the Armed Services Committee, he had consistently done his homework on a wide range of issues. As a consequence, he had mastered many complex military subjects. His approach to them was generally cautious, fair, and scholarly. On most occasions it represented a refreshing change from the superficial and often self-serving efforts of many members of Congress who served on the Authorization and Appropriations committees. Since he had recently been conspicuous for his support of efforts to continue the economic embargo of Iraq rather than the military confrontation selected by the president, his written statement to the media was of widespread interest. Because Congress had not given formal approval to the steps being taken by the president, it became the subject of even greater interest.

FOR IMMEDIATE RELEASE
August 21, 1990

Senator Nunn's Statement on Reserve Call-Up Decision
. . . I support the decision by the president to order members of the reserve and national guard to active duty under the reserve call-up law. As the principal sponsor of this legislation in 1976, my intent was to deal with the type of situation we have

in the Persian Gulf where reservists are needed for a limited period and can be activated without a formal declaration of war or national emergency.

As I stated in a Senate floor speech on April 20, 1990, concerning the reluctance over the years to exercise a call-up of reserves, "such political reticence to selectively mobilize reserves has led military planners justifiably to question the accessibility of forces that depend on reserve personnel."

The President's action . . . to exercise this authority will enable military planners to have greater confidence in the availability of the reserves for future military contingencies. In the short-term, the reserve and guard personnel will provide much-needed capabilities. In the long-term, it sends a clear signal to active and reserve personnel alike that the total force is a reality.[28]

On Wednesday, August 22, Secretary Cheney and General Powell flew to the president's oceanside home in Kennebunkport. After a short meeting, and at about two P.M., the president stepped out into the bright sun and to a waiting press corps. After delivering a few opening remarks about the status of deployment of troops to the Persian Gulf, the president said the following:

. . . our forces continue to arrive, they can look forward to the support of the finest reserve components in the world. We are activating those special categories of reservists that are essential to completing our mission.

The United States considers its reserve forces to be an integral part of the total military command. These essential personnel will soon be joining the cohesive organization required to support the military operations in and around the Arabian peninsula, and I have the highest confidence in their ability to augment the active forces in this operation.[29]

Earlier, the president had signed Executive Order 12727, authorizing the secretary of defense and the secretary of transportation (with respect to the coast guard when the latter is not operating as a service in the Department of the Navy) "to order to active duty units and individual members not assigned to units, of the Selected Reserve," for the conduct of operational missions in and around the Arabian peninsula. A related written statement by the White House press secretary made it clear that the actual number of reserve personnel that would be called to active duty would depend upon the operational needs of the armed forces.

Fortune shined brightly! Unpredictable circumstances now presented the opportunity for which I had long hoped. America had clearly demonstrated its confidence in the ability of its citizen warriors to stand shoulder to shoulder with career professionals in the defense of Saudi Arabia. For the first time since some 26,000 naval reservists, army reservists, and army national guardsmen were activated over twenty-two years earlier to support the government during the New York City postal strike, the bugle had sounded for America's reservists. This time the enemy would not be late mail. This time the enemy would be a nation 8,000 miles away; a nation estimated to have 900,000 combatants organized into sixty-three divisions, armed with Soviet-made T-72 tanks, missiles, rocket launchers, 155mm heavy artillery, and other modern systems; a nation ruled by a ruthless dictator capable of the mass murder of his fellow citizens.

Only twenty days had elapsed since the first Iraqi formations had entered Kuwaiti territory. Only twenty days in which the threat to American interests had been measured, a means of response planned and developed, the need to involuntarily activate tens of thousands of American reservists fully evaluated, and the likely consequences considered. I wondered whether a matter of this nature, of this importance, and of this complexity could be decided any faster within a great democracy. I hoped that the myth of civilian refusal to rely upon the nation's reserve forces was now dead.

Curiously, I began to feel a strong sense of relief and calm as the intense activities of recent days faded quickly into memory, and the catalogue of the challenges that lay ahead began to slowly form in my mind. I knew that all across the land, men and women in thousands of offices, shops, classrooms, clinics, and firehouses would soon and suddenly be pulled away from their civilian jobs, their families, and their many civilian pursuits, to don the battle dress uniform. Now a new myth had to be challenged—the myth that these part-time soldiers were not prepared for their forthcoming ordeal.

One of the many ironies associated with the debate about the capabilities of the reserve forces was the widespread use by the National Guard and certain of the other reserve components of the symbol of the Minute Man. To generations of Americans, the Minute Men of the battles of Lexington and Concord—citizen warriors of the early militia who were ready to defend their communities at a moment's notice—were the standard of military preparedness. In August 1990, however, more than a few senior military professionals harbored doubts about the responsiveness of the reserve components if called. But responsiveness to a call to arms was only the first step. Would the reserve components be ready to fight?

Only a year earlier, Gen. John R. Galvin, a brilliant soldier who was then serving as Supreme Allied Commander of NATO forces in Europe, had noted the distinction of the two questions. In a new edition of his earlier book *The Minute Men,* Galvin had inadvertently prophesied a principle that applies as directly to the modern citizen warrior as it did to his colonial fathers: "Readiness means more than keeping one's musket close at hand. It means, as the minute men knew, that the ready force must be well-organized, well-equipped, well-trained, and mentally prepared to fight."[30]

Were America's reserve forces "ready to fight"? We would soon find out.

CHAPTER II
Roundout Brigades, Early Policy Decisions, and Questions of Readiness

"In no other profession are the penalties for employing untrained personnel so appalling or so irrevocable as in the military."

—*General Douglas MacArthur,*
Army Chief of Staff Annual Report,
1933

The increasing pace of events soon signaled that the reserve call-up authority delegated by the president would not be consigned to a back shelf for later use. It would be promptly exercised. Early in the morning of August 23, the day after the president's announcement, Secretary Cheney appeared on CNN and the network news programs to explain why a reserve call-up was necessary. Much of the initial media reaction had already been to characterize the president's action as politically risky, and there was clearly no better time to explain it.

In his classic *On War,* the Prussian general and military writer Karl von Clausewitz expressed his well-known dictum that war is a continuation of politics by other means. By that he undoubtedly meant much more than that war is merely another tool of the statesman. Rather, the dictum expresses what history teaches—that politics pervades war and its preparation. Clausewitz also asserted that it is senseless to consult soldiers on plans for war in such a way as to permit them to pass purely military judgments on what political leaders have to do. But when ministers of government decide upon a course of action for their nation, a successful outcome is likely to depend not only upon the merit of their decision, but also upon the integrity with which it is explained.

The political decision to use military force to achieve a political objective is very likely the most important and difficult decision a government can make. In making it, political leaders must not permit temporary fluctuations of public mood or a desire to be universally popular to interfere with their judgment of the long-term interests of the nation. Churchill made this point in his remarks to the House of Commons in November 1932, when he spoke of the dangers of disarmament while the Nazi movement was gaining strength: "Tell the truth to the British people. They are a tough people, a robust people. They may be a bit offended at the moment, but if you have told them exactly what is going on, you have insured yourself against complaints and reproaches which are very unpleasant when they come home on the morrow of some disillusion."[1]

This hard lesson had been learned too late by American leaders during the war in Vietnam.[2] That mistake would not be repeated in this conflict. The administration would have policy disagreements with several members of Congress in ensuing weeks, but in all of our congressional hearings and public statements we would speak with candor about the call-up. The wisdom of the approach was soon evident. On November 22, a writer in the *Washington Post* observed that the administration looked "honest and open by comparison to the effort by [President Lyndon] Johnson's White House 'to go to war without arousing the public ire' in the telling phrase attributed to [Johnson's secretary of defense] Robert McNamara by historian Barbara Tuchman and others."[3]

At seven thirty A.M. on the same morning as Cheney's television appearances, his personal secretary telephoned to invite me to a nine o'clock meeting in the secretary's conference room next to his office. This room had been the scene of many contentious policy and budget decisions during my almost three years in the government. Now we were to discuss the question of how actually to implement the call-up of reserve forces. I had no reason to expect that this subject would be any less controversial.

Arriving a few minutes before the hour, I quickly surveyed the landscape to see who else the secretary had invited. While we waited for Cheney, the early arrivals engaged in the type of light conversation that usually preceded meetings whose content was expected to be heavy. The Joint Chiefs of Staff were present, including Colin Powell, the chairman; Gen. Carl Vuono, the Army Chief of Staff; Gen. Al Gray, the Commandant of the Marine Corps; and the two new service chiefs, Gen. Mike Dugan of the air force and Adm. Frank Kelso, the Chief of Naval Operations. The secretaries or under secretaries of the army, navy, and air force were also present. In addition to myself, the office of the secretary of defense was represented by Deputy Secretary Don Atwood; Paul Wolfowitz, the under secretary for policy; Chris Jehn, the assistant secretary for force management and personnel; Terry O'Donnell, the department's general counsel; Pete Williams, the assistant secretary for public affairs; Patty Howell, from the Office of Legislative Affairs; and David Addington.

Two initial matters were quickly decided. After very brief preliminary remarks by the secretary, I urged upon him the need for policy uniformity in connection with the reserve call-up. I described the October 1987 test call-up and the problems that can arise when each military service is given unfettered discretion to establish policies and standards for granting exemptions from a call-up.

In anticipation of the president's action, we had already prepared and submitted to Cheney proposed policy guidance to the services on a range of matters. The proposed guidance would, for example, require that reserve units that had been organized to serve as units be activated as units. But a "unit" would now be defined to include any group or detachment of two or more individuals organized to perform a particular function.[4]

The policy guidance would further direct that the 90- or 180-day period of service for activated reservists be measured from the date their active duty actually commenced, without regard to either the date of the president's action or the date upon which other reservists were activated. The military services would also be instructed that neither the importance of a particular reservist's civilian occupation nor the amount of any financial hardship that might be sustained as a result of the call-up would be justification for release from active duty. We recognized that certain reservists who earned a high income in their civilian occupations might have to make serious sacrifices in order to live off their more limited military income, but they were all volunteers, and the middle of a conflict was not the time to permit individuals to reconsider their commitment. Moreover, it was critically important that any deferments that might be granted be equitable. The deferment of high-income individuals on that ground alone could not meet that standard.[5]

Finally, the proposed guidance would establish a uniform interpretation of the many statutory protections and benefits available to reservists under the Soldiers and Sailors Civil Relief Act of 1940, the Veterans Reemployment Rights Law, and other legislation and policies. Cheney made it clear that he wanted policies established to ensure that each military service was "doing the same thing." In fact, he had already approved our proposed policy guidance.

I next raised the issue of the department's "key position" policy. In order to insure that the Ready Reserve is composed only of members who are available immediately for active duty in the event of a crisis, the Department of Defense had adopted a policy several years earlier requiring all federal agencies to designate certain employment positions as key positions. An employment position was a "key position" if it was sufficiently important that it could not be vacated during a mobilization or national emergency without seriously impairing the capability of its agency to function effectively. Because of the essential nature of the positions, agency heads were required to ensure that they were not filled by employees who were members of the Ready Reserve. By definition, the vice president and all officials in the order of presidential succession occupied a key position and were, therefore, key employees. So too, were members of Congress, federal judges, and the heads of all federal agencies appointed by the president with the consent of the Senate.

Over the preceding several months I had vigorously pushed enforcement of the policy, but it was clear that many federal employers were reluctant to make the tough management decisions required to designate positions as key. If a position was currently filled by a valued employee who was also a ready reservist, the employee would be presented with the unattractive choice of leaving his civilian employment or terminating his service in one of the reserve components. Since no reservist had been involuntarily called to active duty in years, many federal employers had assumed that their employees would never be called and had failed to implement the policy.

I had no doubt that when the war tocsin sounded, every reservist upon whom the nation depended should be activated, whatever his civilian position. On the day that I assumed office as assistant secretary, I had myself transferred from the Ready Reserve to the Standby Reserve to avoid any appearance of a conflict of interest in the policy decisions I would have to make. But before and after Desert Storm I consciously permitted George Kundahl, my principal deputy, to remain active in the Army Reserve and I was prepared to see him called to active duty.

I suspected, however, that once we began to issue orders to reservists, many federal employers would suddenly plead that they couldn't afford to lose particular employees. For these reasons, I recommended to Cheney that if a position had not been designated as a key position prior to August 22, the date on which the president signed the executive order authorizing the reserve call-up, it could not be so designated until the current crisis had passed and all reservists had returned home. He promptly agreed.

Paul Wolfowitz then offered the suggestion that we rely upon European forces for the combat service support of the combat troops that were being deployed. The proposal was not per se unreasonable since we had long planned on logistical support from European "host nations" in the event of an armed conflict between NATO forces and the nations of the Warsaw Pact. I nevertheless objected to it. I suspected that the idea had been urged upon Paul by someone whose real agenda was to avoid use of reservists to the greatest extent possible. It was obvious that as soon as the Gulf crisis ended, the ongoing, internal policy debate over the most appropriate future mix of active and reserve forces would continue.

My main objection, however, related to the fact that in excess of sixty percent of the army's combat service support units were in the Army Reserve and the Army National Guard. Having invested major resources in the army's reserve components so they could perform just such missions, I did not believe that we should turn around and pursue a course of action that might at least appear to be an effort to actually avoid reliance on those components. The secretary agreed with me in words to the effect that he did not want to change the plans for the use of the reserve components that had been made pursuant to the Total Force Policy.

Each of the military service representatives reported large numbers of reserve volunteers. General Dugan noted that several thousand air force reservists and air national guardsmen had volunteered. Unfortunately, the military skills of the volunteers often did not correspond to the needs of the air force. The service chiefs then described their respective reserve requirements, which Cheney approved. He noted that he had already signed a memorandum delegating authority to the secretary of the army to order to active duty as many as 25,000 selected reservists, including national guardsmen and reservists; to the secretary of the navy to activate as many as 6,300 members of the Naval Selected Reserve, and 3,000 members of the Marine Corps Selected Reserve; and to the secretary of the air force to call as many as 14,500 members of the Air Force Selected Reserve.

After discussion, Pete Williams was directed to announce at the regular Thursday noon news briefing that the call-ups would begin as early as the next day, that they would be phased in to match service needs, and that the numbers announced for each service were only through October 1. By implication, more could be called later, as needed. At my suggestion, and in order to give the civilian employers of the activated reservists as much planning certainty as possible, it was further agreed that reservists should be publicly informed that while they would initially be activated for 90 days, they should plan on remaining on active duty for the full 180-day period authorized by law.

The meeting had lasted for over an hour. Just before we adjourned, the secretary addressed the group in words that suggested a favorable effect of my briefing to him and the other participants in the meeting the previous month of the Defense Planning and Resources Board. After observing that the Department of Defense had designed a Total Force Policy, that for over a decade we had allocated the department's resources in accordance with the policy, and that we had planned on using reserve forces as part of the policy, he said that to the greatest extent possible, he wanted us to rely upon it. To that end he directed that there would be no exemptions from the call-up except on the basis of demonstrated personal hardship, and that the same criteria for judging hardship among active career personnel would be applied to the reservists.

As the meeting broke up, Cheney quietly asked me to join him for a second, smaller meeting in his office. I had no idea what the subject of the meeting would be. Little did I know that the issue for discussion was already the subject of an argument between Schwarzkopf, the theater commander, and Vuono, the Army Chief of Staff—an argument that Schwarzkopf would later describe in his autobiography as "heated."[6] Certainly, I did not anticipate that I was shortly to be asked my opinion on an issue that has since been described as "one of the most enduring controversies surrounding Desert Shield";[7] that the issue would be the focus of intense discussion during my future congressional hearings; that it would be the subject of a report by the army inspector general and an investigation by the General Accounting Office of Congress; that it would become the source of widespread bitterness among many army reserve component leaders; and that, despite the disproportionate amount of media attention that the issue would receive, it would be a subject about which there would long be misunderstanding. The issue: whether to deploy to the Gulf three Army National Guard "round-out brigades." Unfortunately, the matter was considerably more complex than many of the antagonists on either side would admit.

As a consequence of both the Total Force Policy and the army's decision in the early 1980s to limit the numbers of its active forces and to rely more on its less expensive reserve components in order to meet the high cost of equipment modernization, the relative size of the Army National Guard and the Army Reserve had increased substantially.[8] By 1990 the combined numbers (end strength) of these two reserve components exceeded the end strength of the active career professionals, and the reserve components provided over one-half of the army's combat power and two-thirds of its support capabilities. Of the army's eighteen active divisions, six were organized with fewer active brigades than the number called for by the army's divisional structure and were "rounded out" by reserve brigades of approximately 4,000 soldiers each. Typically, a roundout brigade was the third brigade of a division otherwise composed of two active brigades.

During the latter stages of the Cold War, the United States had made a political commitment to its NATO allies that it would place ten divisions on the ground in Europe within ten days of the commencement of an armed conflict with the nations of the Warsaw Pact.

The commitment was unrealistic from an operational standpoint because of the lack of sufficient airlift and sealift to move such large forces so quickly, but it was treated seriously. To fulfill the commitment, it was expected that the roundout brigades would deploy shortly after the active army units. This assumed relatively high readiness of the brigades, since their readiness was critical to the overall readiness of the divisions to which they were assigned.

The initial order to deploy combat forces to the Persian Gulf had been issued on August 6. On August 10, the first elements of the Army's 24th Infantry Division (Mechanized) began to be loaded aboard a fast sealift ship in Savannah, Georgia.[9] Time was of the essence. Intelligence reports of Iraqi attack preparations continued to be received. The 24th Division was the only heavy division assigned to the army's contingency corps, and its armor units were needed urgently to add fighting power to airborne units already in the area. It would take until mid-September for the division and its M-1 series Abrams tanks and M-2 series Bradley infantry fighting vehicles to be unloaded at Ad-Dammam. Meanwhile, the 1st Cavalry Division was commencing its deployment. Plans called for the two divisions to be "rounded out" by the Army National Guard's 48th Infantry Brigade and 155th Armor Brigade respectively.

No decision had yet been made by the president to involuntarily activate Selected Reserve units. As a result, and because many army leaders doubted both the willingness of the civilian leadership to call up the reserves and the ability of the National Guard brigades to fight effectively in the short term, the army had decided to deploy the 197th Infantry Brigade (Mechanized) as the roundout brigade for the 24th Division. By August 23, General Schwarzkopf, the theater commander and former commanding general of the 24th Division, was continuing to object to the scheduled deployment of the roundout brigades. His objections were to be considered at the meeting in Cheney's office.

Schwarzkopf's objection was not without basis. Given the 180-day restriction on the reserve call-up and the time required to complete a certain amount of postmobilization training of the brigades and ship the soldiers and their equipment to the Gulf area, it made no sense, he argued, to use them at all. By the time they arrived, he asserted, he would have to worry about sending them home, and he did not want any untrained troops in the theater. The Goldwater-Nichols legislation had given operational commanders in chief like Schwarzkopf new authority, especially in wartime, to decide what units to accept or reject. Because of Schwarzkopf's opposition, Cheney had thus far restricted the army's call-up authority to support units.

This was the situation as the meeting in Cheney's office began. By this time Colin Powell had left to attend to another matter. The small group included Army Secretary Mike Stone, General Vuono, Air Force Lt. Gen. Mike Carnes, the director of the Joint Staff and Powell's representative, and David Addington.

Vuono characterized the issue for discussion as involving two major elements: a "war fighting" element and a "Total Force" consideration. He expressed his judgment that it would take approximately sixty days to train the first of the roundout brigades, the 48th, to the level needed for combat against the formidable and battle-tested Iraqi fighting force.[10] It was implicitly understood that Iraq had one of the world's larger armies and that its ground forces were the largest in the Gulf area. Within days the Iraqi forces in Kuwait alone would consist of ten divisions, 1,350 tanks, 900 armored personnel carriers, and 650 artillery pieces. Another twelve divisions would be just across the border in Iraq.[11] Vuono conceded that when the training time was added to travel time, the brigades would be able to remain in the combat area for only ninety days unless a national emergency was formally declared by the president, triggering a new level of mobilization. He and Mike Stone nevertheless seemed to take the view that the brigades should be activated and deployed as planned.

In retrospect, there is more than a little reason to believe that Schwarzkopf had never supported the roundout concept. He later fumed that Vuono's desire to deploy the roundout brigades was merely a Washington "political problem" that should not have interfered with his own preferences.[12] It was true that several members of Congress from the states from which the brigades were formed were applying pressure on the army to deploy them. It was also true that the statutory provision that provided authority to the president for this call-up—with its limiting provision of 180 days of reserve service—was much different from the authority a president would be expected to have from a declaration of war by Congress for a major conflict in Europe.

Nevertheless, the strong working presumption had always been that the roundout brigades would deploy as scheduled after the deployment of the remainder of their parent divisions. The brigades had been trained and equipped for just this purpose. No one contended that they were part of any "rapid deployment" force that would be expected to be deployed in the very earliest hours of a conflict. Rather, in the war plans that had been prepared for a war in Europe, the brigades were to be a part of "early reinforcing" forces, i.e., those that would deploy to a crisis area between thirty and ninety days after its commencement. No evidence had yet been presented in the meeting that the brigades could not meet that schedule.

Mike Carnes argued that we should not utilize the roundout brigades because it would appear that the active units could not do the job. I countered that anyone who knew anything about the Total Force Policy at all would understand that we had planned on the use of the brigades, and that their use was no reflection on the relative abilities of the active forces. Carnes's comment suggested that considerable misunderstanding of the Total Force Policy remained at senior levels.

Adding to the complexity of the problem was the historical tension that exists with varying intensity—depending upon the circumstances—between the nation's regular, or professional career, (active) forces and its reserve forces. These tensions are not unique to American shores, but our history is full of examples of the dislike of professional soldiers for the "amateur" soldiers who constitute most of the reserve forces. Normal tensions are usually exacerbated in times of severe fiscal constraint.

The leaders of the American Revolution believed that the new nation needed land defenses even less than did Great Britain, and the British antimilitary tradition took firm root here. "I believe," wrote James Madison, "there was not a member in the Federal Convention who did not feel indignation" at the idea of a professional standing army.[13] Consequently, at a time when Napoleon and other European military leaders were turning to massed, conscript armies, the new American nation rejected conscript service and turned to a militia system that had been characterized as obsolete by European standards for two hundred years.[14] Since that time, the concept of citizen soldier has been a prominent feature of American military policy.

Tension between the leadership of the army's active forces and the leadership of its reserve components had been greatly reduced during the first half of the 1980s as military budgets ballooned. By 1990, however, the historical tension had reappeared as various elements of the army competed for a decreasing share of the defense pie. Suspicions were especially high among National Guard leaders that the army leadership and Colin Powell were seeking ways to avoid use of the reserve components in order to justify a shift of resources to active forces. A refusal to use the roundout brigades as planned would undoubtedly be perceived with great alarm throughout the army's reserve community, unless the merits of any such decision were obvious. Since Schwarzkopf and Vuono, both career army general officers, appeared to be in such disagreement over the issue, it seemed hardly likely that the eventual decision would be accepted without question.

In this context I advised Cheney that if a roundout brigade of the caliber of the 48th Brigade—purportedly the best of the roundout brigades—was not used, and for no apparent reason, the effect on future recruiting and retention of national guardsmen for combat units might well be unfavorable. I further counseled that while no one could reasonably assert that "war fighting" considerations were not the most important of all, we should be careful to avoid an arbitrary definition of "war fighting" that would be outcome-determinative. In short, our decision should be based on the ability of the roundout brigades to perform well and on the merits of whatever would give us the most effective fighting force to meet the objectives laid out by the president in this conflict. But I cautioned that those who opposed the use of the roundout brigades as previously planned should bear the burden of proof to demonstrate why the plans should not be implemented. Cheney was noncommittal, and the meeting adjourned.

A few minutes later I walked with Secretary Stone and General

Vuono down the Pentagon's E-Ring corridor to their offices in the army headquarters suite. Stone seemed frustrated that a clear decision on the issue had not yet been made. I suggested that if it was the best professional judgment of the Army Chief of Staff that the 48th Brigade should be deployed, then Stone should draft a personal memorandum to Cheney that included "bullet" style arguments in support of the deployment. I did not, however, believe that Vuono was correct in framing the issue as one of war fighting versus Total Force considerations. I suggested that the theme of the memorandum should be that the use of the 48th would not be for "political" reasons, but rather because the war-fighting plans call for its use and because it was ready—assuming that it was ready. I further urged that the combat capabilities of the brigade should be addressed with specificity. Mike indicated his general support of the idea.

Cheney's decision on the near-term use of the roundout brigades was predictable. While it may have been largely implicit in nature, the president's clear guidance was to achieve the military objectives of the conflict with minimum casualties rather than to achieve the objectives in the shortest possible time frame. Given the strong preference of Powell, the president's senior military advisor, and Schwarzkopf, the commander on the scene, for fully ready ground forces that could remain indefinitely in the combat area, and Cheney's own strong inclination to defer to Powell's judgment on such matters, it came as no surprise that the roundout brigades would not be immediately activated. The tale of the roundout brigades, however, was not over.

The announcement on August 23 of the imminent first activation of reserve units immediately focused public attention on what I have previously characterized as the "twin myths" of reserve opposition to activation and of the inability of reservists to perform their assigned wartime missions. In a front-page article in the *Washington Post* on the morning of August 24, veteran correspondent George Wilson observed that if past reserve call-ups were a guide, Bush might encounter such problems as "reservists and their families going on television to complain that the wage-earner was forced to leave home, only to sit idle at a military base; reservists going to court to contend their call-up was illegal, or that they were not trained for their jobs."[15] The point that was missed, of course, was that there was little reason to rely upon the evidence of previous call-ups—made under significantly different circumstances—as a guide for a call-up of the volunteer and substantially more capable reserve forces of 1990. With much greater justification, Wilson quoted an analyst at the Brookings Institution for the proposition that the call-up would be "a real test for the whole future of the reserves." How the reserve units performed would go a long way toward answering "whether this unprecedented dependence on reserve forces is a reasonable option for protecting our national security."[16]

The question of whether the reserve components were ready and capable of performing the major new wartime responsibilities that had been assigned to them in recent years was, of course, fundamental to the entire Total Force concept. If they were not ready and could not be made ready, it made no sense to rely upon them.

When I assumed office in October 1987, I had not yet had a full opportunity to examine the combat readiness of each of the reserve components. Only a few months earlier, however, Gen. Bernard W. Rogers, the Supreme Allied Commander in Europe, had informed Congress that many reserve units whose wartime mission was the reinforcement of active combat forces in Europe were "undermanned, underequipped and unable to perform the tasks for which they were formed."[17] It was well known that the readiness of many of the army's support forces, especially those in the Army Reserve, was even worse.

I had made every effort to leave no doubt as to the importance of the readiness problem among my own set of priorities. During my confirmation hearing, I declared:

> My primary focus . . . will necessarily be on the combat readiness of the Guard and the reserve. The importance of reserve readiness to the credible deterrence of war, and to the winning of war if deterrence fails, has never been greater. The Total Force doctrine is a reality, and we are continuing to increase our reliance on our ability to rapidly mobilize, to deploy, and to utilize combat-ready Guard and reserve units anywhere in the world. I understand the manpower and the other difficulties we

face with complex, difficult, worldwide commitments in an era of severe budgetary constraints, and I pledge to you that I will consider any policy that will improve combat readiness. In the final analysis, the single question to which I believe the president, the Congress, and the American people must have an unequivocally affirmative answer, is: "Are they ready?"[18]

The initial challenge was one of definition. Readiness had traditionally been viewed as one of the four "pillars" of military capability, the others being the proper organization and structure of forces, modern equipment, and the ability to sustain effective performance. The measurement of combat readiness is not, of course, an exact science, but some standard is necessary if only as a benchmark of progress or decline. The Joint Chiefs of Staff had defined readiness as "the ability of forces, units, weapons systems, or equivalents to deliver the outputs for which they were designed, including the ability to deploy and employ without unacceptable delays."[19] I had found such definitions too similar to the cumbersome models and formulas of economists to be of much working value.

In 1987, a new Status of Resources and Training System (SORTS) had been adopted, but it did little more than indicate the status of certain resources within a particular unit at a given point in time.[20] From my own reserve service, I knew that the capabilities of reserve units with the same resources varied widely. I believed that evaluations of unit capability needed to rely more upon operational readiness inspections, mobilization tests, and other criteria related to actual performance, i.e., upon the demonstrated ability of a particular unit or groups of units to perform specific missions.

During congressional testimony in early 1989, I had noted that readiness includes both tangible components such as the number of people assigned to a unit, and certain intangible components—the presence of which makes some units perform beyond expectation—such as good leadership and high morale.[21] Tangible problem factors, such as the number of people in a unit and the type and amount of equipment on hand, are usually identifiable and correctable. Intangible problem factors are often less obvious and more difficult to correct. I had emphasized, however, that the foundation of combat readiness is training.[22]

At the beginning of the 1980s, the readiness condition of the reserve components had been dismal by any standard. The all-volunteer force was only a few years old and it was not working. It was difficult to recruit high-quality personnel. Many of the best reserve officers and noncommissioned officers were leaving military service, too often because the existing rewards of reserve service were outweighed by the sacrifices that were required in their civilian workplaces and their private lives. A combination of austere procurement budgets during the previous decade and a de facto defense policy of allocating almost all first-time equipment to the active forces had created both obsolescence and a major shortage of equipment throughout the reserve forces. Fiscal constraints had prevented full correction of some of the readiness problems in the reserve forces, but many others—especially those relating to training—were the result of factors that are unique to reserve units and individual reservists.

The amount of training required of individual reservists for technical skills positions was also a constant challenge. In order to identify positions within units by specialty and skill level, the armed forces rely upon a military job classification system. A soldier's or sailor's individual military occupational skill, such as "tracked vehicle mechanic" or "fire control technician," is that which he is trained to perform to assist his unit in the performance of its wartime mission.

The length of the training courses required to achieve these skills in 1990 ranged from several days to several weeks. While many reservists, especially unit commanders and senior noncommissioned officers, were routinely spending far more time on active duty each year than the law required, reserve component training was, in fact, mandated by law and set at thirty-eight days per year for reservists and thirty-nine days per year for national guardsmen.[23] Thus, even when reservists could obtain time away from their civilian employment for individual training, that training had to compete with their unit's training and, in the case of the Guard, with civilian emergencies and other peacetime operations in the individual states.[24]

Geographical limitations were also a challenge. In order to reduce unprofitable travel time, Defense Department regulations limited the mandatory assignment of reservists to units within a normal commuting area of 100 miles, or 50 miles if temporary military quarters were not available. And unlike active personnel who could easily be assigned to new units that required their military occupational skills, most reservists had to be trained to fill a limited number of available positions in a reserve unit near their civilian home. Many trained military personnel were also leaving active duty only to find that they were untrained for the only position that was available in the local reserve unit they wished to join. Similar problems were caused when reservists received civilian job transfers or moved for other personal reasons. Ironically, the introduction of new weapons systems into reserve units caused additional readiness problems. Members of units often had to be retrained in new military occupational specialties in order to operate complex new systems.

All of these problems were further complicated by our insistence that reserve units use the same training methods, the same performance standards, and the same readiness criteria as full-time active soldiers. The strict requirements were, however, necessary. While many reserve units would inevitably have to train on fewer tasks because of time limitations, field commanders had to have the assurance that for those tasks, the reserve units could meet the levels of performance expected of the active forces with which they would be fighting. Much work had yet to be done on the determination of which tasks were essential to the performance of assigned missions.

In addition to the problems that were the result of limited training time, geography, lack of modern equipment, and certain other factors unique to reservists, others were caused by lack of management attention. In the army, for example, there were continuous changes and resulting turbulence in the CAPSTONE alignment process by which reserve units were assigned wartime missions and schedules. Some changes required the creation of entire new units or the disestablishment of existing units. Each change required a different focus on training. Efforts were under way to eliminate or at least reduce the turbulence, but those efforts were only beginning to bear fruit.

Other obstacles to the improvement of reserve readiness were less understandable—and much less acceptable. One such impediment was the rigid and often obtuse attitude of a few uniformed officers in the Pentagon who were eager to avoid close civilian scrutiny of the problem. Another impediment was the endless bureaucratic in-fighting by civilian and military policy makers who had concurrent jurisdiction over matters that affected readiness. During my first days in office, for example, I asked for information on the readiness condition of the small number of reserve units that had been randomly selected for the test call-up during the weekend of 24–26 October 1987. To my amazement, a lieutenant general on the Joint Staff came to my office to complain about my interest in the issue. My limited patience with his objection was severely tested as I strained to explain calmly that since the law made me responsible and accountable for the reserve components, absolutely nothing would interfere with my own analysis of reserve readiness.

A few months later, and as a consequence of a "first to fight, first to equip" policy that had been established almost six years earlier by then Secretary of Defense Caspar Weinberger, I became interested in the readiness condition of those reserve units that would be among the early deploying units for any of the most likely conflicts. It was, of course, impossible to ensure that units that would be the first to fight had received the priority in equipment dictated by the policy unless the equipment readiness of those units was examined. In order to do that, I had to first know which reserve units would be the first to fight. Once again a stone wall was encountered.

In order to circumvent such problems, I decided to elevate the importance of the reserve readiness issue by taking it directly to the secretary of defense. Throughout 1988 I met privately with then Secretary of Defense Frank Carlucci to brief him on various reserve readiness issues. His easy accessibility to me and his other senior advisors on matters of importance made him a pleasure to work for. Eventually, he suggested that we ask the Joint Staff to include an update on the readiness condition of each reserve component in its weekly intelligence briefing to him. He invited me to join him at the briefings, and I did so until a turf-conscious Joint Staff persuaded Adm. Bill Crowe, the chairman of the Chiefs of Staff, to pointedly comment that the intelligence briefings were intended to be restricted to the secretary and deputy secretary of defense.

Similar obstacles were routinely encountered with civilian policy makers. During a June 1989 review by senior Pentagon officials of the execution of certain budgetary programs, for example, I proposed a clarification of the "first to fight" policy in light of projected budget constraints and ambiguities that permitted conflicting interpretations of the current policy. Some of my colleagues were more interested in controlling the implementation of the policy than in ensuring its soundness.

The readiness condition of units in the individual reserve components varied. There were several reasons why. Active duty experience varied widely. While ninety-two percent of the Naval Reserve officers had served on active duty, a much smaller percentage of Army National Guard officers had similar experience. The match between required military skills and civilian job skills was also much closer for certain reservists than for others. It is obviously much easier for airline pilots who are assigned military airlift missions, civilian emergency room doctors who are assigned to combat medical units, and civilian truck drivers who are assigned to military transportation units to maintain their military proficiency than it is for the crew of an M-1 Abrams tank or a sonar operator on a frigate.

Some reserve units had higher attrition of trained reserve personnel. The broad geographical dispersion between individual reservists caused readiness problems in others. The readiness of yet other reserve units was affected by the numbers and quality of "full-time support" personnel who helped them organize, train, recruit, and maintain equipment, and who performed administrative and planning functions so that the limited time available to unit members could be devoted exclusively to training.

Despite the range of problems affecting reserve readiness, recent trend lines had been very good. A series of legislative and policy initiatives since 1981 had brought about measurable improvement in all areas. More and more units were receiving modern equipment. Bonuses and other financial incentives were reducing recruiting and retention problems. Training obstacles were being slowly but steadily removed.

As we entered the year 1990, the nation found itself in the midst of what was formally characterized as "historic . . . transformations in the global security environment."[25] Only seven weeks earlier, the Berlin Wall had been opened. Other revolutionary events were already taking place in Eastern Europe. The threat of a sudden attack by the Soviet Union was greatly reduced, and intelligence analysts believed that we would have a substantially greater warning of any such attack than in previous years.

But early signs of the instability that would later dominate many parts of the world were already becoming evident. American armed forces had entered Panama in Operation Just Cause on December 20. National Guard and reserve volunteers had contributed in many ways there, but in limited numbers. I visited the scene of the conflict during a trip to Panama over the weekend of January 19, 1990, to observe their performance and to discuss it with Gen. Max Thurman, the innovative and highly respected commander in chief of the Southern Command. I was pleased with what I saw.[26] But I knew that the performance of a limited number of volunteers, however brilliant it may have been, said little about the combat readiness of most of the nation's 1,170,000 selected reservists or the approximately 470,000 members of the Individual Ready Reserve.

By April 1990, four months before the Iraqi invasion of Kuwait, I was able to report to Congress that the combat readiness of the reserve forces was continuing to improve. I didn't rely entirely upon readiness data for that conclusion. I had firsthand knowledge. I had spent a great deal of time personally observing reserve soldiers, sailors, marines, and airmen in action. I had flown with them in Air Force F-15s (fighters), Marine Corps TAV-8Bs (attacks), Army Cobra helicopters, and other aircraft. I had watched them conduct amphibious landings on cold Norwegian beaches, cut roads through the mountains of Honduras, set up field hospitals on the plains of Germany, and engage in combined arms exercises. I had talked at length to them as they trained on the decks of aircraft carriers, in the desert hills of the army's National Training Center, near the demilitarized zone in South Korea, in National Guard armories and reserve centers all over the nation, and in dozens of other training locations.

I remained concerned, however, about a general lack of understanding by too many policy makers, military leaders, and molders of public opinion of precisely what was and could be fairly expected of national guardsmen and reservists. Too much of the public discussion of the question was still being dominated by special interest groups who, though often well intentioned, had agendas that were not necessarily in the best interests of the armed forces as a whole. Too much of the debate was uninformed, or at least insufficiently focused.

I pointedly reminded Congress that given the limited training time of part-time national guardsmen and reservists, as well as the constrained budgetary environment in which the Department of Defense was being required to operate, it was unrealistic to attempt to make every reserve unit the absolute equal in terms of readiness and capability of the best active units. The long-term objective was, rather, to integrate the capabilities and strengths of active and reserve units in the most cost-effective manner, i.e., one that provided the most total military capability and flexibility possible within the limitations of what the American people were willing to pay for defense.

Fate did not give us more time to pursue long-term objectives. The president's Executive Order 12727 of August 22, 1990, had set into motion a massive activation of the nation's reserve forces. Now we would see for the first time whether the efforts of recent years to build a Total Force had been successful; whether part-time citizen warriors could in fact perform important wartime missions with minimum postmobilization training; whether our unprecedented reliance on national guardsmen and reservists was sound policy or inexcusable folly!

CHAPTER III
Mobilization and Deployment—Phase One

"Leaped to their feet a thousand men, Their voices echoing far and near; 'We go, we care not, where or when'; 'Our country calls us, we are here!'"

— *"The Seventh," verses by an unknown author in* Harper's Weekly, *April 27 1861 (in honor of the New York Seventh Regiment when it was called to the colors to go to the defense of Washington, D.C.)*

Although it was, by law, technically an "augmentation" of active forces for an "operational mission," the de facto mobilization of reserve forces now proceeded with alacrity. On August 24, the secretary of the air force announced the first actual call-up. Military airlift units of the Air National Guard and Air Force Reserve were activated to supplement the reserve volunteers and active personnel who were already engaged in strategic airlift missions with C-141B and C-5A aircraft. The following day, the secretary of the navy announced the activation of a large number of medical, port security, minesweeping, and other Naval Reserve units, and the secretary of the army alerted dozens of Selected Army National Guard and Army Reserve units of their possible activation. Most of the army units had support missions such as transportation, maintenance, supply, water purification, and distribution and would be used for other logistical functions.

Additional controversy regarding the call-up did not wait long to appear. By letter dated August 24, Congressman Sonny Montgomery wrote to Secretary Cheney to urge the mobilization of reserve combat units as well as support units. In a news release three days later, he broadly rejected all suggestions that reserve component combat personnel needed any additional training, and he asserted that "they are well prepared right now, and could be on the job alongside the active forces in a matter of days."[1] On August 28 he wrote again to Cheney, urging a call-up of F-15 and F-16 Fighter squadrons from the Air National Guard and Air Force Reserve and the activation of two of the Army National Guard's six roundout brigades: "I have checked on both the 48th Armored Brigade and the 155th Armored Brigade. They are trained and ready."[2] The same day, and in response to a letter he had received from Montgomery, President Bush wrote in general terms to say: "As usual, your advice was right on the mark—the activation of Guard and reserve units was clearly called for. Like you, I have total confidence in the ability and dedication of the men and women of our reserve forces. They will do an outstanding job."[3]

Shortly thereafter, a twenty-two-member delegation of the House of Representatives left for a four-day "study mission" to Bahrain, Saudi Arabia, and Egypt that included visits with military personnel. The group included Montgomery, Representative Les Aspin, the chairman of the House Armed Services Committee, and Representative Bill Dickinson, the ranking Republican on the committee. Upon their return, Aspin announced that "we want to see . . . how good the [reserve] combat units are. This is a test for the future."[4] Dickinson was quoted as saying that he regretted the decision not to immediately activate the roundout brigades. Montgomery proclaimed: "I love the old generals and admirals, but they still go with active forces before they go with reservists. There's no shooting war. Let's find out if you can mobilize and see how many will show up."[5]

On the afternoon of September 5, Dave Gribbin, the assistant secretary of defense for legislative affairs came to my office. He had traveled with the congressional delegation to the Gulf and wanted to brief me on the results of both the trip and a meeting in the White House that morning in which the president hosted the delegation. I was particularly interested in Dave's discussion of the briefing that Schwarzkopf had given the delegation at his temporary headquarters at Dhahran. Dave described as "vigorous" a discussion that followed a question by the delegation of why the 48th (roundout) Brigade had not been activated when its parent 24th Division was sent to Saudi Arabia. Schwarzkopf had argued that the 48th needed additional training and that he was concerned about a potential morale problem if a National Guard brigade was rotated out of the combat area at the end of their 180-day activation period, while active units remained.

The same question had been raised with the president that morning by several members of the delegation. Les Aspin had informed the president that he was being lobbied by "outside organizations," and he argued in effect that we ought to "try it."[6] Congressman Newt Gingrich, from the 48th's home state of Georgia, and the man who had replaced Cheney as the Republican whip in the House, had argued along the same lines. The president had been noncommittal.

The following day, Aspin and Montgomery were joined by two other important House Democrats in yet another letter to Cheney urging the activation of National Guard and reserve combat units: "We recognize that there is considerable resistance within the [A]ctive component to utilize the [R]eserves for combat missions. Active duty generals want to command infantrymen and tank crews, not supply sergeants and truck drivers." Four days later a similar memorandum was sent to Cheney and others by Gingrich.

It was, of course, a fact that many reserve combat units, especially within the Air Reserve components, were fully ready for immediate deployment. It was also true that not all reserve units were ready and that many of the best reserve units would not be needed because the particular wartime missions for which they had been trained did not need to be performed. And the fact that Saddam Hussein was momentarily content to digest the fruits of his invasion of Kuwait was hardly a basis for concluding that a "shooting war" would not immediately start if he should suddenly covet the oil fields of Saudi Arabia. The challenge was to establish clearly defined military objectives and to make honest judgments on the military need for particular reserve units—consistent with Total Force planning—to meet those objectives. If a reserve unit was needed and was capable of performing its mission, military commanders should not hesitate to use it. If it was not, it was important for us to ignore pressures to do so.

On September 11, Colin Powell formally presented his views to Congress on the activation of the roundout brigades. In response to a series of questions by Senator Trent Lott about the 48th Armored

Brigade from Georgia and the 155th Armored Brigade from Lott's own state of Mississippi, Powell informed the Senate Armed Services Committee that the matter remained an open question.

> But the fact of the matter is when you do mobilize them they do require some time after mobilization before they're ready for deployment. The problem we have right now, what we're looking at, is when do we really need those kinds of units in the theater? We haven't made a decision yet as to when we will need them.
>
> But, when we do decide to call them up and send them, should it become necessary, we have to consider the amount of pre-deployment training they would need before you could ship them over. And one of the concerns we have is: if you call them up and send them to the training we think is required, and if you're only going to use the president's 200,000 call-up authority, which gives you 90 days plus another 90 days, total of 180 days, you have to think twice before you send that unit all the way over to the Persian Gulf if you're only going to get about 60 to 90 days worth of utilization out of them once they arrive in theater.

> We have not decided not to call them up. We have not yet decided to call them up. It is a matter that is under active consideration. We have been discussing it with General Schwarzkopf, as to his need and as to our ability to put their equipment in to the flow of equipment going to the Persian Gulf. So, it is still an open question as to whether they should be called up, and when they should be called up."[7]

Meanwhile, I found it necessary to confront certain members of Congress and a federal judge on a collateral matter that had policy, political, and even constitutional implications. The genesis of part of the problem lay in the fact that the merits of service in uniform had long appealed to candidates for elective office. For many candidates, military service was simply the duty of all Americans. For others, it was an important ingredient of electoral success. Long after

World War II, individual members of Congress had continued to take great pride in remaining formally associated with one of the reserve components. Soon after he left active duty in November 1945, Sen. Barry Goldwater personally formed the Arizona Air National Guard. He retired from the Air Force Reserve as a major general in 1967, three years after he received the Republican nomination for president. Sonny Montgomery served as major general in the Army National Guard. Senator Strom Thurmond rose to the rank of major general in the Army Reserve. Former senator Gary Hart sought to fill a conspicuous gap in his résumé by obtaining a commission in the Naval Reserve when he was contemplating his campaign for president. At the time, he was forty-five years old and seriously overage. Many questioned why he had not volunteered for military service when he was of draft age during the Vietnam War, but he apparently felt that American voters would prefer "late" rather than "never." There were many additional, similar stories.

Since the adoption of the Total Force Policy in the mid-1970s, however, reserve forces were no longer merely forces to be held in reserve during a conflict. Many National Guard and reserve units were organized, trained, equipped, and assigned wartime missions that required early, if not immediate, deployment. Under such circumstances, and for the reasons I explained in the previous chapter, it made little sense to continue to permit members of Congress and the federal judiciary to serve in the Ready Reserve. The policy requiring them to be screened out of the Ready Reserve had been adopted before I arrived at the Pentagon in late 1987, but it made eminent sense to me. Members of the Ready Reserve have to be instantly available for active duty, and it is far easier to replace one member of a reserve military unit than it is to replace an elected representative of the people or a judge who has been nominated by the president and confirmed by the Senate. There is also an inherent conflict in the military service of those who are charged with civilian control and oversight of the armed forces. It was for this reason that I had requested my own transfer out of the Ready Reserve on the day that I assumed office as assistant secretary, even though it meant the loss of several years of credit for military retirement and any realistic prospect of later promotion to flag rank.

Unfortunately, no one in the Pentagon had attempted to seriously enforce the policy. The individual military services and reserve components were exceedingly reluctant to bite hands that could be counted on to feed them during periods of tightly constrained defense budgets. When I discovered this some time before Desert Shield and asked the flag and general officers who were then serving as the chiefs of the reserve components to immediately screen out of their components all persons who occupied such "key" positions, the cloud that filled the room was darker than the center of a major thunderstorm!

It was in these circumstances that I read with some unhappiness the headline in the August 23 edition of the *Washington Post* that "13 House Members Belong to Military Units."[8] Five days later, one of the congressmen telephoned the Pentagon to inquire whether he would be included in his unit if it was activated. Upon looking into the matter, I learned that all but four of the congressmen had been transferred to the Standby Reserve in accordance with our policy directive.

A delicate constitutional issue was presented, however, by the apparent conflict between the reserve service of the thirteen congressmen and the language of Article I, Section 6, Clause 2 of the Constitution. That section provides in pertinent part that "no person holding any office under the United States shall be a member of either House during his continuance in office."[9] In 1971 a U.S. District Court had held that a reserve commission is an "office under the United States" within the meaning of the constitutional prohibition, but the court had declined to order the removal of members of Congress from the reserves.[10] No appellate court had ever ruled directly on the issue, and on at least two subsequent occasions the Department of Justice had recommended that the resolution of the matter be left to Congress, on the ground that each house of Congress is the judge of its members' qualifications.

After discussing the question with the Department of Defense general counsel, I became convinced that the middle of a conflict that might soon erupt into a war was not the time to address a constitutional issue that had lain dormant for years and that would have no effect on the outcome of the conflict. Consequently, I concurred with the general counsel's recommendation to Cheney that no member of Congress be involuntarily called to active duty during the present crisis. Separately, however, I recommended to Cheney that the remaining members of Congress who were members of the Ready Reserve be informed that as a matter of *policy,* they were being transferred to either the Standby Reserve or the Retired Reserve. When Cheney failed to give any indication of his views on the matter, I continued my pressure on the military departments to take this action.

The later case of the federal judge presented a different and unusual twist on the same issue. The forty-two-year-old judge was a captain in the Marine Corps Reserve and the son of a marine combat veteran who had been wounded in World War II. He was assigned to a reserve civil affairs unit that was activated in November 1990. After he had completed approximately three weeks of postmobilization training, and on the eve of the unit's departure for Saudi Arabia, the Marine Corps discovered that he occupied a "key" position and that it had failed to screen him out of the Ready Reserve pursuant to existing policy.

Eager to serve with his unit, the judge requested a waiver from the Marine Corps, wrote to a member of Congress seeking assistance, personally appealed the matter to an assistant secretary of the navy, and shared his plight with the media. When I learned one day that he was in the Pentagon working on the request for a waiver, I invited him to discuss the matter with me.

I had met the judge on a previous occasion and had formed a high opinion of him. I had no doubt of his strong patriotism or of his desire to follow in the footsteps of his father, whom he obviously admired greatly, and who had only recently suffered a serious illness. I was soon to be contacted by several distinguished lawyers from the judge's home area who were mutual friends and who asked me to consider a policy exception for him.

Upon examination of the matter, the Marine Corps had determined that because of his status as a key employee, he never should have been assigned to the Ready Reserve in the first place. He had received a "direct commission" in the corps and had never completed the six-month course at the marine basic school in Quantico that is required of all marine officers. For these reasons, the Marine

Corps directed that he be transferred to the Standby Reserve. The action was concurred in by the Department of the Navy.

Despite the judge's admirable motives, I could find no reason to grant an exception to the established policy. I could hardly enforce the policy against members of Congress whose political support we needed and grant an exception to an individual with whom I was personally acquainted and whose military service was not needed. Reluctantly, therefore, I informed the judge of my decision and reminded him that by his important public service in the federal judiciary, he was already sharing in what justice Oliver Wendell Holmes had referred to as the "action and passion" of our times. A few months later I made arrangements for the judge to be the guest of the commanding officer of the U.S.S. *Guadalcanal* during a celebration of the World War II Battle of Guadalcanal, a battle in which his father had fought in establishing the very proud tradition of service by his family.

By the end of August, and even though the president's executive order was only days old, National Guard and reserve volunteers had already made significant contributions to the deployment of forces to Southwest Asia. Air force reservists and air national guardsmen had flown forty-two percent of all the strategic airlift missions and a third of the aerial refueling missions. Thousands of volunteers in each of the other reserve components had made similar contributions.

Despite the absence of any recent precedent upon which to rely for guidance, fortune smiled upon the efforts to effectively manage the complex business of deciding which units should be activated. Experience gained in recent war-gaming exercises was invaluable. A mobilization guidebook which my staff had recently completed provided a good roadmap.

The procedures adopted for deciding which units to activate involved far more than the mechanics of selection. This was the first involuntary activation of reserve units since the nation adopted the all-volunteer force and the Total Force Policy. Congress had not yet voted on the president's commitment of troops to the Gulf. Public support of the president's actions had been favorable to date, but no shots had been fired at American forces, and the deployment of troops was still in its early stages. It was important that the selection process be, in fact, and equally important, be perceived to be, fair. It was also important that it be based upon the war-fighting needs of the theater commander, and not skewed toward or away from particular reserve units.

Several lessons could be learned from history. Shortly after the passage of the National Defense Act of 1916 that substantially increased the degree of federal control of the National Guard, the question arose as to the likely reliability of the National Guard in combat overseas. An army general staff study concluded that the Guard should not be used and that some 500,000 men should be drafted into the regular army instead. Douglas MacArthur, then a thirty-seven-year-old major in charge of the Bureau of Information in the War Department, disagreed. He believed that the Guard's strength could be increased by voluntary enlistments, and that full strength units could be made combat-ready. He convinced Secretary of War Newton Baker and then President Woodrow Wilson to employ the Guard fully. In describing the incident almost a half century later, MacArthur forcefully observed: "I steadfastly shared my father's long-held belief in the citizen-soldier."[11]

Even after Congress had formally declared war on Germany in the First World War, the actual selection of National Guard units to be sent to France had required political sensitivity since, as Secretary of War Baker would later recall, "public psychology was still an uncertain and mystifying factor."[12] There was concern both that guardsmen in some states would be resentful if they were not given an early crack at the Germans, and that the families of guardsmen who *were* called would object to their sons being singled out for sacrifice.[13] The solution was the formation of the famous 42nd "Rainbow" Division consisting of troops drawn from several states.

Geographical diversity was not as much a concern to me during the Gulf conflict. In fact, only three days after an August 28 inquiry by Cheney, I was able to report that by September 30, some reserve forces from all but six states and two territories would be activated or engaged in the process of activation. I was much more concerned with the imperative of not flinching from the use of reserve units so long as the best military judgment deemed them ready. The process that was quickly adopted for the selection of units to be deployed, did, with minor exceptions, meet this requirement.

When General Schwarzkopf and other unified commanders around the world requested specific types of units to meet identified needs, the requests were passed through the Joint Staff to the individual military departments. The military services would then decide whether to fill the need with an active unit or to activate a reserve unit for the mission. Reserve leaders within each service had the opportunity, to varying degrees, to influence each decision. In some cases, active component units were selected to deploy to the theater of operations from Europe, the continental United States, or elsewhere, and reserve units were activated to "backfill" the active units. This was more common with medical units, but the procedure caused no small amount of irritation with some reservists, who much preferred to go to the scene of conflict to provide needed medical care to combatants than to leave their own families and civilian professional obligations to simply provide care to military dependents and retirees.

Once a reserve unit was tentatively selected for activation, approval of the appropriate service secretary was obtained and deployment orders were prepared. The deployment orders would then be coordinated with elements of the Joint Staff and the office of the secretary of defense, including my office, and then delivered to the secretary of defense for his approval.

In order to closely monitor the number of reservists being called to active duty, I asked each of the military departments on August 29 to provide daily information on the status of its call-up. The information was to include details about each unit activated. The data obtained proved to be important not only for daily policy and operational decisions, but also for keeping Congress and the public informed. The next day, a Crisis Management Steering Group was formed within the secretary of defense's Crisis Coordination Center. Several individual reservists with special skills, commonly known as "individual mobilization augmentees," were activated to man the center and to screen the hundreds of messages and questions arriving daily.

As the call-up proceeded, I was flooded with anecdotal stories demonstrating the lengths to which American reservists were willing to go in order to participate in Desert Shield and the pride associated with their military service. One of my favorites involved Army Reserve SSgt. Mirtha Maria Reyes Alonzo. A native of Ecuador, Sergeant Alonzo had come to the United Sates as a child. She was employed as an accountant at a New York bank and had applied for American citizenship when her reserve unit, the 139th Transportation Detachment at Fort Dix, New Jersey, was notified that it was being activated. With the prompt aid of her unit, the Immigration and Naturalization Service, and U.S. District Judge Nicholas H. Politan, Sergeant Alonzo became an American citizen in a special emergency session of the court. After taking the oath of citizenship dressed in her battle dress uniform, she was quoted in the local newspaper as saying "If I die, I would like to die for the United States as a citizen."[14]

Meanwhile, a series of new matters required attention. As individual guardsmen and reservists left their homes and civilian occupations to report to their military units, they and their families were left with many unanswered questions. Inquiries began to flood in about such matters as home mortgages, installment contracts, residential leases, continuation of education programs upon termination of the conflict, insurance, and reemployment rights. Less than forty-eight hours after the president had authorized the call-up, the chairman of the Senate Veterans Affairs Committee joined the chairman of the Subcommittee on Manpower and Personnel of the Senate Armed Services Committee in a letter to me requesting legislative proposals for the amendment of outdated statutes regarding these and related matters. Since the individual military services have responsibility for implementing existing laws with their respective services, I was also asked to evaluate and summarize the effectiveness of the implementation within each service. It was further requested that my responses be received no later than September 10.

Fortunately, work had already begun on the questions raised. The Soldiers and Sailors Civil Relief Act was the first target. The statute had been passed by Congress in 1940 with the objective of temporarily suspending the enforcement of civil liabilities and obligations against individuals who were called to active duty. The act provided for forbearance and reduced interest on home mortgages and other obligations incurred prior to activation, and it restricted both default judgments against persons activated and evictions of their dependents.

In the intervening fifty years, certain developments had made the statute inadequate. I was particularly concerned with the need for professional liability insurance protection for physicians and other professionals who would be activated. Premiums for malpractice liability had risen steeply in recent years and a strong shift toward "claims made" policies was under way. Once a professional was activated, he was usually no longer covered by his civilian liability insurer unless he continued paying the premiums. The premiums for some professions actually exceeded the pay and allowances that members of those professions received while in military service. Consequently, if a claim was made against a reserve doctor during his military service by an aggrieved former patient, he might have no insurance protection even though the conduct for which the claim was made may have occurred before his military activation. Since this problem had been identified earlier as one that could affect our efforts to improve the readiness of reserve medical units, we were already preparing a proposed legislative remedy.

Another area of concern involved reemployment rights. Over eighty percent of the enlisted members of the Selected Reserve and nearly ninety percent of the reserve officers had civilian jobs. Existing statutory protection provided a basic set of reemployment rights for reservists and set minimum standards of employer conduct, but certain provisions of the statutory scheme required clarification. I had been working with the Department of Labor for two years to develop a comprehensive proposal to revise and update the existing legislation. At a September 12 joint hearing before the House and Senate committees on Veterans Affairs, I urged its favorable consideration by the Congress as soon as it had been coordinated within the Administration.[15] Since one of every four enlisted members of the Selected Reserve was engaged in academic or vocational programs, I also urged an amendment to cover the reimbursement or crediting of tuition for reservists whose schooling was interrupted by their unexpected active service.

Several additional actions were also taken to provide immediate assistance for the families of activated reservists. By September 7, a booklet had been prepared for families which provided answers to the most commonly asked questions regarding pay, medical care, family assistance, and other benefits.[16]

Within three weeks of the president's authorization of the reserve call-up, it was becoming increasingly clear that the actual activation was proceeding smoothly. On the morning of September 10, at his first full senior staff meeting since the Iraqi invasion, Cheney expressed the view that the call-up was going extremely well. He also made clear the president's "don't screw around" approach to the use of U.S. forces. We would send to the Gulf whatever forces were needed to eliminate any doubt about the outcome of the crisis.

Cheney's remarks left me wondering. To date, our overall policy had been to provide a shield for Saudi Arabia through deterrence and containment. While we waited to see the effect of the economic sanctions against Iraqi, we would attempt to contain Saddam Hussein's aggression by our buildup. It seemed to me, however, that even if we succeeded in preventing further aggression, the president was unlikely to accept permanent Iraq control of Kuwait. The dislodgement of Iraq from Kuwait would require much larger forces than those required for defensive purposes, and the "don't screw around" doctrine would likely require the activation of much greater numbers of reservists than those discussed to date. Coincidentally, a little-noted development the previous week had helped open the door for an expanded activation.

On September 5, the Congressional Research Service of the Library of Congress had sent a memorandum to the House Armed Services Committee in response to an August 31 inquiry. The issue was whether President Bush's August 2 declaration of a "national emergency" for the purpose of invoking the asset-blocking authority conferred by the International Emergency Economic Powers Act would also support a partial mobilization of reserve forces pursuant to Section 673 of Title 10 of the U.S. Code, the provisions of which required such a declaration.

At the time, it had merely been the intent of the president to demonstrate U.S. disapproval of Iraqi aggression in Kuwait by placing Kuwait's assets beyond Iraq's reach. If, however, he did not wish to be limited to a call-up of 200,000 selected reservists, or if he wished to activate reservists for a period in excess of 180 days, a declaration of a national emergency would be required. Such a declaration would permit the call-up of as many as one million ready reservists for as long as a full year. It would also permit the activation of members of the Individual Ready Reserve, as well as the better trained units of the Selected Reserve. The domestic political consequences of a new public declaration of national emergency for this purpose would, of course, have to be weighed by the president.

As a legal and political matter, the issue became somewhat moot with the opinion of the Congressional Research Service that the law did not require an additional declaration of a new state of national emergency.[17] The president could merely specify in a subsequent executive order that on the basis of his previous declaration, he intended to exercise the authority granted to him by Section 673. As a result of the Congressional Research Service legal opinion and the congressional pressure to deploy additional reserve forces, it was becoming increasingly clear that at least for the moment, there would be little if any opposition within Congress to a broader call-up of national guardsmen and reservists.

That fact did not immediately influence the attitude of Cheney and Powell. In a September 18 letter to the House Armed Services Committee that appeared to be carefully crafted by Pentagon lawyers and that neither I nor the service secretaries saw until it was released, Cheney announced his support of a Total Force Policy "that maximizes the nation's military capabilities."[18] No one could argue with that definition of the policy in wartime, but it differed from the more common description of the policy as one that seeks the most cost-effective Total Force. If cost considerations are not relevant, maximum military capability can be obtained for many missions by total reliance on full-time active component units and personnel.

Cheney had further asserted in the letter that he had not authorized the call-up of army combat units for two reasons. First, because his senior military advisors had not advised him that the call-up of the units was necessary; second, because the statutory limits on the use of Selected Reserve units imposed "artificial restraints on their employment."[19] He concluded the letter with the pointed observation that "Congress has within its power the ability to lengthen the period of maximum service under Section 673b [of Title 10], to permit more effective use of Selected Reserve units."

Thus, almost a month after the president's authorization of reserve forces, a peculiar situation had developed. More than 500 reserve component support units had already been successfully activated. Only 3 of the nearly 27,000 reservists called up had failed to report. Congressional leaders were urging greater use of combat units in the army's reserve components. And the Congressional Research Service had even provided a legal justification for the activation of as many as a million reservists for as much as one year of service under the provision of Section 673. Nevertheless, the secretary of defense and the chairman of the Joint Chiefs of Staff were continuing to justify their reluctance to use the troops not on readiness grounds so much as on the basis of the limitation contained in the much narrower provisions of Section 673b and the apparent military view that the troops were not needed.

As the political pressure increased, I continued to defend Cheney's position. On September 26 I was interviewed by a group of twenty-five defense reporters. I had anticipated that most questions would be about my recent work in developing and overseeing the department's several new counterdrug programs and policies. The entire one-hour-twenty-minute session was in fact devoted to the reserve call-up. After explaining the department's position in considerable detail, I predicted that we would eventually send reserve combat units to the Persian Gulf. I also stated that there was no reluctance by the civilian leadership of the department to call up whatever reserve units were requested by military commanders on the scene and other senior military advisors. I was quoted later as saying that "we'll be guided by military necessity, and . . . we'll deal with the politics later."[20]

As the call-up proceeded into October, its overall success and the continuing controversy surrounding the Army National Guard roundout brigades continued to dominate the news. In remarks delivered to the National Guard Association on October 3, Army Chief of Staff Gen. Carl Vuono tried to provide reassurance to the leaders of the Guard. Observing that the matter went "to the heart of the Total Army concept," Vuono asserted that the roundout concept was alive and well. He went on to say, however, that no one should argue that the 48th and 155th Brigades were then ready to go directly into combat. He pointedly noted that from its inception, the roundout concept was based upon an assumption that the roundout brigades would have sufficient time to go through a period of intense, focused training with their parent units to ensure their readiness for war.

The following day I met with Secretary of the Army Mike Stone to discuss his trip to Saudi Arabia the previous weekend and his discussions with Schwarzkopf on the roundout brigades. Mike informed me that while obviously unenthusiastic, the general continued to be ambivalent and noncommittal about the use of the brigades despite Stone's suggestion that Cheney needed a specific recommendation one way or another. The Department of the Army had recommended the activation of the 48th Brigade, but Cheney had made no response and given no direction on the issue. He was unlikely to do so unless Schwarzkopf requested or at least agreed to it.[21] The tradition of "hands off" deference by political leaders to field commanders on operational matters had roots in sound policy.[22] Vietnam veterans Schwarzkopf and Powell were particularly of this view. As a veteran of the Vietnam conflict myself, I shared their feelings.

But this issue was not solely operational in nature. It also involved the question of who should make the decision of what particular manpower resources should be sent to the operational commander. Traditionally, the military departments had made such decisions. While Congress had taken steps in recent years to strengthen the role of theater commanders, we were in somewhat of a gray area. Since Powell was opposed to the use of the roundout units, Stone agreed with my assessment that it would be very difficult for a civilian secretary of defense who had no personal military experience to reject the advice of his senior military advisor on this kind of issue unless the military commander in the field gave him strong grounds to do so, or the Department of the Army presented an absolutely convincing case for the use of the units.

By October 9, Cheney appeared to recognize the inevitable. His years in Congress has sensitized him to the powerful winds that blow there, and if anything, he was a smart, practical politician. Moreover, it was no secret that the increasing pressure for greater use of reserve combat forces was bipartisan. Consequently, he telephoned and wrote to Congressman Sonny Montgomery to express his support of a "prompt extension of the duration of the president's authority" that would permit the activation of reservists under Section 673b for as much as two consecutive 180-day periods.[23] I strongly supported the action.

In an October 16 news release entitled "Anti-Reserve Bias Behind Combat Unit Absence," members of the House Armed Services Committee increased the pressure on us to call up reservists under the existing legislation. Representative Les Aspin, the chairman of the committee, was quoted as saying:

> A national debate is beginning over the role of the reserves in our forces of the future, but the debate is being fueled by conjecture when it could be based on fact.
>
> We've heard a number of reasons for not sending Guard and reserve combat units, but they're about as solid as sand. I suspect the most important factor is the active force prejudice against using reserve forces.[24]

Representatives Beverly Byron and Sonny Montgomery expressed similar views. Mrs. Byron summed up the issue succinctly. "The nation has a right to know whether our investment in the reserve has been the right answer."[25] She also suggested the obvious resolution of the issue: "We can recall combat units and evaluate them without committing them to combat, so safety is not a threat to recall. It is a threat-free exercise that I believe will confirm our faith in the citizen-soldier."[26]

During the week of October 22, two significant developments occurred that would have an immediate impact on the call-up. Early on the morning of the 22nd, I left on a trip to Central and South America. My objective was to view firsthand the implementation of our new policies against illicit drug producers in Panama, Colombia, and Bolivia. The same day, Don Atwood, the deputy secretary of defense, signed an important directive relating to the call-up. Don had received a letter from Rep. Jack Murtha, a Democrat hawk from Pennsylvania who had served with distinction in Vietnam as a marine reservist. Murtha had complained about an alleged recent degradation in the quality of medical care at Bethesda Naval Hospital as a result of the deployment of medical personnel from the hospital to the Gulf.

Rumor had it that Murtha's conclusion was based on little more than anecdotal evidence represented by a personal visit to Bethesda for some treatment for which he received less than first-class service. But he was important to the Pentagon for several reasons. As an influential Democrat, his continued support of the president's actions in the Gulf would be essential should future congressional approval be requested. As the chairman of the Defense Subcommittee of the House Appropriations Committee, his support of the president's defense budget was also essential. Nevertheless, I was surprised at Atwood's response. The new policy required the military services to call to active duty as many reservists as were necessary "to ensure that there is no degradation in the quality or quantity" of medical services available in the military medical facilities in the United States.

The goals of the effort were admirable. Neither military dependents nor retirees should be required to accept substantially less medical care, even in a time of a potentially large war. I had the gnawing concern, however, that in a rush to placate Murtha, little thought had been given to the implications of the policy for reservists. Full coordination of the new policy within the department had not even been attempted. Substantially larger numbers of physicians and other reserve medical personnel would now have to be activated. And many of those activated would not be sent to the Gulf to care for combat casualties. Instead, they would be sent to military hospitals in the U.S. to handle routine medical appointments for retirees and dependents. I suspected that the prospect of making substantial personal sacrifices for the less glorious work would not improve the attitude of the physicians toward future reserve service.

Two days later the second development occurred. In the final moments before Congress adjourned, the following amendment to the Conference Report accompanying the House (Defense) Appropriations Bill was adopted by both the House and the Senate:

> Sec. 8132. During fiscal year 1991, in exercising the authority provided . . . under section 673b of Title 10, . . . the President may use that authority in the case of orders to active duty

in support of operations in and around the Arabian Peninsula and Operation Desert Shield as if "180 days" were substituted for 90 days" . . . Provided, that this section applies only to Selected Reserve combat Units.[27]

One more obstacle to the call-up of the roundout brigades and other combat units from the army's reserve components had been eliminated.

In mid-October it was becoming increasingly clear that a continuation of economic sanctions against Iraq was unlikely to cause Saddam Hussein to withdraw from Kuwait. The Iraqi buildup was continuing and Iraqi forces in Kuwait now included at least ten divisions of troops, 2,250 tanks, 650 pieces of artillery, and 900 armored personnel carriers. Major reinforcements were poised just across the border in Iraq. The forces in Iraq were also starting to engage in activities that suggested a plan to dig in for a fight. As a result of these developments, very closely guarded planning began for the possible conduct of offensive operations into Kuwait. As increasing numbers of reservists were activated, however, the public posture necessarily had to continue to be that they were to be part of the forces needed to defend Saudi Arabia, which was true. Should Iraq learn of the plans for possible offensive operation and launch an attack upon Saudi Arabia, the question of any such operation would immediately become moot.

By the end of October, the army had activated some 24,000 national guardsmen and reservists in 235 combat support and combat service support units. The soldiers had been drawn from forty-four states and Puerto Rico. More than 5,000 air force national guardsmen and reservists from 32 units and approximately the same number of naval reservists from 355 units had also been activated. And after intentionally avoiding a reserve call-up to demonstrate its ability to deploy for sixty days without one, the Marine Corps had activated a unit of 157 marine reservists to replace an active unit that was leaving for the Gulf from Hawaii.

On Monday, October 29, Secretary Cheney's executive assistant telephoned me to say that representatives of the 56,000-member National Guard Association of the United States (NGAUS) wished to schedule a meeting with Cheney. No purpose had been stated and she indicated that she would either schedule the meeting or not, as I recommended. I suggested that the meeting be scheduled and that I attend.

The meeting took place during the morning of October 31 in Cheney's third floor E-Ring office above the river entrance to the Pentagon. In addition to the secretary and me, the participants included only the adjutant general of Florida, who had recently been elected president of NGAUS, the association's executive director, and the adjutant general of Georgia, the home of the 48th (roundout) Brigade. Two of the three were then serving as uniformed general officers of the National Guard. The executive director was himself a retired lieutenant general in the National Guard. They were not there in their military capacity, but rather as representatives of an association that had unusually strong influence with members of Congress.

Little did they know that only the previous afternoon, the president had decided to ask King Fahd and our other coalition partners to agree to the offensive operation. As we sat around Cheney's small round table, the NGAUS representatives made an emotional appeal for the use of Army National Guard combat units. Cheney explained that immediately after the invasion of Kuwait, and because it was feared that Iraqi forces would continue into Saudi Arabia, the primary military objective had been to place as much force as possible on the ground in Saudi Arabia, and as soon as possible. I reminded the group that at the time the 24th Division was sent to the Gulf, the president had not yet authorized an involuntary call-up of reserve forces. Cheney added that he did not wish to authorize the deployment of any combat forces, active or reserve, that were not judged to be fully combat-ready. When he was asked directly, the adjutant general of Florida conceded that the 48th Brigade would need at least "three to five weeks" of training before it could be deployed.

The meeting adjourned with no immediate decision having been requested or made, but I was pleased. I knew from dealing with Cheney that he almost never divulged his thinking on a matter until he had decided it, but his comments suggested to me that he had not ruled out the use of combat troops from the Army National

Guard and reserve. Given the president's as-yet-unannounced authorization of an offensive operation, and his further agreement to Schwarzkopf's request to almost double the U.S. forces in Saudi Arabia, Cheney had no choice but to keep our manning options open.

The mere fact that the meeting had taken place was constructive. In addition to the advice that he was receiving from Powell, Schwarzkopf, Vuono, and other active army commanders, the secretary had now received advice directly from senior Army National Guard leaders. Equally important, he had been personally exposed to the strength of the frustration being felt by voluntary National Guard and reserve warriors who had trained for years for the opportunity to catch a glimpse of what British military historian John Keegan has characterized as the "face of battle."[28] I was hopeful that whatever future decisions were made on the use of combat units from the army's reserve components, they were likely to be made and met with better understanding by all concerned.

By the morning of Monday, November 5, the imminent call-up of the first reserve combat units had already been picked up by the media. The *New York Times* reported that the anticipated activation of reserve combat units would mark "the first test of the military's largely unproven concept of integrating active-duty combat forces with their part-time counterparts."[29] The Associated Press characterized the expected use of reserves in combat jobs as "politically sensitive because it can be viewed as putting the country on a wartime footing"[30]—which was, of course, precisely where the country should be if its armed forces are about to engage in war!

When I entered my office after attending Cheney's early morning senior staff meeting, I learned that *ABC Evening News* wanted to interview me on the subject. I preferred that all new activations of reservists be treated in a low-key fashion. If they were not, they would never be perceived as "routine." Consequently, I turned down this and all other media requests. That night the president signed the Defense Appropriations Bill, which gave him new authority for the purposes of Operation Desert Shield only, to activate reserve combat forces for two consecutive periods of 180 days.

Now only one obstacle remained to the activation of combat units in the Army National Guard and Army Reserve—need. The readiness condition of the roundout brigades might prevent their actual deployment to the Gulf, but their readiness condition could not be effectively gauged unless they were activated and had an opportunity to complete the planned postmobilization training. Only a handful of people were aware that the answer to the question of need had effectively just been determined by the president's decision to send sufficient forces to the Gulf to drive Iraq out of Kuwait.

Tuesday, November 6, was Election Day. At his regular noon news briefing, Pete Williams routinely announced the immediate call-up by the Marine Corps of 824 reservists, including combat personnel, for assignment to the 5th Marine Expeditionary Brigade, then training at Camp Pendleton, California. Since no limitations had been placed on the activation by the Marine Corps, navy, or air force of reserve combat personnel, the call-up was within the scope of the authority previously granted by Cheney's August 23 memorandum to the service secretaries. The fact that this was the first activation of reserve combat troops by *any* of the military services was soon lost in a flood of questions about whether Cheney's continued failure to authorize a call-up of Army Guard and reserve combat personnel reflected a lack of confidence in their training and capabilities. Pete did not handle the questions with his usual deft manner, and after reviewing a transcript of the news conference, I regretted my earlier decision not to discuss the activation with the media myself.

On Wednesday, Deputy Secretary Don Atwood and I flew to Fort Bliss, Texas, to meet with law-enforcement officials and the leadership of the new military Joint Task Force Six, which had been created to coordinate military support of counterdrug operations near the southwest border. As we were approaching Andrews Air Force Base in Washington on our return the next afternoon, the president announced that he was ordering 200,000 additional American troops to the Persian Gulf area. The troops were to join the 230,000 already there and the roughly 100,000 troops from our coalition partners in order to "ensure that the coalition has an adequate offensive military option should that be necessary to achieve our common goal."

When I heard the president's words later that evening, my thoughts turned to the man who had administered the oath of office of assistant secretary to me, former Secretary of Defense Cap Weinberger. In a highly regarded November 28, 1984, speech to the National Press Club, Cap had laid out detailed principles which he believed should govern the use of military power. Anyone familiar with his World War II service on the staff of General Douglas MacArthur and his deep admiration of Winston Churchill would not have been surprised at his second principle: "If we decide it is necessary to put combat troops into a given situation, we should do so wholeheartedly, and with the clear intention of winning. If we are unwilling to commit the forces or resources necessary to achieve our objectives, we should not commit them at all."[31]

At a four forty-five P.M. briefing in the Pentagon news room, Secretary Cheney and General Powell outlined the details of the president's decision. A few minutes into his opening remarks, Cheney made the announcement that established yet another milestone in the hard march of the army's citizen-soldiers to assume their place in the front ranks of the nation's warriors:

> There will clearly be a need to call up further reserve units, and we will also be calling up for the first time combat units of the Army National Guard . . . ; specifically that will include the 48th Infantry Brigade Mechanized out of Georgia; the 155th Armored Brigade out of Mississippi; and the 256th Infantry Brigade, Mechanized, out of Louisiana.
>
> These last three units . . . are roundout brigades for various army divisions.[32]

A few moments later, and in response to a question about the readiness of the brigades, Cheney added:

> I want to be absolutely certain that before we send combat units, drawn from the Guard and reserve, that they have had the opportunity for the additional training that our people think is required so that they would be prepared to operate in the environment that they'd be sent into.
>
> I think it's important . . . that I rely upon the best advice and judgment I can get from a military standpoint on the quality of the units that we send.

And then if [the roundout brigades] meet the necessary standards, they will be available for deployment.[33]

The debate was over. Over the course of the past three and a half months, every conceivable argument for and against the use of ground combat forces from the army's reserve components had been advanced. Military advice on the question had been badly divided. National Guard leaders and some of their supporters in Congress had consistently taken positions that were based too much on false pride and an unrealistic understanding of the complexity and difficulties of the combat that American soldiers would face in Kuwait and Iraq. In exercising admirable and prudent concern for all possible casualties, some active force commanders had focused too much on the weaknesses of the Guard and reserve troops. Their reluctance to even call up the troops, much less deploy them to the Gulf, had reminded me of the comments of Prime Minister Winston Churchill during a visit to Algiers in November 1943. Someone had remarked that the Chiefs of Staff system was a good one. Churchill responded: "Not at all. It leads to weak and faltering decisions—or rather indecisions. Why, you may take the most gallant sailor, the most intrepid airman, or the most audacious soldier, put them at a table together—what do you get? The sum total of their fears!"[34]

I had been careful during this period not to lose my poise as I attempted to fill several different and often competing roles. As the Bush administration's senior reserve official, I had to publicly explain and defend policy decisions and actions taken by the president and the secretary of defense that involved or affected reservists. As the secretary's senior advisor on reserve matters, it was important for me to help him understand the strengths and weaknesses of each of the reserve components, and to advocate the use of reserve forces where the use was appropriate and the forces were ready. I had to scrap daily to ensure that he received full and accurate information before he made important decisions affecting reservists. Cheney's personal operating style did not make it easy. Although his informed and highly credible news briefings, interviews, and other public comments would prove to be a major cause of the public's confidence in the administration's handling of the war, Cheney was a very private individual. Colin Powell would later describe him as "the lone cow-boy."[35] He preferred to deal with as few people as possible, and his distaste for meetings was legend.[36] His special assistants could also be counted on to try to limit access to him.

As the debate on the call-up of the reserve ground combat units had proceeded, I had been intensely engaged in a separate internal fight over the question of the future structure and active-reserve mix of the armed forces. Many reserve leaders held the view that military force planners and senior civilian policy officials who opposed the idea of greater reliance in the future on reserve forces did not want to give reservists any unnecessary opportunity to demonstrate their capabilities in the current conflict. I could not know with certainty whether those perceptions had any basis in fact, but I was determined not to permit the separate agendas of anyone to interfere with the opportunity of reserve units to demonstrate their capabilities. I was far more familiar with the true capabilities of reserve combat forces in each of the military services than any other civilian official, but I had avoided a direct challenge to the military advice Cheney was re-ceiving. I recognized his need to rely upon the judgment of his se-nior military advisors. It was critical, however, that those judgments be based upon actual recent demonstrations of capability rather than on outdated opinions about Reserve forces generally, or on limited data that might give distorted pictures.

Now the words and gestures of the Total Force Policy had been backed by action. Now the matter would be put to proof. For the first time, the military services were totally free to activate any combat or support unit in any reserve component. If the roundout brigades and other ground combat forces could successfully meet the rigors of their postmobilization training, they would be considered for de-ployment to the Gulf on the same basis as active forces. If they could not, it was far better that we learned that fact on the peaceful train-ing grounds at home than in the middle of a battlefield 8,000 miles away. Stern work lay ahead.

CHAPTER IV
Mobilization and Deployment—Phase Two

"Requests from National Guard officers and from Governors for the early acceptance of their State units poured into the War Department.

"The most important question that confronted us in the preparation of our forces of citizen soldiery for efficient service was training.

"It was one thing to call . . . men to the colors, and quite another thing to transform them into an organized, instructed army capable of meeting and holding its own in the battle. . . ."

—General John J. Pershing,
commander in chief, American Expeditionary
Forces in World War I, Memoirs, 1931

As the nation entered the last two weeks of November 1990, the mobilization gained momentum. On November 13, the president issued an executive order extending the service of reservists already activated for an additional ninety days. The following day, the military services were given authority to call up an additional 72,500 reservists to a total of 125,000.[1] At a November 30 press conference, the president outlined the stakes involved in the crisis and the objectives of the military operation. He then explained to the public the rationale for the large deployment of forces.

I've been asked why I ordered more troops to the Gulf. I remain hopeful that we can achieve a peaceful solution to this crisis. But if force is required, we and the other twenty-six countries who have troops in the area will have enough power to get the job done. In our country, I know that there are fears of another Vietnam. Let me assure you, should military action be required, this will not be another Vietnam. This will not be a protracted, drawn-out war.

. . . there will not be any murky ending. If one American soldier has to go into battle, that soldier will have enough force behind him to win . . . .[2]

Few words could have conveyed a more welcome message to those who were likely to be ordered to go in harm's way.

Even though public support of the president's handling of the Gulf crisis had declined in recent weeks, surprisingly few problems had been encountered in the reserve call-up. It was yet too early to label it a success, but there was a general perception of real progress. During a conversation with Colin Powell at a November 14 reception for the South Korean minister of defense, I made a reality check of my own perception. When I asked him how he thought the call-up was proceeding. Powell quickly responded, "Very well."

With each passing day, war had become more likely. Discussions were continuing between the president and congressional leaders about the need to call a special session of Congress and to seek formal approval of any decision to exercise the offensive option—an option that was becoming more viable as increasing numbers of U.S. troops deployed to the Gulf. On November 29, the United Nations Security Council voted overwhelmingly to adopt a critical resolution proposed by the United States. The resolution stated simply that unless Iraq fully complied by January 15 with previous council resolutions relating to the conflict, member states would be free to "use all necessary means . . . to restore international peace and security in the area."

Meanwhile, urgent new developments on different matters seemed to occur hourly. Operation Desert Shield was not the only major challenge then facing the Department of Defense, and the intensity which always characterizes some activities in the Pentagon had become routine.

November 16 was a typical day. After morning meetings on family support and other administrative problems associated with the call-up, I focused on matters relating to the soon-to-be-completed study of the Total Force Policy. This included force structure–force mix alternatives to the Base Force concept that had been developed by Colin Powell and the Joint Staff. Late in the afternoon, I briefed Cheney, Atwood, Powell, and other officials on two recent proposals by Bill Bennett, the drug czar,[3] for inclusion in the next annual statement of the president's national drug control strategy. Yet later, I worked on several other counterdrug matters.

Other defense officials were simultaneously focusing on the chaos in the Soviet Union, the preparation of a new post–Cold War military strategy, the development of a six-year defense plan, and the supporting defense budget that had to be submitted to the president the following month. Work was also proceeding on the restructuring of the armed forces and the other regular work of the Department of Defense, all of which defied characterization as "routine." Few senior officials were surprised, therefore, when Cheney observed at the November 19 senior staff meeting that "the next few months could possibly be the most difficult in the history of the department."

On Saturday, December 1, Secretary Cheney and the Joint Chiefs of Staff went to Camp David to brief the president on the status of the deployment. As I looked out of my office window above the Pentagon helicopter pad to watch their return, I suspected that we would soon be calling additional reservists to supplement the almost 97,000 that had been activated since August 23. At five forty-five P.M., Cheney's special assistant showed me a draft of a proposed memorandum from the secretary to the military departments that would authorize the army to activate an additional 35,000 selected reservists; the navy, an additional 20,000; and the Marine Corps an additional 8,000. I promptly endorsed the memorandum. It was signed by the secretary shortly thereafter.[4] The military departments now had authority to activate as many as 188,000 selected reservists.

Meanwhile, all over the country individual reservists and their families were dealing in their own ways with the realities of the call-up. Most national guardsmen had experienced local call-ups by their governors to respond to forest fires, devastation caused by hurricanes, and other domestic crises, but the overwhelming majority of guardsmen and reservists had never before been involuntarily activated for a foreign crisis, much less one that was likely to ripen into an armed conflict. Even as they were preparing to report to their mobilization sites, many reservists were frantically making arrangements for their families.

Unlike the families of career professionals, who usually live on or near a military base, most reserve families do not. They cannot easily talk to a military office about health care, commissary, and other benefits to which they become entitled when their family member is activated. They do not typically have a military support group. Many reserve families in 1990 did not fully understand the kind of part-time military work their family member performed or the duties they would be expected to perform when activated. Many were suddenly faced with the prospect of a military income considerably smaller than the civilian salary to which they were accustomed. That fact alone was causing understandable anxiety and strain. Bills did not stop arriving merely because the bill payer had a reduced income as a result of important service to the nation.

One unusual problem was already causing hardships in reserve families. As greater numbers of women entered the armed forces in recent years, a new social phenomenon had become increasingly common—the dual-service military family. For thousands of couples, reserve service by one spouse while the other pursued an active military career was attractive financially and in other ways.[5] Despite instructions to make provision for the care of children in the event of a reserve activation, however, many families had not. As more and more reservists were activated, pressures on the Pentagon to establish broad policies limiting active service to one family member increased rapidly. To his credit, Secretary Cheney did not budge. Across-the-board policies would not be adopted. Reservists who had been paid to be ready when the nation called would be presumed to be eligible for activation. Requests for exemptions from the activation would be handled by the military services only on a case-by-case basis. Reserve units needed all hands to perform their missions. Except in highly unusual circumstances, they would have them.

All of these problems were being exacerbated by rumors that activated reservists might have to serve a full year instead of the six months that had already seemed to be the most likely outer limit of

continuous service. In fact, that possibility was great for most reservists. There were several reasons upon which one could base the
hope that the crisis in the Gulf would be resolved in the near or intermediate term. But it was taking several months to transport troops
and their huge logistical train to the Gulf, and after the conflict was
resolved in some way, it would take several months to bring it all
home. Military specialists with medical, transportation, linguistic,
and other support-related skills would continue to be important.
Most of these specialists were reservists.

On Monday, December 3, Cheney and Powell appeared before the
Senate Armed Services Committee. Cheney's testimony was the first
by an administration witness since the dramatic November 8 expansion of the deployment to the Gulf. He repeated the president's
earlier statement of U.S. policy objectives in the Gulf, which included
the complete and unconditional withdrawal of all Iraqi forces from
Kuwait, restoration of the legitimate government of Kuwait, protection of American lives, and improvement in the security and stability of the Gulf region. In prepared remarks that would prove important in helping activated reservists and their families understand
why their lives were being so severely interrupted, he explained the
complex web of principles and interests that lay behind the president's policy. They included the prospect of further aggression by
Saddam Hussein, the dangers associated with Saddam's domination
of the world's oil supplies, and the need to forcefully demonstrate
that Iraq's aggression could not stand as an unpunished precedent
in the post–Cold War world.[6]

In his own remarks, Powell characterized the deployment to the
Gulf as one of the largest and most successful deployment operations
in the nation's history and one that could not have been even contemplated by any other country. By way of illustration, he noted that
by the sixth week of Operation Desert Shield, the Military Airlift
Command had already moved by air the equivalent of the entire
Berlin Airlift of 1948, an operation that had taken place over a period of sixty-five weeks.

Powell then reminded Congress that Desert Shield involved the
first large-scale practical test of the Total Force Policy. There was no
doubt about the test results to date: "The success of the Guard and

reserve participation in Desert Shield cannot be overemphasized. Their participation has been a significant factor in affording us flexibility and balance and reinforces the policies and decisions made over the last ten years to strengthen the Total Force concept."[7]

The week after his testimony, Cheney chaired a series of meetings of the Defense Planning and Resources Board (DPRB), as part of the preparation of the fiscal year 1992 defense budget. The purpose of the meetings was to evaluate the recommendations of each of the military services regarding both the structure of the forces they desired (i.e., the number of ground divisions, air wing equivalents, ships, etc.) and the active/reserve mix of those forces, within the broad constraints of the "base force" concept that had already been approved by the president[8] and the previously defined budgetary "topline."

I was already concerned about the army's position. A few days before the first meeting, I had been alerted by telephone calls from both the Army Vice Chief of Staff, Gen. Gordon Sullivan, and the assistant secretary of the army for manpower and reserve affairs, Kim Wincup, that the army was going to recommend a much lower future force structure for its reserve components than I thought wise. While all army forces were being reduced, the army was apparently going to recommend a disproportionate cut of its reserve components.

This did not make much sense to me. It was undisputed that we faced a greatly reduced threat from the Soviet Union and its allies. It was also undisputed that reserve forces are less expensive than active forces. A great deal of uncertainty remained about the most likely future threats to our security, but I remained unpersuaded by the arguments being advanced by some that the post–Cold War world required relatively greater numbers of active forces. As a collateral matter, I was also convinced that the expected army recommendation was not politically realistic and would be rejected by Congress even if Cheney and the president accepted it. On December 10, Lt. Gen. Denny Reimer, the deputy chief of staff (Operations) of the army, came to my office to confirm the army's position. Ironically, later the same day the army announced an additional call-up of National Guard and reserve personnel for Desert Shield.

The first meeting of the DPRB commenced on the afternoon of December 12 in Cheney's conference room. Presentations were made by each of the CINCs, i.e., the commanders in chief of the worldwide unified and specified commands, on their respective challenges and budgetary needs. The first meeting would be followed by subsequent half-day sessions in which the secretary and Chief of Staff of each service would present the best prima facie case for their recommended force structure/mix. It was not necessary to wait for the army's presentation to join issue on the proposed reserve cuts. Sabers were drawn during the first meeting.

Powell's successor as commander in chief of the Army's Forces Command, Gen. Ed Burba, opened by expressing his strong reservations about the recommended cuts in both combat and support units in the Army National Guard and Army Reserve. Cheney responded that he had been tremendously impressed with the work of all of the reserve components in Desert Shield, but he reminded Burba that the CINC himself and other army leaders had been reluctant to deploy the roundout brigade with the remainder of the 24th Division.

Without altering his opposition to the proposed broad-based cuts in all units, Burba attempted to answer. He explained that while roundout brigades should not be made a part of the earliest deploying divisions in the type of contingency conflicts projected for the future, the brigades would still be needed to fill out the divisions assigned later deploying reinforcing missions. Suddenly the discussion had veered from the general subject of the army's proposed cuts in various types of reserve units to the specific subject of roundout brigades. Unfortunately, the nature of the ensuing discussion demonstrated that political factors and lack of knowledge were once again interfering with the type of tough-minded, fair analysis of Army Reserve component capabilities and limitations that was needed.

Cheney opined that it was "dumb" to spend significant resources on reserve units that the military services were reluctant to use simply because it was the "politically correct" thing to do. He further stated that decisions on the resourcing and use of reserve units should not be influenced by the lobbying pressures of the National Guard and Reserve Associations.[9] Though he didn't say so, I assumed that Cheney's latter comment was in reference to remarks that had been made the previous day by the leadership of the National Guard Association. At a news conference, the president of the association had challenged the army view that the roundout brigades were not ready for combat and had asserted with evident seriousness that a failure to deploy the brigades to the Gulf would effectively be a vote of no confidence in the readiness of the National Guard generally.

Colin Powell then asserted with some force that "we can't permit Congress and the reserve lobbies to make Desert Shield a test" of the types of reserve forces that would be needed in the future. In his view, the scenarios for the most likely types of future conflict had changed. Roundout brigades had been created when the most likely conflict was a major regional war in Europe that would almost certainly erupt quickly into a global war. He clearly doubted the need for roundout brigades in the future.

I had no disagreement with much of what I had heard. The nation was absolutely entitled to the best collective judgment of the leadership of the department on the size, shape, and use of the armed forces of the future, whether or not that judgment was popular. The soldiers in the roundout brigades were themselves absolutely entitled to an informed judgment about their use in combat. In his famous 1962 address at West Point, General Douglas MacArthur had eloquently reminded the nation that "the soldier, above all other people, prays for peace, for he must suffer and bear the deepest wounds and scars of war."[10] It was no less true that the National Guard soldiers would suffer the deepest wounds of the Gulf War and future conflicts if they were sent into those conflicts unprepared.

The immense political pressure from Congress and the National Guard Association for the immediate use of combat units from the army's reserve components, however, had obviously cluttered and confused the internal debate. Too many senior officials seemed to be overreacting to the pressure, and it was skewing the decision-making process. Even active army leaders continued to be divided on the use of the brigades. A better understanding of the many issues involving their use was clearly needed. I decided to go see them for myself.

Six days before Christmas, I flew to Fort Stewart, Georgia, to observe the postmobilization training of the 48th Infantry Brigade. I talked at length to soldiers of all ranks in the brigade as well as to the active army professionals who were training them. I participated in individual training involving the M-47 Dragon II medium antitank assault weapon, M-60 machine guns, and hand grenades. I observed the field testing of the crews of M-1 Abrams tanks. I received detailed briefings on the training the brigade had already received and would yet receive at its mobilization station, and at the army's national training center at Fort Irwin, in the California desert. I studied the brigade's critical skill and equipment shortages and its maintenance problems. I asked hard questions. I received straight answers.

The ultimate decisions on the combat readiness and use of the roundout brigades would properly be made by military leaders on the basis of their demonstrated performance. As a lieutenant junior grade on a combatant ship in Vietnam, I had reacted with amazement and anger to the stories of civilian officials in Washington, D.C., making decisions on operational matters that were clearly best left to the military judgment of people on the scene. I was not about to impose my views of the combat readiness of the brigades on military professionals. I would, however, have to defend their decisions in Congress and before the public, and it was important to satisfy myself that the evaluation of the brigades' performance was fair and that the eventual military judgments were sound.

I quickly formed three impressions. First, that smaller units of the 48th Brigade were, in fact, being held to the same standards of performance applied to active units and that the active force soldiers who were training the brigade were doing everything reasonably possible to help it succeed. Second, that the training of the National Guard unit corroborated my own reserve experience. The relative stability of Guard units due to fewer personnel transfers and the cumulative effect of the same people training together for several years made many of them much more capable than might reasonably have been expected on the basis of their annual training time alone.

Finally, it was obvious that despite the controversy surrounding their possible use, the morale and motivation of the individual members of the brigade were high. The commanding officer of a combat service support company informed me that his unit included nineteen women, several of whom had small children. Not one had requested an exemption from the call-up. Generally, only four percent of the brigade's soldiers were considered nondeployable and ninety-five percent of those soldiers had medical problems that prevented deployment.

For all of the positive signs, however, a great deal of additional training would be required before the 48th Infantry Brigade would be ready to deploy for war against the fourth largest army in the world. As I would note only a few days later in the final report to Congress of a Pentagon group that was studying the Total Force Policy, the development of unit skills, particularly in large maneuver units, is more difficult in the face of limited training time.[11] Large units need time to train together so that commanders and staffs develop the coordination skills essential for effective mission performance. The officers and NCOs of the 48th Brigade understood the tenets of the army's AirLand Battle doctrine,[12] but as I would later testify to Congress, there was a real challenge in providing all three brigades sufficient training in the synchronization and integration of complex battlefield systems, e.g., air defense, direct and indirect fire support, close air support, command and control, etc.[13]

One problem that later became apparent involved the methodology used by the army to evaluate the capability and readiness (to perform assigned missions) of reserve forces. Army policy required active army officials to validate the combat readiness of all the roundout brigades before they could be deployed to the Gulf. One of the brigades that had recently been evaluated as mission-ready when tested on the range that was normally used for training in its home state was later found to be not ready when it was tested on the range at Fort Hood, Texas. The apparent inconsistency was at least partially explained by the facts that the unit was very familiar with the local range since it trained there often and that the range at Fort Hood was capable of testing the unit under conditions more similar to those likely to be encountered in combat.[14]

Other problems were also present in the roundout brigades. Many of the soldiers lacked proficiency in battlefield survival skills. Others had not been sufficiently trained to fully perform their individual jobs. Difficulty in maintaining tracked vehicles (e.g., tanks and Bradley fighting vehicles) also plagued the performance of the two brigades that would later train at the army's national training center.[15] Ultimately, however, the 48th Infantry Brigade was validated as being ready for combat—ninety days after it mobilized.[16]

The same day that I flew to Fort Stewart, Cheney and Powell arrived in Saudi Arabia for final briefings on the war plans that might have to be executed sometime after January 15. The uncertainty of the situation and their own unexpected absence from home made Christmas 1990 one that the reservists who had already been activated would not soon forget.

Since it was the general practice of senior officials in the Pentagon to avoid trips to Saudi Arabia and the attendant diversion of the attention of military commanders who would be their hosts, I searched for ways to stay in personal touch with U.S. reservists in the Gulf. I could obviously talk to senior reserve officers who traveled to the theater of operations, but a better method was needed. The answer was close at hand. On December 29, my senior enlisted advisor, Naval Reserve MCPO Larry Rhea, led a small group of other senior enlisted reservists on a visit to reserve units already in the Gulf. Their firsthand observations confirmed the many other indications of the excellent reserve performance to date. They also brought to my attention a few administrative problems that were quickly solved. As the new year of 1991 dawned, 325,000 American troops were in the Middle East. Every day some 12,000 additional troops arrived. Almost a fifth of all of the troops were in Selected Reserve units. The Army National Guard had deployed two Field Artillery Brigades, including the 142nd from Arkansas and Oklahoma and the 196th from Kentucky, Tennessee, and West Virginia. The Air National Guard and Air Force Reserve were deploying three tactical fighter squadrons, two special operations squadrons, one special operations group, and a tactical reconnaissance squadron. The Naval Reserve was sending two combat search and rescue detachments, two minesweepers, one Seabee (construction) battalion, four logistics squadrons, and several mobile inshore undersea warfare detachments.

It was becoming increasingly clear that the activation of Selected Reserve units only would not be sufficient to meet all the manpower requirements for the Gulf. Members of the Individual Ready Reserve would also be needed to bring active and Selected Reserve units up to full strength and to serve as individual replacements for combat and other casualties. The likely need would be greatest in the combat support and combat service support units of the army. I was not surprised, therefore, when I was informed by Cheney's special assistant early on the morning of January 3 that the secretary and General Powell had informally discussed the possibility of a partial mobilization.

Under existing legal authority, the president could involuntarily order to active duty as many as one million members of the Ready Reserve, including the Selected Reserve and the Individual Ready Reserve, for a period of up to twenty-four consecutive months. In order to exercise this partial mobilization authority, only two minor threshold obstacles had to be overcome. First, the law required the president to declare a national emergency. Since the Congressional Research Service had itself already opined that the president needed only to specify in a subsequent executive order that on the basis of his August 2 declaration of a national emergency he was exercising his call-up authority, this obstacle did not appear to present a problem.

The second obstacle was more of an internal DoD matter. Some of my own colleagues in the office of the secretary of defense were reluctant to endorse a call-up of individual ready reservists. Their objections seemed to be based on a fairness principle. How could we activate people who technically had a remaining military obligation but who did not receive regular military training, compensation, and other benefits before we exhausted the pool of selected reservists who did? The answer was obvious—military necessity. Many individual reservists had specific skills that would be needed in the Gulf. Many selected reservists did not.

Despite the continuing buildup, by the first week of January there was still no evidence of an Iraqi attempt to comply with the U.N. resolutions. To the contrary, Saddam Hussein's troops appeared to be resigned to war and bracing for an attack. Much work had to be done in the week before the U.N.–imposed deadline of January 15.

Early in the morning of Monday, January 7, Cheney convened a senior staff meeting in the Pentagon. I took my usual seat next to Army Secretary Mike Stone and across from Deputy Secretary Don

Atwood and the seats normally occupied by the other service secretaries. Cheney sat between us at the bottom of a large "T" formed by the conference tables. He opened the meeting with measured words and the observation that intense attention would be focused on all comments by defense officials this week. He cautioned us to speak with one voice and reminded everyone of former House Speaker Sam Rayburn's famous remark that public officials can "never get into trouble for what they don't say."

Before moving on to more routine business, Cheney summarized internal administration debate on whether the president should seek a formal congressional authorization of the use of force. There was still doubt about the outcome of a vote on the issue, and lawyers could not guarantee the president the unfettered discretion that would have made the matter moot. The Constitution clearly gives the commander in chief and the Congress concurrent jurisdiction over the subject of war powers. As recently as the previous evening the issue had been discussed at the White House without agreement. A decision could not wait much longer. Late in the day the Speaker of the House announced that debate on a resolution authorizing the use of force would soon begin in that body.

On Tuesday, January 8, two final, critical actions were taken that would ensure the availability of sufficient military manpower for the armed conflict that was about to begin. Despite the obvious risks involved, the president had decided to seek a clear congressional position on the use of force. A letter was immediately dispatched to the Capitol seeking the political as well as the legal support that only a favorable vote by Congress could give.

The same day, Powell sent a memorandum to Cheney formally recommending that the president exercise his partial mobilization authority. In explaining the basis of his recommendation, Powell was candid in his assessment of the need.

> It is virtually certain that the deployment of forces in at least current numbers will continue well into 1991. Even in the absence of hostilities, we will continue to need units and individual members of the Reserve Components (particularly in the area of combat service and combat service support) to serve on

active duty in current or even higher numbers for the entire period of deployment, particularly if we begin rotating units. Projected requirements for Reserve augmentation to sustain a lengthy deployment at likely force levels are for 500,000 Reservists. . . . If hostilities occur, our need for augmentation from the Reserve Components at both the unit and individual replacement level may increase significantly.[17]

On Wednesday afternoon I sat in the Reserve Affairs Conference Room with senior members of my staff to watch the televised remarks of Secretary of State James Baker and Iraqi foreign minister Tariq Aziz. After several hours of fruitless last-minute discussion, it had become apparent that Iraq had no intention of withdrawing from Kuwait. No other talks were planned.

On Thursday, Congress opened debate on resolutions that would give its formal approval of the use of force against Iraq.[18] The same day, the navy activated the first reservists to be assigned to combat ships in the Gulf. In little-noticed remarks to the Washington, D.C., bar association, Colin Powell again declared that the nation's "citizen soldiers have met the challenge. They have proven that the Total Force concept is alive and well. . . . I am enormously pleased with their performance."[19]

Meanwhile, I was focused on the documents that would have to be signed by the president to authorize the partial mobilization and on the preparation of the policy guidance to the military services that would accompany the exercise of the authority. On Friday evening, Terry O'Donnell, the department's general counsel, telephoned to tell me that the documents had arrived back at the White House after review by the Justice Department and that the president was likely to sign them as early as Monday morning. The next day, both houses of Congress voted to approve the president's use of military force against Iraq.

When I arrived at my office on the morning of Monday, January 14, I found several documents awaiting immediate review. The package had been prepared by Cheney's special assistant and included a proposed memorandum from the secretary that would delegate to the military services the expected presidential authorization to commence a partial mobilization. I spent the morning preparing a memorandum to the secretary explaining certain recommended changes. Later in the day I hosted a meeting that included the senior civilian manpower officials from each of the military departments. Many policy and management problems had yet to be overcome if the implementation of the partial mobilization was to proceed as smoothly as the call-up had to date.

The corridors of the Pentagon were surprisingly calm as the U.N. deadline day of Tuesday, January 15, slowly passed. I worked on a report to Congress on the department's counterdrug activities, presided over a promotion ceremony, and worked my way through the other routine business. It was difficult to concentrate. The exact timing of the anticipated strike by coalition forces was closely guarded to protect operational security, but one could merely observe the atmosphere within the building to recognize that it was imminent. The eve of battle was upon us.

People outside the building could also tell. At ten P.M. I was working at home on a speech to be delivered a few days later to the midwinter conference of the Reserve Officers Association. The telephone rang. An old friend, a distinguished former federal judge, was on the line. "Are we really going to war?" he asked. I had no doubt that most Americans, including the families of tens of thousands of reservists, were asking the same question. They could not know that some five hours earlier, at the direction of the president, the order to execute the attack had been signed by the secretary of defense.[20]

The next day, January 16, was also hectic. I had to attend several meetings devoted to counterdrug matters, but most of my attention continued to be directed at the preparation of the policy guidance that would govern the military services as they implemented the partial mobilization. We had to walk a fine line. Each service had to have sufficient flexibility to meet its unique needs. At the same time, a certain amount of uniformity was essential to ensure fairness. We could not, for example, permit one service to grant exemptions from the mobilization for reasons that were categorically rejected by another. There would also be endless questions about the implementation of the mobilization. They needed to be anticipated beforehand so that the answers would be immediately available to inquiring reservists, families, and the media. While mistakes would undoubtedly be made, everything that could be done had to be done. The war fighters were entitled to receive needed manpower as smoothly as they received munitions.

After a late afternoon break to meet with representatives of the drug czar's office on a contentious matter involving a new National Drug Intelligence Center, I opened a meeting at five P.M. in my conference room. Once again the subject was policy guidance for the partial mobilization. Each of the military services was again represented, as was the department's general counsel and other policy officials.

At seven P.M., just as I was closing the meeting, my military executive, Marine Col. Andy Finlayson, entered the room. He quietly informed me that a CNN television bulletin had just reported an air raid over Baghdad. Six minutes later, the president's press secretary appeared in the White House press briefing room to announce that "the liberation of Kuwait has begun." Forty-three hours later, the president signed the executive order authorizing the Department of Defense "to order any unit, and any member not assigned to a unit organized to serve as a unit, in the Ready Reserve to active duty . . . for not more than twenty-four consecutive months."[21] The secretary of defense immediately authorized the military departments to call as many as 360,000 ready reservists to active duty, including 220,000 from the army, 44,000 from the Marine Corps, 44,000 from the navy, and 52,000 from the air force.

Thus it was that the nation's citizen warriors became engaged in the major armed conflict that history would record as Desert Storm. Thus it was that almost a quarter of a million national guardsmen and reservists found themselves suddenly and unexpectedly pulled from their families, their civilian occupations, their college studies, and the privacy of their individual lives to serve on active duty in support of the Gulf War and the other worldwide military commitments of the United States.

A well-known defense analyst has noted that wars are fought generally "on three synergistic levels: the engagement or tactical level, which involves actual fighting; the theater of war or operational level, which involves a series of such engagements to achieve set objectives; and the strategic level, which involves the use of national power to achieve the objectives of national policy."[22] In his classic *Strategy*, B. H. Liddell Hart, one of the leading military thinkers of this century, gave a specific description of war at the strategic level:

> . . . strategy is an application on a lower plane of "grand strategy." While practically synonymous with the policy which guides the conduct of war, . . . the term "grand strategy" serves to bring out the sense of "policy in execution." For the role of grand strategy—higher strategy—is to coordinate and direct all the resources of a nation, . . . towards the attainment of the political object of the war. . . .
>
> Grand strategy should both calculate and develop the economic resources and man-power of nations in order to sustain the fighting services.[23]

The grand strategy of Desert Storm was now being executed. The nation was employing elements of all of the manpower of its "fighting services," not just the full-time professionals. The mobilization of the reserve components would ultimately become the largest since the Korean War some forty years earlier, and the first major mobilization since the 1962 Berlin Crisis.

In May 1965, over a quarter of a century earlier, while I was participating in an amphibious landing of three battalions of marines at Chu Lai, some fifty-seven miles southeast of Da Nang, Republic of Vietnam, Gen. Harold Johnson, the Army Chief of Staff, had formally presented to the Joint Chiefs of Staff a proposal for the mobilization of reserve forces. Believing that the war in Vietnam could not be won without a mobilization, the chiefs had quickly approved the proposal. In a fateful decision that would burn like hot coal on the minds of military leaders many years later, President Lyndon Johnson had rejected it.[24]

George Bush was not Lyndon Johnson. The leadership of the Department of Defense in 1990 and 1991 included many veterans of Vietnam. The military renaissance that had taken place in the 1980s had resulted in a Total Force that bore almost no resemblance to the U.S. armed forces of 1965.[25]

Only a few days after he had decided to send military forces to the Gulf, the president had formally authorized the call-up of Selected Reserve units. He had subsequently authorized the activation of increasing numbers of reserve units, including combat units. He had now authorized a mobilization which, if fully implemented, could result in the activation of as many as one million reservists, including individuals not assigned to units for as long as two years. Secretary of State James Baker would later observe that the activation of so many reservists was designed to reinforce the credibility of our commitment and to produce a quick and overwhelming victory.[26]

More than 400,000 U.S. military personnel were now in the Gulf. In excess of 146,000 reservists had already been activated, including 16,558 marines, 102,828 soldiers, 11,390 sailors, 14,806 airmen, and 641 coast guardsmen. Some 64,000 reservists, or sixteen percent of the total U.S. forces in the area, were already serving in the theater of operations.[27] There would be no graduated response to Iraq's aggression. The president had personally experienced combat in World War II. Since then he had acquired the statesman's experience. He was now demonstrating the resolve of a Churchill, and the profusion of yellow ribbons on coat lapels, around trees, and on the doors of homes suggested a level of national support not seen since Vietnam.

As I paused briefly to reflect upon the start of the war, my eyes came to rest upon the remains of an old point-detonating fuse that sat on a bookshelf in my office. It had been taken off of the warhead of a five-inch rocket that had misfired during an action in Vietnam. I remembered the anxiety with which my shipmates and I had waited while the rocket crashed into gun mounts and other objects. Until it came to rest, we had not known whether the rocket would explode immediately above the ship's munitions magazine, an almost certain death for everyone. I could only imagine how many of America's current warriors, active and reserve, were feeling the same kind of anxiety as the nation entered its first major armed conflict since Vietnam.

A critical question remained. How would the all-volunteer Total Force, including thousands of part-time citizen warriors, perform in combat against the fourth-largest military power in the world? Could they hold their own against an Iraqi Order of Battle that the Defense

Intelligence Agency estimated to include 540,000 troops, more than 4,200 tanks, more than 2,800 armored personnel carriers, and approximately 3,100 artillery pieces? Would the Total Force Policy prove to be as sound during the chaos and destruction of war as it had been in peace? The nation would soon find out!

CHAPTER V
Combat!

"This victory belongs . . . to the regulars, to the reserves, to the National Guard. This victory belongs to the finest fighting force this nation has ever known in its history."

—President George Bush,
address to the Congress, March 6, 1991

"It was a great team effort."

—General Colin Powell,
chairman of the Joint Chiefs of Staff,
handwritten note to the author,
March 5, 1991

═══════════════

In previous conflicts, American forces had often lost the first battle before going on to win the war. Students of Desert Storm would later point out that this conflict was different. With relatively small volunteer forces, no draft to provide replacements for large, unexpected losses, and coalition partners of uncertain capability, American forces would have to fight like veterans from the first shot.[1] The danger was real. Whatever the intelligence estimates of Iraqi competence, no one could deny that that country had been on a war footing for almost a decade, or that its army had engaged in large battles in recent years, or that it had a substantial chemical and bacteriological warfare capability.[2]

Saddam Hussein's apparent war-fighting strategy was of intense defense, conceding no inch of ground without a hard fight. The higher the costs that could be imposed on coalition forces, the more likely those forces would be to accept peace on terms that could be characterized as a victory for Iraq.[3]

To implement the strategy, Iraq designed what some writers

have characterized as a "massive defensive line"[4] and what even the writers of the Pentagon's official report of the war described as a "formidable array of defenses."[5] In a manner that reflected the success of their defensive strategy in the recent war with Iran, the Iraqis constructed two major defensive belts. The first belt included minefields roughly five to fifteen kilometers inside Kuwait, and boobytrapped barbed wire, deep antitank ditches, twenty-foot-high berms, and trenches filled with burning oil, all intended to cover key avenues of approach.[6] The second belt, up to twenty kilometers behind the first, mirrored the first.

Iraq's front-line infantry divisions were to defend in sector from prepared positions and they were to be backed up by a corps reserve that would counterattack the penetration by coalition forces into any sector. Operational reserves, primarily armored forces, would be to the rear of the corps reserve to either counterattack or occupy blocking positions. A theater reserve would be deployed in southern Iraq to destroy the coalition's main attack line of march.[7]

Great reliance would also be placed on Iraq's ability to commit sufficient forces to prevent the coalition from achieving what classical combat theory and most conventional wisdom believed necessary for success—a ratio in force strength against the entrenched forces of at least three to one.[8] Saddam believed that the coalition would ultimately fold because its members lacked the endurance to fight a war of exhaustion and to accept the level of casualties that Iraq had incurred in its war against Iran.

The U.S. Air Force Tactical Air Command (TAC) wanted to use Air National Guard and Air Force Reserve fighter squadrons in the Gulf, along with active squadrons, specifically to prove that the Total Force concept would work in combat as well as in peacetime. As a result, it asked each of the two reserve components to identify a fighter squadron that was ready to deploy. Selection was difficult. Several squadrons were ready.

The 706th Tactical Fighter Squadron, home-based in New Orleans, Louisiana, was one of the best fighter units in the Air Force Reserve. As recently as March 1990, its parent unit, the 926th Tactical Fighter Group, had received the air force outstanding unit award. The commander of the 926th TFG, however, had a lot on his mind. Colonel Bob Efferson, an air force reservist from New Orleans, had flown F-105s in Southeast Asia. After almost six years of active duty, he had transferred to the Air Force Reserve as an air reserve technician.[9]

Now he was the pilot of an A10-A Thunderbolt II, and he knew that he would soon be going into combat again. His ungainly fighter-attack aircraft, affectionately known as a "warthog," had little in common with the stealth fighters and other high-tech weaponry that would soon capture the imagination of TV viewers around the world. The air force wanted to replace most A-10s with faster F-16s and convert the others to forward air-control aircraft. The A-10 appeared to most casual observers as an unexplained remnant of a much earlier time. Casual observers would not know that it was a tough old bird that had a reputation of surviving heavy attacks by surface-to-air missiles and antiaircraft ground fire. Casual observers would not know that it could carry six 500-pound bombs, cluster bombs, air-to-air missiles, a 30mm cannon, and an electronic countermeasures pod, and that it was an ideal killer of tanks and SCUD surface-to-surface missiles.

Efferson's immediate concern, however, was all of the reserve A-10 crews in the 706th TFS. He had to ensure their readiness for the combat operations that could start any moment. He knew that he was operating under a microscope. The 926th TFG/706th TFS would almost certainly be the first Air Force Reserve fighter squadron in history to participate in combat. It was already the first such unit to be mobilized and deployed for combat duty. Aircraft from the unit were assigned the critical mission of destroying Iraqi ground-controlled interception radar and other early warning sites during the opening daylight hours of the war.

Even though the unit had not received formal notice of its impending mobilization until late November 1990, contingency plans had been made in late August and early September in anticipation of a possible activation. Unit personnel had been encouraged to update their wills, powers of attorney, child custody arrangements, and similar personal matters.[10] Having advertised that the unit could mobilize and deploy within three days of receiving orders to do so, members of the unit had been eager to demonstrate that the commitment could be met.

On December 29, the 706th had been officially called to active duty. Three days later, its eighteen aircraft had been deployed to the Gulf. Within four additional days, its aviation support package, including elements of the 926th Consolidated Aircraft Maintenance Squadron, operations, and other support personnel, had deployed to King Fahd International Airport, Saudi Arabia, the expected base of operations. Altogether, 450 of the 1,200 personnel assigned to the 926th TFG had deployed. After arriving in the theater a little more than a week prior to the commencement of hostilities, the 706th was promptly integrated into the active wing and made fully operational.

The 926th was a typical Air Force Reserve unit. Many of its members were combat veterans of Vietnam. Many had substantial experience on active duty. Several of the pilots had civilian jobs with commercial airlines. Some were lawyers. Others were businessmen. Competition among the pilots was rugged.

On January 16, Efferson moved from King Fahd IAP to Al Jouf, a remote civil airfield in the northwest region of Saudi Arabia, to supervise ground refueling and other operations there. The following day, pilots from the 926th flew their first combat missions.[11]

It soon became apparent that Al Jouf would be an excellent forward operating location, and a pattern developed in which aircraft and crews would rotate through Al Jouf for periods of four to five days. It also became quickly apparent that the destruction of fixed launch sites and mobile launchers of the Iraqi Scud ballistic missile would be a continuing attack priority. Scuds mattered because every hit had a major political impact.[12] Every Scud that caused casualties in Saudi Arabia raised questions among the Saudis about the decision to fight Iraq. Every Scud that fell in Israel increased the likelihood of retaliation and the end of Israel's forbearance. Such an action would inevitably threaten the unity of coalition forces.

For fifty-two days, and until the temporary cease fire went into effect, the 706th TFS engaged in combat operations. Using intelligence from coalition special forces units in Iraq and their own binoculars, pilots from the 706th flew armed reconnaissance missions in search of Scuds and other targets of opportunity. Although the A-10 was designed to provide close air support of ground forces, one pilot of the 706th shot down an Iraqi helicopter, the first combat air-to-air kill by an A-10. Another team of two A-10s destroyed twenty Scud launchers, ammunition warehouses, and miscellaneous other targets in a single day. Efferson's aircraft was riddled with 378 holes from Iraqi 57mm antiaircraft fire on one sortie, but he managed to fly it back to Al Jouf.[13] Ultimately, 706th pilots flew over 1,000 combat sorties without a single personnel casualty or lost aircraft.[14]

At the same time in November 1990 that the 926th TFG/706th TFS was receiving formal notice that it would be activated, similar notice was being given to the marines of Bravo Company, 4th Tank Battalion, a reserve unit based in Yakima, Washington. To date, the Marine Corps had stubbornly followed its policy of not activating any Marine Reserve units or individuals during the first sixty days of a contingency operation, but it had no choice when the decision was made to liberate Kuwait as well as to defend Saudi Arabia. The active Marine Corps had already been fully committed.

Like their Air Force Reserve counterparts, the marines of Bravo Company brought an interesting array of civilian experience to their military service. The company commander, Ralph Parkinson, was a wine seller. Members of the unit also included an eighth-grade history teacher, farmers, an agent of the U.S. Immigration and Naturalization Service, plumbers, and several college students. Unlike their air force counterparts, the officers of the Bravo Company did not have active duty experience with the equipment with which they would have to fight. While they did have active duty experience in other combat branches, not one had served in tanks prior to joining the unit.[15]

In the fall of 1990, few members of Bravo Company had been closely following the debate in Washington about the efficacy of economic sanctions. Fewer still were aware of Congressman Les Aspin's assertion that if war became necessary, it could be ended in three weeks by air attacks alone. The marines were aware, however, that one of the primary means of overcoming the strength of a defensive line is to smash through it with armored forces.

When Bravo Company was officially activated on December 15, it faced an unprecedented situation. Several weeks earlier, the Marine Corps had decided that if a ground war against Iraq occurred, marine tank crews would be far safer and have a much greater chance of success if they engaged Iraqi armor with the new M1A1 Abrams tank instead of the M60A1 tanks that were stored in maritime prepositioning ships.[16] Bravo Company had been selected to transition to the new tank. It had also been decided to fight the company in three platoons of four tanks each instead of the two five-tank platoons to which it was accustomed.[17] The difficulties of fighting with a new weapons system using a new tactical organization would be challenging enough. Adding to the problem were severe time constraints. In order to deploy a battalion of M1A1s to the Gulf by January, the new equipment training course would have to be drastically shortened.

Two days after it was activated, Bravo Company arrived at Twentynine Palms, California, Marine Corps base for intense training over the Christmas holidays. On the day that the air war commenced, the company arrived in Saudi Arabia. After a few days bringing the tanks to combat readiness and practicing basic tactical movements, the company practiced the breaching operations that would be required to pierce the defensive lines that the Iraqis had been preparing for months. Meanwhile, Saddam Hussein was repeatedly declaring to his public that the ground war for control of Kuwait would be the "mother of all battles."

H-hour for the commencement of the ground assault was four A.M. on February 24. At four fifty-eight A.M., Bravo Company entered Kuwait in a rain and commenced breaching operations. By two forty-five P.M. the company had passed through two minefields and was engaging the enemy. Much of the first day's effort was directed to the 396 Iraqi prisoners taken into custody, and it was not until two hours after midnight that the company's thirteen tanks circled for the night.

A half hour before sunrise on the second day, some of the marines on watch heard familiar engine noises that sounded like those of enemy tanks. As the marine tank crews raced to man their battle stations, the M1A1's thermal image sighting system confirmed the first impression. At least twelve Soviet-made T-72 tanks were moving toward them on both sides of a road. Since the road was on the crest of a ridge, it took a few moments for the marines to realize that two more columns of Iraqi tanks were about to come over the ridge.

By the time the Iraqis were detected, Bravo Company had lost the range advantage provided by the M1A1's 120mm gun, but for the few minutes that remained before daylight, the imaging system would allow the marines to at least see their targets. Time was of the essence, less for surprise than for effect. Whichever tanks fired first were most likely to be able to fire a second round.

The ensuing battle was over quickly. In the first seven minutes, more than thirty enemy tanks and personnel carriers were destroyed. Within another fifteen minutes, several additional enemy vehicles were picked off. When the sun rose and the dust settled, the extent of the victory became more visible. Bravo Company had surprised an entire battalion of Iraqi tanks that were moving with two mechanized infantry battalions to attack a marine supply convoy. Without suffering a single casualty itself, the company had destroyed thirty T-72 tankers, four T-55 tanks, and seven personnel carriers.[18]

Writing to an acquaintance from St. Helena in 1817, Napoleon remarked that "you medical people will have more lives to answer for in the other world than even we generals."[19] The obvious importance of medical personnel to success in combat, to say nothing of the imperative of ensuring the best possible care of the nation's warriors, had not, however, attracted the focused energy of many of America's generals and admirals in the months preceding Desert Shield.

As defense resources were being reduced in 1988 and 1989, there was always strong advocacy in the Pentagon budget planning process for more high-tech weaponry, but there were few champions of items such as deployable medical equipment and little priority had been placed on bringing sufficient numbers of surgeons and nurses into the force structure. By July 1990, the Pentagon bureaucracy hadn't even agreed upon the number of combat casualties that would likely result from the conflict in Europe that America had planned for over a period of forty-five years. Fortunately, the performance of military medical personnel in the Gulf War and the remarkably quick success of the nation's combat units prevented this potential problem from becoming lethal. The work of naval reservists was an important part of the story.

Even before the president had authorized an involuntary call-up, many Naval Reserve medical personnel had voluntarily left their civilian jobs to assume active duty responsibilities. There was much to do. No one could yet predict with certainty how the United States would respond to Iraq's armed aggression, but even the potential prospect of a war so far away and in so hostile an environment was sobering. Unlike a conflict in Europe, where host NATO nations could be expected to provide hospitals and other critical types of support, medical facilities that could handle the numbers of casualties that might be expected in a Mideast war simply did not exist.

After the conflict in Vietnam, the navy had no deployable medical assets except medical battalions in the Marine Corps and a few ships that could be used as casualty receiving vessels. Recognizing a gap between the forward edge of battle areas and permanent medical facilities located outside of the theater of operations, the navy developed the Fleet Hospital Program to expand its afloat medical capabilities to "in-theater" treatment facilities. Using expandable modular personnel tents, modern medical equipment transported to a war zone by maritime prepositioning ships, and medical teams of as many as 22 surgeons, 5 dentists, and a 448-member medical staff, fleet hospitals had become essentially self-sufficient by the late 1980s. They were equipped with sufficient supplies to operate thirty days without logistical support. More important, they had developed the capability to provide most medical and dental services to as many as 500 patients each.[20]

By December 16, 1990, some 3,591 naval reservists had been activated and were already staffing two fleet hospital units.[21] As active duty career personnel were rushed to the Gulf area from some eighteen stateside medical facilities, reservists also began arriving at those facilities to augment staffs that had been cut to the bone. Other reservists reported aboard the hospital ships USNS *Mercy* and USNA *Comfort* operating in the Persian Gulf, the Red Sea, and the Gulf of

Oman, doubling the patient care capability of each of the 1,000-bed floating hospitals and bringing to their tasks a wide range of valuable experience in private practice and academia.

Ultimately, over 10,000 reserve medical personnel were called up for Desert Storm, half of all the naval reservists activated. Fortunately, the operational success of U.S. forces and the president's policy decision to minimize casualties rather than to force the earliest possible ejection of Iraqi forces from Kuwait prevented a full test of the capabilities of the many medical units of all the services in the theater. Naval reservists had, however, formed an important part of the largest and best medical force deployed to the Middle East since World War II. They had deployed to one of the harshest environments in the world even as they simultaneously helped to maintain all other worldwide navy medical care commitments. Even though they were ready for much more tragic circumstances, Naval Reserve medical personnel ultimately spent far more of their active service treating dehydration, minor injuries, and routine medical problems than life-threatening battle wounds. Not one American combatant complained.

At three A.M. on November 15, 1990, a week after the president had announced the additional buildup of U.S. forces in the Gulf, and only hours after the secretary of defense had authorized the army to activate as many as 80,000 reservists, Oklahoma Army National Guard major Jim Doyle, the administrative officer and S-3 of the 1st Battalion, 158th Field Artillery, was awakened by a telephone call at his home in Lawton, Oklahoma. The call was from the executive officer of the 45th Field Artillery Brigade and it didn't come as a surprise. The call went straight to the point. First Battalion was being placed on alert for activation. All full-time support personnel of the battalion and ten percent of the unit's key personnel were ordered to immediately report to their armories.

The troops of the 1st Battalion and all other artillery units did not know at the time just how badly their fire support would be needed. When the decision was made to send the army's VII Corps from Europe to the Gulf to provide sufficient offensive combat power to liberate Kuwait, insufficient field artillery remained in the active army to provide the level of support prescribed by the army's operational doctrine.

The army's leadership decided quickly to rely upon National Guard artillery battalions. The risk was not great since it would not be necessary to involve the battalions in the fire support planning or coordination process. The units would be used in a general support-reinforcing role and fire on targets selected by other artillery units.

Major Doyle's unit was not just another National Guard unit. Unlike many other units assigned wartime missions requiring skills that could be applied with equal effect to domestic missions, 1st Battalion would not be helping the victims of a natural disaster or controlling a riot. It was one of only five battalions in the entire army that fired the powerful long-range rockets of the multiple launch rocket system (MLRS). As recently as June, the three firing batteries of the battalion had engaged in desert training with the MLRS in Utah.

Six days after Doyle's call, all 370 soldiers of the battalion were mobilized and placed under federal control. Because they constituted only eighty percent of the unit's required strength, they were joined over the next several weeks by 39 volunteers from other Guard units and 54 career soldiers.[22]

On November 24, the battalion moved to its mobilization site at Fort Sill and quickly began the essentials of the mobilization routine. Physical and dental examinations had to be conducted; financial records had to be corrected; wills had to be prepared; 253 vehicles and other pieces of movable equipment belonging to the battalion and its associated units had to be painted the desert sand color that would soon become so familiar to American TV viewers; and soldiers had to be given inoculations. By December 9, the unit's equipment had been loaded aboard railroad cars for shipment to appropriate seaports and the unit could concentrate its efforts on individual and unit training.

After several delays in the sealift of its equipment, the nine launchers and 122 personnel of the battalion's Battery A arrived in Saudi Arabia on January 23. The main body of the battalion arrived nine days later.

The general object of the 158th's mission was no secret—Iraqi artillery. Modern by any standard, it had been effective in the Iran-Iraq war and it outranged the guns of several of the coalition forces. Unless it was neutralized, it might have a powerfully disruptive effect on the ground assault by coalition maneuver forces, delaying breaching operations long enough for Iraqi units to counterattack.[23] There was also substantial concern that Iraqi commanders might use artillery-delivered chemical weapons.[24] The tangible danger of this threat would later be summarized by Lt. Gen. Walt Boomer, the commander of all marine forces in Central Command: "During the 1972 [North Vietnamese Easter] offensive, we had to fight against tanks. What I learned from those battles I carried into the Gulf: An infantryman can deal with tanks. What you can't deal with is if you are outgunned by enemy artillery."[25]

The final ground offensive plan of the U.S. Central Command involved several interrelated operations, but the army's VII Corps would conduct the main coalition effort.[26] In order to avoid most defenses, the main attack would be designed to sweep west, then drive to the north and east to envelop Iraqi forces.[27]

On February 13, and as part of the VII Corps deployment to the west, the 158th's A Battery sent an advance party on a ninety-five-mile motorized march across the desert. On the afternoon of February 16, the battery attacked six enemy targets with almost a hundred rockets, becoming the first Army Guard unit to deliver hostile fire in the war. Additional raids were conducted over the next several days by the launchers of the battalion's B and C batteries.

On February 23, Doyle and Lt. Col. Larry Haub, 1st Battalion's commander, were briefed on the unit's mission for the day the ground offensive was to begin. The battalion would join elements of III Corps's 75th Brigade in preparing the battlefield for the assault by attacking Iraqi artillery positions and other targets as a prelude to the move by maneuvering forces into Kuwait. The preparatory fire was expected to last two and one-half hours. Additional missions would depend on subsequent developments. That night the battalion staff met for the last time. Anticipating that the unit would receive counterfire from Iraqi forces using chemical munitions, plans were made for the disposition of unit casualties. The battalion's chaplain read the Ninety-first Psalm, and the meeting concluded with a prayer.

Fortunately, the preparatory fire mission on the 24th was completed without incident or casualties, and the battalion quickly moved through the Iraqi defensive line. Shortly thereafter, the unit began to receive firing requests from various commanders. During the next several hours, elements of the battalion moved alternately in column and abreast formation through four divisional sectors to respond to the requests with great effect. They participated in Joint Air Attack Team missions that required rigorous coordination as fighter aircraft, attack helicopters, the MLRS, and other ground combat units hammered enemy positions in waves.[28] The 158th's Battery A was detached to support the move into Kuwait of the United Kingdom's 1st Armored Division. The British commander of the 4th Armored Brigade later reported that an Iraqi artillery commander had informed him after the war that ninety percent of the Iraqi artillery crews had been killed or wounded during the initial bombardment in support of the British units and that Iraq had lost more than seventy guns in the space of an hour.[29] By the end of the second day of ground combat, the 158th had fired almost 900 rockets.

Over the course of the next seven weeks, the battalion traveled hundreds of kilometers throughout Kuwait and Iraq in support of VII Corps operations. On April 15, the 158th began its withdrawal from Iraq, and shortly after noon the next day, the battalion's last vehicle moved through the same cut in the sand berm in the Saudi Arabia–Iraq border through which the battalion had moved fifty-one days earlier.

Reflecting upon the Gulf War over two and a half years after the fighting had stopped, the highly respected defense editor of *The London Daily Telegraph* observed that the war "was a triumph of incisive planning and almost faultless execution. The logistic achievement alone, which effectively brought the army meant to fight the Warsaw Pact to the eastern Saudi ports from a standing start in four months, bears comparison with that which preceded D-Day."[30]

Historians and military professionals may recognize that "the logistician's trade is an essential element of the art of war" and that a force is "only as combat capable as the effectiveness of the logistics support it receives,"[31] but few others do. The subject of logistics has rarely ever been appreciated fully, and it almost never competes for attention with subjects like grand strategy, tactical innovations, high-tech weaponry, and leadership.

If it was anything, however, the Gulf War was a logistics war. Without the superbly qualified airlift, sealift, supply, maintenance, ground transportation, procurement/contracting, and other support personnel, the success that marked the combat performance of coalition forces simply could not have been possible. *Business Week* called the war the largest military logistics operation in history. Reservists were indispensable to it.

When America committed its armed forces to the defense of Saudi Arabia, it assumed not only the risk of possible combat. It also assumed the herculean burden of deploying large numbers of troops and huge amounts of material to an area 8,000 miles away, where we had no established bases, few prepositioned resources, no logistics infrastructure or transportation network, and no established alliance support relationships. One informed observer compared the task to moving the entire city of Richmond, Virginia.[32] The challenge was made more difficult by the urgency with which the logistical mission had to be performed. Iraq had already completed its invasion of Kuwait, and it was critically important that we place sufficient combat force in Saudi Arabia to deter an invasion of that country.

As an important part of the Total Force Policy, the military services of 1990 relied heavily on their reserve components, especially for certain combat support and combat service support functions. Many reservists had civilian skills that related directly to their military assignments. And as we noted in our 1990 report to Congress on the Total Force Policy, functions that require high levels of activity in wartime but comparatively low levels in peacetime are particularly well suited for reservists.[33]

Individual reservists were integrated into the active forces in the Gulf crisis even before the president authorized the involuntary call-up on August 22, 1990. By that date thousands of volunteers were already serving on active duty supporting deploying active combat forces. Their work was crucial to the early sustainment of those forces, and it included tasks such as providing port security and cargo handling services, air- and sealift, water purification, storage and distribution, and ground transportation. Many of the tasks were assigned almost exclusively to reservists.

Within days of the president's decision to help defend Saudi Arabia, the sea- and airports of that country had become the hub of a massive logistics network. Troop and supply flights began arriving every fifteen minutes and cargo ships lined up to discharge ever-increasing amounts of war material. In the first 30 days of Operation Desert Shield, 38,000 troops and 163,581 tons of equipment were landed and processed.[34] Within the first 120 days, more than 210,000 personnel and 1.6 million tons of equipment and supplies were moved, breaking every existing logistics record.[35]

The movement of people and supplies was only the first part of the logistics effort. A "bare-bones infrastructure" which could sustain life in the harsh desert environment during the brutal heat of late summer had to be promptly established.[36] Before arriving troops could even begin to focus on the specifics of defending Saudi Arabia, the more fundamental needs of food, water, shelter, and sanitation had to be met.[37] Water was particularly critical. Even when it was available, if it was left unrefrigerated in the 120-degree desert sun, it soon became undrinkable.

The arrival of reserve support personnel in the theater of operations had an immediate effect, especially on army ground forces. As a result of the effort years earlier to increase the percentage of combat units in the army's forward-deployed active forces, especially in Europe, a high percentage of its support forces resided in its reserve components. By 1990, over two-thirds of the army's entire aggregate combat support and combat service support resided in the Army Reserve and the Army National Guard.[38]

The "tooth-to-tail" ratio of combat to support troops had also changed considerably in the last two decades. In Vietnam, it was 1 to 2.3. As a result of improved individual soldier productivity, the ratio in Desert Storm was only 1 to 1.[39] Consequently, the arrival of each reserve soldier was felt.

With the arrival in the theater of the army's VII Corps from Europe in November, it became clear that the overall mission in the Gulf was likely to change and that coalition forces might have to conduct offensive operations to eject Iraq from Kuwait. This presented a whole new set of logistical challenges. Thousands of combat troops and all their equipment would have to be trucked hundreds of miles across the desert. They would have to be sustained with ammunition, fuel, food, water, and other necessities. The supply network would have to be movable and sufficiently flexible to respond to the constantly changing needs of the combat units. The existing theater force structure would have to be tailored to meet the new demand by the addition of substantial numbers of reservists who had not yet been mobilized. That is exactly what happened.

When the ground assault began on February 24, in excess of 2,700 miles of main supply routes had already been established, and peak traffic at an important checkpoint on the northernmost of the supply routes "approached eighteen vehicles per minute, seven days a week, twenty-four hours a day."[40] That volume of traffic continued for almost six weeks.[41] By the time that Desert Storm had concluded, the United States had sent 560,000 troops through the theater. Some 1,200 tanks, 1,800 aircraft, and 100 naval combatants had been deployed,[42] along with staggering quantities of ammunition, fuel, equipment, and other supplies. The most difficult challenge was yet to come—the redeployment home of all the troops, equipment, and supplies. Reservists would also be critical to this phase of the conflict.

The magnitude and complexity of the logistical challenges that were met and conquered in Desert Shield/Desert Storm are still difficult to grasp. General Schwarzkopf summed up the accomplishment as well as anyone: "Operation Desert Shield was the fastest buildup and movement of combat power across greater distances in less time than at any other time in history. It was an absolutely gigantic accomplishment, and I can't give credit enough to the logisticians and transporters who were able to pull this off."[43]

When Lt. Gen. William G. "Gus" Pagonis, the Chief of Logistics for the ground forces of Desert Shield, visited me several months after the conclusion of the war, he described in some detail the importance of reservists to the logistical success. He subsequently made the same observation in a more public manner:

> I owe much of the success of my command to the talents of
> . . . flexible and well-trained reserve components (National

Guard and reserve units). Those talents came to the Army as a direct result of the Total Force approach. At the height of the Gulf conflict, the 22d Support Command drew a full 70-plus percent of its personnel from reserve units; and we're lucky that we were able to do so. Reserve logisticians entering the theater thoroughly understood pertinent military doctrine, and also possessed the intellectual flexibility to use doctrine as a jumping-off point for innovation. They were fully confident in their ability as leaders—and in fact, many had been leaders in the private sector—and they accepted broad responsibilities eagerly.[44]

On Monday evening, February 25, all the success achieved and the sacrifices made to date by reservists were forgotten. In a metal warehouse in the Dhahran suburb of Al Khobar that was being used as a barracks, several army reservists of the 14th Quartermaster Detachment were settling in for the night. The detachment included soldiers with a predictable array of civilian backgrounds from the Greensburg, Pennsylvania, area. After a month of training in Virginia, the unit had arrived in Saudi Arabia less than an week earlier. Its mission was water purification.[45]

At about eight thirty P.M. a single Iraqi Scud missile hit the barracks. The reservists had almost no warning. Thirteen of the sixty-nine members of the 14th Quartermaster Detachment, including a young woman who had joined the Army Reserve to save money for college, perished. The unit's casualty rate was seventy-five percent. Fifteen other army reservists who had been sharing the barracks were also killed, and ninety-eight soldiers were wounded. The twenty-eight fatalities would be recorded as the largest number of casualties from a single attack during Desert Storm.[46]

The cease-fire on February 28 brought an end to forty-three days of sustained combat. Over a million men had faced off in battle in a war that would later be described as one that involved "a new breed of highly skilled professional soldiers."[47] National Guard and reserve soldiers, sailors, marines, and airmen, from Vietnam veterans to high school youths, had answered the call to colors and soldiered alongside their active force counterparts. The verdict on the performance of all of the nation's warriors was immediate and direct: "In terms of military objectives conquered, allied casualties minimized and popular support on the home front sustained, the war was that rarest of prizes in the age of relativity; an absolute victory."[48]

On March 5, 1991, five days after the cease-fire was entered into, I received a handwritten note from Colin Powell. Many of the books that would be subsequently written about the Persian Gulf War would say little or nothing about the specific contributions of America's citizen warriors. Those who had fought the war would understand why. In the heat of battle, where active and reserve troops fought shoulder to shoulder, all that mattered was performance. Powell's brief but eloquent note said it all: "It was a great team effort." He would later refer to the importance of the Desert Storm reservists in similar fashion: "We could not have gone to war without them, and they were to perform superbly."[49]

On the evening of March 6, President Bush addressed a joint session of Congress and the American people. His concluding words will long be recorded in the martial history of the nation whose first president established the precedent on these shores of citizen warrior.

> This victory belongs . . . to the regulars, to the reserves, to the National Guard. This victory belongs to the finest fighting force this nation has ever known in its history.[50]

There was little time to savor the victory. The very suddenness that characterized the end of the fighting now unleashed new problems. The families and civilian employers of the citizen warriors who had contributed so much to the victory now sought their immediate return. The mobilization and combat performance of the nation's reserve components in Desert Storm was already a part of history. The story of their return home, their demobilization, and their reentry into the world of their civilian pursuits had yet to be written. Hard lessons would be learned in the process of writing it.

CHAPTER VI
Civilian Employment and Demobilization

"Give your employees the freedom to protect ours."
                                            —*Tag line of national*
                                        advertisements produced
                                    through the National Ad Council

Let love and friendship on that day, hurrah, hurrah!
Their choicest treasures then display, hurrah, hurrah!
And let each one perform some part
To fill with joy the warrior's heart,
And we'll all feel gay when Johnny comes marching home.
And we'll all feel gay when Johnny comes marching home.
                                    —*"When Johnny Comes Marching Home"*
                                            by Patrick S. Gilmore

On the very day that the United States entered into a formal cease-fire arrangement ending our involvement in the Vietnam War, the nation abruptly ended the draft.[1] The move toward a new all-volunteer force had begun in 1969 when President Nixon appointed a commission chaired by his secretary of defense, Thomas S. Gates, to study the feasibility of manning the armed forces with volunteers only. In preparing its report, however, the commission concentrated mainly on manpower supply, civilian substitution, and equity issues, giving little attention to the question of defense manpower requirements.[2] In recommending an end to the draft, the commission concluded that so long as the armed forces did not exceed three million personnel, a volunteer system would meet anticipated requirements.[3]

The shift to a volunteer force and the subsequent adoption in 1973 of the Total Force Policy placed new pressures on military recruiters and manpower officials. Political opposition to the war, competing civilian job opportunities, and a host of other factors made it difficult to attract and to retain qualified people to a life of part-time military service in the National Guard or the reserves. As reliance on the reserve components began to increase under the Total Force Policy, the time demands for training also increased, placing additional burdens on the civilian careers and private lives of reservists.

It was clear that a formalized effort was required to educate civilian employers, managers, and supervisors of the new importance of reservists in the nation's defense strategy. Although most employers were accustomed to their employees serving in one of the reserve components as an alternative to the draft, it was assumed that employers would look at voluntary service with much less enthusiasm and might even question the necessity of the service.

Overt pressure on employees who served in the National Guard or in one of the federal reserve components was prohibited by the Veterans' Reemployment Rights Act (VRRA).[4] Since 1940, Congress had provided reemployment rights to reservists, and in a 1946 opinion, the Supreme Court had sustained the protection by ruling that "he who was called to the colors was not to be penalized on his return by reason of his absence from his civilian job."[5]

Subtle pressures on employee reservists, however, such as slow promotions, infrequent pay raises, and poor assignments could send an unmistakable message. They would also be much more difficult to detect. Moreover, even where a violation of a statute by an employer was clear, few employees who wished to continue in their civilian jobs would be likely to commence costly litigation against their employers.

To carry out the massive effort of educating the nation's employers about the importance of national guardsmen and reservists, the office of the secretary of defense chartered the National Committee for Employer Support of the Guard and Reserve (NCESGR) in 1972. The national committee was given the specific task of finding ways to minimize conflicts between part-time military duties and full-time civilian career responsibilities. Initially, the national committee consisted of a small group of business, labor, government, and military leaders who focused their efforts on senior executives of large corporations and the heads of large government agencies.

By the late 1970s it had become evident that a broader effort was required. Surveys of reservists who were leaving the reserve components indicated that they were leaving because of actual or perceived "employment conflict." Consequently, in 1978 the national committee began to build a nationwide network of local volunteers within each state. The network would be supported by a small staff of military and civilian personnel in Washington, D.C. After Congress created the new position of assistant secretary of defense for reserve affairs in 1983, responsibility for the management of the national committee was assigned to the new official.

When I assumed office in October 1987 as the second assistant secretary, I was already familiar with the merit of the employers support program. I remembered vividly my own experience when as a young, new lawyer, I had the unpleasant task of informing a very senior partner of the firm I had just joined that he had no choice but to grant me a leave of absence for my training with the Naval Reserve.

In early 1988, however, it became apparent to me that the program was floundering. Over eighty percent of the enlisted members of the Selected Reserve and nearly ninety percent of the officers were employed in the civilian sector, but few employers fully appreciated either the nature or the importance of the new missions being assigned to the reserve forces. Fewer still understood that the VRRA required employers to grant a leave of absence to employees who participated in reserve training and that it further required the reinstatement of employee reservists upon their return to the same "seniority, status, pay, and vacation" as they would have had but for the leave of absence.[6] The employer support program had grown rapidly within a relatively short period of time, but it lacked guidance and was poorly managed on a day-to-day basis.

After initial resistance from the permanent Pentagon bureaucracy, I elevated the position of the executive director of the NCESGR support staff to one that required that it be filled by a member of the new senior executive service. I then replaced the incumbent executive director, defined goals, issued strict and detailed new management guidelines, and placed responsibility for the regular oversight of the program in the hands of my principal deputy.

I also commenced an aggressive effort to persuade the Advertising Council, Inc., to continue its support of the work of the national committee. When I met with the council's leadership in New York in 1988 to plead our case, however, it was far from clear that our employer programs would continue to receive that support. Since the council is a nonprofit organization that addresses a wide range of social problems through public service advertising, the tug of other deserving programs was strong. It was also undisputed that no reservist had actually been involuntarily activated since the adoption of the all-volunteer force.

To its great credit, the council agreed to continue its support. Over the next five years, the council and Ross Roy, Inc., a volunteer advertising agency, produced millions of dollars of pro-bono mass media advertising through a national campaign that included creative and production quality television, radio, billboard, and print media public service announcements. Some of the ads appealed directly to the patriotism of employers. Others demonstrated the training that employees receive while on military duty and the other tangible benefits to employers.[7] The television and radio spots always ended with the same message to employers: "Give your employees the freedom to protect ours."

Well-intentioned advisors suggested to me from time to time that civilian employers who actively supported the service of their employees in the reserve components should receive some form of tax break. This carrot, so the argument went, would balance the stick of enforcement presented by the VRRA. Several members of Congress supported the idea. I was not persuaded. In early 1988 I had participated in the difficult process of reducing the defense budget by $33 billion. In such circumstances, revenue-reducing mechanisms were suspect in the absence of a clearly defined need. The carrot might be needed in the future, but it was not yet.[8]

Other, less controversial forms of incentive were at hand. In May 1988 the Naval Reserve sponsored a "boss lift" aboard the aircraft carrier U.S.S. *Independence* (CV-62) that demonstrated the possibilities. Some 1,200 employers from Pennsylvania, Delaware, and New Jersey embarked on the ship for a series of briefings and discussions on the current role and importance of the Naval Reserve. By 1990 the national committee was using routinely scheduled aircraft training missions to transport almost 3,000 employers per year on "boss lifts" to observe field training of national guardsmen and reservists.[9] Individual awards and other forms of recognition for supportive employers were also increasingly employed.

By the early summer months of 1990 I felt much more confident about the quality and level of our employer support efforts, but I had no way to actually gauge the likely response of the nation's employers to a mobilization of their employee reservists for any of a wide range of possible crises. And my confidence was somewhat tempered by the fact that as recently as my January 1990 trip to Panama to meet with the volunteer reservists who were then serving in Operation Just Cause, I had encountered lingering problems. Several of the reservists had related stories of unhappy confrontations with their employers when the employers realized that the employee had volunteered for service in Panama. Whatever the degree of improvement, another opportunity to measure our progress in educating the nation's employers was not long in coming.

Shortly after the invasion of Kuwait, a twenty-four-hour telephone watch was immediately established in the offices of the national committee to handle the thousands of telephone calls that were expected if a call-up was announced. The 3,700 volunteer civilian members of the national committee were asked to personally visit previously assigned reserve units within their respective states to answer questions about employer-related issues. They were also encouraged to seek interviews by hometown newspapers and television and radio stations on the reemployment rights of reservists.

At the national level, articles were written for public and military periodicals and newspapers. The Advertising Council continued to be particularly helpful. The national committee was the recipient of $49 million worth of pro-bono mass media advertising in 1991 alone, and the creative public service announcements produced during the conflict were aired on television and radio stations all over the nation.

A separate effort was made to protect the educational opportunities of the reservists who were being activated. Many reservists had joined the armed forces principally because of the tuition and other assistance available under the G.I. Bill. On January 29, 1991, Cheney

wrote to all state governors soliciting new state legislation and policies to protect the rights of reservists to return to their college upon
completion of active service, and for refunds of tuition and fees that
had been paid by activated reservists for the semesters they were unable to complete.

The efforts paid off. Between August 1990 and September 1991
the national committee received over 6,500 telephone inquiries per
month, but the number of reservists who experienced reemployment
problems was an exceptionally small percentage of the total number
who were activated.[10] Indeed, a February 1991 survey[11] determined
that Baltimore-Washington, Chicago, Houston, Milwaukee, and Min-
neapolis–St. Paul area employers generally exceeded the requirements of law. Almost a third of the companies surveyed elected to
pay their employers an amount which, when added to their military
pay, equaled their regular civilian income. Twelve percent of the employers said they paid their employee reservists their full civilian
salaries for periods of time ranging from one month to the entire
length of the period of activation regardless of the amount of military pay the reservist received.

In December 1991 another survey was conducted by Ross Roy, Inc.
The survey was directed at the supervisors of employees who served
in the reserve components. Its findings were very encouraging.
Some ninety-five percent of the respondents knew that an employee
cannot be denied a promotion because of the obligations imposed
by service in the reserve components; eighty-seven percent said they
normally have sufficient notice to plan for the absence of their employee reservists; only three percent reported problems of mobilized
employees returning to work from active duty. Most important,
ninety-nine percent of the respondents said that other things being
equal, they would hire someone knowing that the new employee's
reserve commitment might periodically require an absence from the
workplace.

On February 19, 1991, a month after the air campaign had begun
in Desert Storm, and only five days before the ground assault commenced, a little-noticed action of great consequence to the employer-
employee/reservist relationship was taken by the United States

Supreme Court. In a seventeen-word memorandum order, the court granted the government's petition for certiorari in the case of *King v. St Vincent's Hospital*.[12] The highest court of the land would now decide whether an employee reservist's statutory right to a leave of absence to serve on active duty was conditional on the reasonableness of his request.

The issue presented by this case had troubled me for some time. Opinions in recent years by U.S. courts of appeal in two judicial circuits had established some form of "reasonableness" test to be applied to requests for leave. Such a test was implied at best since the law passed by Congress to establish the reemployment rights of reservists contained no words to that effect. The U.S. Court of Appeals for the Eleventh Circuit had ruled in 1990 that a reservist's protection under the VRRA depended on the length of the leave request, the conduct of the employee in requesting the leave, and the burden placed upon the employer as a consequence of the employee's temporary absence.[13] Two years earlier, the U.S. Court of Appeals for the Third Circuit had adopted a "totality of the circumstances" reasonableness standard in reviewing leave requests.[14] That court had identified various factors by which the reasonableness of the employee reservist's request should be judged. They included the nature of the military obligation, the length of the leave request, the employer's needs, the employer's workload during the leave period, and other factors.[15]

Aside from my objection as a matter of principle to judicial intrusion into military judgments that the courts had traditionally and properly avoided, I knew that we simply could not live with the uncertainty created by these decisions. When the war tocsin sounds and citizen warriors are called to the colors, military commanders cannot afford to wait for a judicial balancing of the nation's needs against those of a private employer.[16]

To attack the problem, I pursued two courses of action. First, I spurred the work of the departments of Defense, Labor, Commerce, and Veterans Affairs to draft a proposed amendment to the VRRA. The piecemeal changes to the statute over the years had made it complex and difficult to interpret. The ambiguities were a standing invitation to litigation. Since 1988 I had invested considerable personal effort in the difficult work of an interagency committee that was drafting new legislation to clarify and improve the law. As a result of the recent court opinions, language was added that would eliminate the judicially inspired "reasonableness" test. The administration's proposed Uniformed Services Reemployment Rights Act of 1991 was finally forwarded to Congress on February 21. During the week of May 13, 1991, H.R. 1578, a bill that encompassed the essence of the administration's proposal, was passed unanimously by the House of Representatives. Election year politics temporarily slowed the legislative momentum in 1992, but the bill was finally signed into law on October 13, 1994.[17]

Second, and as I had in connection with an earlier dispute of constitutional law between the federal government and Governors Dukakis of Massachusetts, Perpich of Minnesota, and others, I called upon the Justice Department, and Solicitor General Kenneth Starr.[18] I impressed upon Ken the urgency with which I felt the case had to be resolved. When the government formally petitioned on December 17, 1990, for Supreme Court review of the case, tens of thousands of national guardsmen and reservists were being involuntarily activated as part of Operation Desert Shield. Whenever the conflict with Iraq was resolved, I did not want those reservists to return to their civilian workplaces in a cloud of uncertainty.

Unfortunately, problems existed with respect to both the proposed legislation and the pending court case. The rigid protection that would be afforded reservists under the proposed new law might pose an unintended but real hardship on some small-business employers. To meet this objection, I offered in testimony before the Senate Veterans Affairs Committee on May 23, 1991, to explore policy changes within the Department of Defense to alleviate any inequities that might arise.[19] No one was interested in protecting a reservist who took advantage of the new law by intentionally abusing the economic interests of his employer.

The facts of the court case were also less than ideal. The national guardsman who was the subject of the case had been employed since 1979 as manager of the hospital's security department. He was also a thirty-five-year veteran of the Alabama National Guard. In 1987 he applied for a position in the Active Guard/Reserve (AGR) Program.

Participants in the program provide full-time support of the training, recruiting, administrative, and maintenance needs of the part-time members of the Ready Reserve. The tour of duty was for three years. There was substantial evidence that he had solicited the duty assignment.

After he had been selected for the position, his employer denied his request for a three-year leave of absence on the ground that such a lengthy period of military leave was unreasonable. The hospital also initiated litigation seeking a declaratory judgment by the federal court that in denying the request, it had not violated the VRRA. Both the trial court and the Court of Appeals had sustained the employer's action.

In an effort to sharpen the government's position, I met with Solicitor General Starr and his staff at the Justice Department to discuss the policy as well as the legal issues that were at stake. As part of their usual thoroughness, Ken and his staff spent many hours studying the likely manpower and war-fighting consequences of an adverse court decision. On October 16, 1991, I sat next to Ken in the Supreme Court chamber as he presented oral argument in support of the government's position.

Our efforts succeeded. On December 16, 1991, a unanimous Supreme Court ruled that the VRRA placed no limit on the length of a tour of duty after which a reservist may enforce his reemployment rights.[20] The veterans of Desert Storm and all other reservists ordered to active duty for a crisis or even peacetime training would thereafter be absolutely entitled to return to their civilian jobs no matter how long they were gone.

The temporary cease-fire ordered by President Bush took effect on February 28, 1991. Even as the talks between the U.S.–led coalition and Iraq on the terms of a permanent cease-fire continued, and long before they took effect, pressure began to build rapidly for the prompt return of reservists from the Gulf, and for the release of all activated reservists.

Much of the resulting confusion was due to a lack of understanding by reserve families, employers, and even members of Congress of the nature of the missions that were being performed by activated guardsmen and reservists. Additional confusion resulted from the well-intentioned but not well-considered policies of field commanders. A third element was what one observer has described as "the American propensity for running, never walking, through a demobilization."[21] It soon became clear that the same intense effort that had characterized the mobilization of reservists would be necessary during the process of demobilization and the transition of guardsmen and reservists back to their civilian lives.

Demobilization in America after armed conflict, especially after the two world wars, has usually been a dynamic process involving two primary aspects: bringing the nation's warriors home from the battlefield, and economic reconversion. The transition from war to peace in a democracy is rarely achieved with the smoothness and efficiency sought by military and political leaders, but Desert Storm began and ended with such alacrity that no significant change in the industrial base was required.

The process of bringing the warriors home, however, involved much more than arranging transportation. In addition to the movement home of half a million troops, all equipment and supplies had to be accounted for, sorted, cleaned (and in the case of tanks being shipped back to Germany, painted), labeled, packed, and loaded onto cargo ships and aircraft. The materials then had to be shipped to American military bases all over the world. Lt. Gen. Gus Pagonis, Schwarzkopf's army logistician who had so brilliantly orchestrated the delivery of cargo to the theater of operations, would later describe the remaining logistical challenge in vivid language: "After exhausting, flat-out exertions to support the war effort, we logisticians now had to throw our enormous machine into reverse. Our fire hose now had to be a vacuum cleaner."[22] The magnitude of the task ahead would not be fully appreciated by many until much later. Only then would analysts realize that within the first 120 days after the ceasefire, in excess of 117,000 wheeled and 12,000 tracked vehicles, 2,000 helicopters, and 41,000 containers of supplies had been shipped out of the theater.[23]

The United States also had other and continuing worldwide commitments; Saddam Hussein was still unpredictable; a new humanitarian effort to protect and feed the Kurdish population of northern

Iraq was soon to begin. These and the other challenges facing U.S. field commanders soon ran head-on into congressional demands for an early return of all reserve forces.

History has illustrated with particular vividness the impatience of Americans during the demobilization of their citizen warriors. When the shooting stops; when the objectives of war are achieved; and when the crusade that compelled the sacrifices of the conflict is ended, Americans want the troops brought home immediately.[24] In World War II, groups of American soldiers had actually held "demobilization rallies" and other protests in several cities around the world, requiring the government and military leaders to take extraordinary steps to restore a measure of calm and confidence.[25]

The pressures for rapid demobilization in Desert Storm came from many points on the compass. Considerable political heat was generated by community leaders who needed the services of reservists who had been activated. A letter we received from a member of the Senate Armed Services Committee was typical. The senator asked us to respond to the administrator of a small hospital in one of the rural areas of his state. The administrator knew little of the medical needs of our forces in the Gulf, but he did not hesitate to complain that the activation of the only reserve orthopedic surgeon in his county was unfair to the community. Similar complaints were being voiced by community leaders where significant numbers of local police or fire-fighting forces had been activated.

Many governors and many more members of Congress wrote on behalf of reserve constituents who were fearful of financial ruin if they were retained on active duty. Others were eager for the prompt return of reservists who were mothers of small children. On the very day that the temporary cease-fire took effect, the governor of Vermont wrote to urge that National Guard and reserve units from his state be returned at the earliest opportunity. He requested specifically that they not be required to participate in the rebuilding of Kuwait.

Reacting to congressional pressure for rapid demobilization following World War II, President Truman had declared that "members of Congress are going to have to take the heat in order to . . . be sure we know exactly where we are going when the demobilization takes place."[26] Few members of Congress in 1991 wanted to take such heat.

Some of the concerns expressed by the reservists themselves could be met simply. An informational pamphlet entitled "Released from Active Duty—What Now?" was promptly completed and distributed to all activated members of each reserve component. The guide included information on veterans benefits, educational assistance, reemployment rights, family services, legal assistance, taxes, and other similar matters of concern to reservists and their families. But while they were well received, administrative actions such as this did not begin to address the more fundamental question of when the reserve forces would return home.

The most heated concern expressed by members of Congress demonstrated the lack of consensus that could still arise on the application of the Total Force Policy in specific circumstances. Shortly after the temporary cease-fire took effect, a "first-in first-out" policy had been adopted by General Schwarzkopf's staff. Operational requirements would be the primary factor in the determination of when units would be released from the theater of operations, but if they were not needed, those units—active or reserve—that had arrived in the theater first would be the first to be released. Even though the individual military services had traditionally been given responsibility for the choice of how to supply the military manpower necessary for the performance of the operational needs of field commanders, the services had made no objection to the "first-in first-out" idea.

On its face, the principle seemed equitable enough. It also appeared to be an excellent application of the Total Force Policy. Active and reserve units would be treated exactly alike. I had long urged elimination of as many as possible of the differences between the active and reserve components as a means of fuller integration. And, there was a need to promptly return certain active combat forces to their home bases, such as the army's 82nd Airborne Division and other elements of the XVIII Airborne Corps, so they could assume responsibility as a "Strategic Reserve" in the event of another unanticipated conflict.

Unfortunately, the application of the principle was not as simple as the theory. It failed to take into account the fact that many reservists bear a disproportionate personal burden in conflicts for which they have been activated. Unlike their active counterparts, each day that reservists are on military duty, they are absent from their primary occupation. Often, this absence does in fact cause significant financial hardship. Even in circumstances where the first-in first-out principle was being fairly applied, operational commanders were encountering difficulties in setting specific dates for the release of each reserve unit. When dates were announced, they were too frequently changed.

Rumors also began to spread of unfair treatment of reserve personnel by active personnel. One anecdotal story involved two soldiers, one active and one reserve, who arrived in the theater the same day. The active soldier was sent home first in order to participate in the first days of a training course he needed. Whether such stories were true or not was less important than the need to develop a general demobilization plan that would meet our military needs and was, and appeared to be, fair to reservists under all of the circumstances.

Any such plan would necessarily have to involve a heavy dose of publicity. Few people realized the importance of the continuing reserve missions. The seventy percent of the army's combat support and combat service support units that were in its reserve components included transportation units, maintenance units, port operations and depot support units, medical units, and units with other logistical skills. Many of those units were precisely the type that were required for the huge task of preparing hundreds of shiploads of cargo for redeployment from Saudi Arabia to the United States.

More than a million and a half tons of equipment, ammunition, and spare parts had to be packed. The Marine Corps alone had over fifty percent of its total ammunition and eighty percent of its mechanized capability in the Gulf.[27] Thousands of tracked and wheeled vehicles had to be scrubbed to comply with Agriculture Department regulations and to eliminate as much as possible of the fine-grained sand that could wreak havoc with bearings and other movable parts. It had taken seven months to transport the troops and equipment to the Gulf under the spur of an invasion of Kuwait and what appeared to many to be an imminent invasion of Saudi Arabia. There was little reason to believe that it would take much less time to bring our forces home. The senior British commander in the Gulf had already declared that it could take "perhaps as much as a year" before the British could get all of their supplies, equipment, and troops out of the region.[28]

An outside limit on the length of time any reservist would be required to remain on active duty had been established weeks earlier. On January 19, 1991, three days after the air war began, Secretary Cheney had informed the secretaries of the military departments and the chairmen of the Joint Chiefs of Staff that the period of service of all members of the Ready Reserve (i.e., Selected Reserve and Individual Ready Reserve) ordered to active duty would be of whatever duration the secretaries decided after coordination with the chairmen. Cheney had further directed that no member of the Ready Reserve would be required to serve in excess of twelve consecutive months, including any period of service subsequent to August 2, 1990.

By the middle of April, the armed forces were coming under increasing congressional criticism for what appeared to be a too-rigid application by Schwarzkopf's command of the first-in first-out principle. Employing the same tool it had used after the Japanese surrender in World War II to seek answers with which to reply to aroused constituents, Congress scheduled a series of hearings. On April 18, the vice director of logistics on the Joint Staff was called for testimony before the House Armed Services Committee. The same day, the director of the Joint Staff, Air Force Lt. Gen. Mike Carns, called me. He said that he was calling on behalf of Colin Powell to ask that I help them defend the policy. I told Mike that it was becoming more difficult each day to defend it.

Our conversation became somewhat testy as I explained my view of how the demobilization process should work. I agreed that the operational and other military needs of field commanders in the theater should continue to be the primary factor in the determination of what tasks had to be performed before reserve units could be released, but I suggested that senior commanders be required to validate perceived operational needs. I did not want junior commanders who were focused on the performance of their immediate operational responsibilities to have absolute authority on a question as sensitive as that of whether or not to release a particular reserve unit.

I also agreed that the first in first-out principle was reasonable. But,

I asserted, it should be applied with discretion and with the objective of returning reservists home at the earliest practical time. Private contract personnel in the Gulf area, qualified military volunteers, and active force personnel should be used to the greatest extent possible to ensure the expeditious release of reserve units and individual reservists. New reserve units should be activated and sent to the Gulf so that some of those already there could be rotated out if the other alternatives proved to be impractical.

I further argued that prompt improvements were needed in the dissemination of information about the time frame in which reservists could expect to be returned home and/or released from active duty. An announced date that was disappointingly late because of operational requirements would be far more welcome to reservists and their civilian employers and families than no information at all.

I reminded Mike of the uniform policy on demobilization that had just been established.[29] The guidance required that to the extent possible consistent with operational requirements, reserve units and individuals who were banded together and ordered to active duty as units should be released from active duty as units. Aside from more general considerations such as unit esprit de corps, it is an element of theology among most reserve commanders that reserve units should remain together. The fear is that if they do not, active force commanders and policy makers are more likely to treat reservists as bands of individual replacements rather than cohesive and effective fighting units. Moreover, much of the strength of the best reserve units is directly related to the long periods of time the individuals in those units have trained together. Historical experience is instructive. After the November 11, 1918, armistice, American troops were demobilized by unit. In the less successful and rapid demobilization that followed World War II, individuals, not units, were demobilized.

The issue was not going away. The next day, Les Aspin wrote to Cheney to request the department's views on the nonbinding House Concurrent Resolution 122. That resolution expressed the sense of Congress that all activated reservists should be returned home no later than July 4, 1991.[30]

On Monday, April 22, Cheney held his first senior staff meeting in a month. In the course of brief remarks on Operation Provide Comfort, the new relief effort for Kurdish refugees in Turkey and northern Iraq, he noted that one-half of the U.S. forces that had been deployed to Desert Storm were already home. A few minutes later he acknowledged the heat from Capitol Hill on the issue of the early return of reservists, but he urged the representatives of the military departments to resist the temptation to tell Congress that reservists were coming home first. That was, of course, precisely what many in Congress wanted to hear. In a letter to Cheney the next day, Sen. John McCain, a decorated Vietnam veteran and respected former prisoner of war, framed the issue in unequivocal terms: "It is unacceptable that any reserve component unit should remain deployed longer than active component units."[31]

On the morning of April 24, I was joined by the chiefs of each of the reserve components at a hearing before the Senate Armed Services Committee on this and several other issues. I informed the committee of the views that I had expressed to Mike Carns a few days earlier. I was unaware that the same day, Lieutenant General Pagonis had finally completed a partial redeployment schedule. His schedule listed an approximate date of redeployment for each army unit, but it did not include return dates for reservists in the reserve components of the other services. Unfortunately, while the general had ensured that a copy of the list be given to Congressman Sonny Montgomery on April 25, no similar effort had been made to place a copy of the list in the hands of those in the administration who were straining to defend his redeployment procedures before Congress.

Tension continued to build. On April 30, a bipartisan group of sixty members of the House of Representatives wrote to Cheney to urge the publication of a redeployment schedule. On May 1, I appeared before the House Armed Services Committee once again to defend the demobilization procedures that had been adopted by the Central Command and the Joint Staff. At the time, two months after the end of hostilities, thirty-three percent of the total number of reservists who had been activated had been released from active duty. Some 80,000 remained in the theater of operations, 11,000 were serving in other areas outside of the United States, and 73,000 were on duty at stateside bases.[32] I decided to focus greater attention on the issue within the Pentagon.

The following day I sent a memorandum to Cheney noting that some of the reserve units that remained in the area of operations, such as the National Guard field artillery brigades, had no obvious relationship to current logistical requirements. I further noted that whatever the merit of the first-in first-out policy in the abstract, there was a widespread perception within the reserve community that the policy was being slavishly adhered to, all to the detriment of reservists. I recommended a prompt meeting with Colin Powell to review all our demobilization policies as well as the manner in which they were being presented to the public. Chris Jehn, the assistant secretary for force management and personnel who had policy responsibility for personnel matters affecting the active forces, joined in my recommendation. Cheney responded that he had discussed the matter with Powell, the army, and General Pagonis and that he believed they were doing the best they could given the requirements.[33]

My memorandum had, however, had the desired effect. During the course of the routine coordination of the memorandum before it was delivered to Cheney, the Joint Staff became aware of the importance attached to the issue by the Pentagon's senior civilian manpower officials. And the same day that the memorandum was sent to Cheney, the secretary of the army informed him of the army's plans to use a small, predominantly active component residual force, augmented by a civilian contractor force, to meet remaining operational requirements in Southwest Asia. Only "as a last resort" would army national guardsmen and reservists be used.[34] The other military services soon followed suit.

At the latest in the series of congressional hearings on the demobilization issue on June 11, I cautioned the Senate Armed Services Committee against unrealistic expectations by reminding its Manpower and Personnel Subcommittee that like war, demobilization is not a clean, neat, and easy operation. As a practical matter, however, and as the pace of demobilization quickened and increasing numbers of reservists returned home, the political pressure began to quickly and predictably dissipate. By the time of the hearing, only

20,000 of the 106,000 reservists deployed to the Gulf remained there. Over 70 percent of the national guardsman and reserve units activated by the army had been released; over 17,000 of the 21,000 activated naval reservists and two-thirds of the activated Marine Corps reservists had returned home. And despite the continuing need for strategic airlift capability, half of the air guardsmen and air force reservists had been released and the air force was hopeful that most requirements after July 1 could be met with volunteers.[35]

Overall, the demobilization of tens of thousands of reservists had gone reasonably well, especially in view of the total lack of experience in demobilization since the all-volunteer force was adopted. Still, problems had been encountered. Action to prevent similar problems in the future needed to be taken while memories were fresh.

One problem that was particularly challenging was the economic losses that many reservists had suffered during mobilization. Military pay received while on active duty often did not equal the combined loss of civilian income and expenses incurred as a result of the mobilization. The losses were substantial in cases involving reservists who were self-employed or who had high civilian incomes like many reserve physicians whose skills were critical. Demobilization did not necessarily stop the loss of patients, clients, customers, and goodwill. Many reserve families had incurred considerable hardships as a result. Congress was concerned about the effect that such losses would have on the future recruiting and retention of reservists, especially medical personnel.[36]

For some time I had toyed with the idea of establishing some form of insurance coverage to protect reservists against economic losses sustained while on active duty, especially when the active duty was involuntary. I had no idea whether significant numbers of reservists would purchase such insurance or even whether any company in the private sector would be interested in offering it.

The idea gained currency rapidly after the shooting stopped in Desert Storm and demobilization began. Eventually, I was asked formally by the Senate Appropriations Committee to pursue the concept. Soon thereafter, I engaged the National Defense Research

Institute of Rand to study the options for addressing the problem.[37]
The results of that work indicated that the actual economic losses incurred by reservists in the Gulf War were more severe than previously
predicted.[38] By 1996, the concept was finally close to reality. The National Defense Authorization Act for fiscal year 1996 contained a
provision that directed the secretary of defense to establish a ready
reserve mobilization income insurance program, a voluntary, self-
funded income insurance plan for reservists who are involuntarily
called to active duty to support contingency operations.[39]

On April 25, 1991, the reserve marines of Bravo company, 4th
Tank Battalion, 4th Marine Division, returned to their homes in
Idaho and elsewhere. On May 15, most of the personnel of the 1st
Battalion, 158th Field Artillery, landed at Altus Air Force Base, Oklahoma, shortly after midnight. Since they still had a sixty-mile bus
trip home, few of the soldiers expected to be met by anyone but
members of their immediate family. When they marched into a
hangar at Henry Post Airfield at Fort Sill at three A.M., 6,000 people
were on hand to greet them.

Two days later I flew to New Orleans to join in the welcome-home
of the 926th TFG/706th TFS. As the aircraft landed and slowly tax-
ied toward the area where the welcoming crowd was assembled, I
watched the families closely. Unlike the families of active forces, who
typically live on or near a military base, reserve families do not usually have the same easy access to military facilities and the accompanying support network. I knew that many reserve families had un-
dergone considerable stress since their loved ones had been
activated. A small girl walked past me carrying a homemade sign that
read THANK YOU, GOD, MY DADDY'S HOME.

After they had an opportunity to spend some time with their loved
ones, I talked to several of the pilots. When I congratulated one of
them for his airmanship in landing an A-10 that had lost all hydraulic
pressure, apparently the first time that the feat had been performed,
he shrugged and replied, "No big deal!" As I talked to others, I
learned of the quiet leadership that had been exercised by the older
members of the squadron. At one point after the unit had been activated, the Vietnam veterans—experienced leaders who had con-

tributed so much to the rebuilding of the armed forces in the last decade—had gathered the younger pilots to simply talk about what air combat was like. Now they could talk about families, civilian jobs, and what they had missed during their five-month absence.

On May 22, I visited the National Defense University in Washington to address a group of new flag and general officers. The new admirals and generals were attending the Capstone course, which had been designed to acquaint participants with military services other than their own as well as the "joint" approach to war fighting. Even though eighteen years had passed since the Department of Defense had adopted the Total Force Policy, this would be the first time that any group of Capstone students were addressed exclusively on the use of reserve forces.

By coincidence, but pursuant to a formal request by Congress, President Bush had issued a proclamation designating the day as National Desert Storm Reservists Day. In calling upon all Americans to observe the day with appropriate ceremonies and activities, the president had declared:

> On this occasion we gratefully salute the members of the National Guard and reserve forces of the United States— dedicated and highly trained men and women who played a major role in the success of Operation Desert Shield/Desert Storm . . . and . . . made a vital contribution toward the liberation of Kuwait.

> When called to active duty, members of the Ready Reserve were suddenly required to leave behind their families and their careers . . . [I]t is fitting that we also honor their loved ones. They too have shown the extraordinary degree of patriotism and courage that we have come to expect of the nation's military families.

> The nation's employers, educators, and other institutions throughout the private sector have provided strong support and assistance to their reservist employees and students who were called to duty on short notice. The National Committee for

Employer Support of the Guard and Reserve . . . has put forth
special efforts to help guardsmen and reservists, as well as their
employers, to understand their job rights and responsibilities.[40]

By August 25, ninety-six percent of all national guardsmen and reservists who had been activated for Operation Desert Shield/Desert
Storm had been released. Only 1,315 reservists, most of whom were
army reservists, remained in the Gulf area. Some 7,874 reservists were
still on active duty in Europe, the Pacific, and at stateside bases. The
significance of these facts becomes more apparent when one understands that the state of national emergency that had been declared by the president on August 2, 1990, to deal with the "extraordinary threat to the national security . . . of the United States
constituted by the actions . . . of Iraq" was still in effect.

On Tuesday, November 19, 1991, the Army Reserve's 1184th
Transportation Terminal Unit—the last reserve unit to remain on active duty other than those that volunteered to do so—returned to its
base in Mobile, Alabama. America's citizen warriors were home!

Summation

In one of the most highly regarded modern studies of the battle-field, British military historian John Keegan has suggested that all battles have something in common; that the common factor is not something strategic, or tactical, or material, or technical; that it is not something that colored maps or collections of statistics of strengths and casualties or readings from military classics will reveal. Rather, "what battles have in common is human: the behavior of men struggling to reconcile their instinct for self-preservation, their sense of honor and the achievement of some aim over which other men are ready to kill them."[1]

The 1990–1991 battle in the Persian Gulf for the defense of Saudi Arabia and the liberation of Kuwait involved the same elements—and more. Three hundred and ninety American men and women died during the conflict, including seventy-two reservists. One hundred and forty-eight were killed in action. An additional 458 were wounded. While it is still premature to proclaim as some analysts have that the victory in the Gulf was a "defining moment in military history; a campaign as momentous in operational terms as Cannae, Agincourt, Waterloo, the Somme, or Normandy,"[2] it is clear at least that the American sacrifices contributed directly to the achievement of the war aims declared by the president. Saudi Arabia was free. Kuwait had been liberated.

Operations Desert Shield and Desert Storm involved what the commander in chief of the U.S. Army Forces Command called "the largest, fastest mobilization since World War II." The fact that it had not been necessary for any president to call reservists to active duty in over two decades had caused many observers to believe that reservists would not be called for any reason short of a global conflict.

Two of the most impressive and rewarding aspects of the Gulf War, however, were the smoothness of the process by which reservists were activated and the responsiveness of citizen warriors in every military

service to the nation's call to arms. Much of the success of the activation was attributable to a recently improved understanding by senior Defense Department policy makers of the law that governs reserve call-ups. Intensive focus on those statutory provisions by a Total
Force Policy Study Group in 1990 and by participants in war gaming
exercises in 1989 and 1990 paid dividends when it became necessary
to actually exercise the authority granted by them.

Even more impressive was the responsiveness to orders to active
duty of units and individuals from the Ready Reserve. When combat operations ceased on February 28, 1991, 202,337 selected reservists and 20,277 members of the Individual Ready Reserve had
been activated. The members included thousands of volunteers.
When the war tocsin sounded, they responded with alacrity and high
motivation.

Some 106,000 national guardsmen and reservists served in the
Kuwait theater of operations. They participated in all phases of the
Gulf conflict, from the initial response through the redeployment
of forces. As the brief vignettes in Chapter V help illustrate, they performed vital missions, including combat missions, combat support
missions, and combat service support missions. They also performed
many important administrative functions. Many served at bases in the
United States and in other parts of the world to replace deploying
active component personnel. Reservists brought to their work civilian experience and skills often lacking in the career military forces.
Reservists fought side by side with the career professionals of the active force. They endured the same hardships. Many of them made
personal, financial, and other sacrifices that were unique. Many of
them made the ultimate sacrifice.

The activation of individual reservists and reserve units from
thousands of communities across the nation also helped to ensure
American public support for the war. In a broader sense, the use and
performance of reservists in the conflict was a major factor in what
has been characterized as the reaffirmation of "the bond between
those in uniform and the larger republic."[3]

Now it was important to look to the future, to decide how American reserve forces could and would be used in national security
crises that were likely to become increasingly difficult to predict. We

did not have much time. The post–Cold War world was changing rapidly and in ways that were not comforting.

A national debate on the future use of the nation's armed forces and on the most appropriate role of its national guardsmen and reservists was inevitable—and necessary. It was essential that the debate be informed and instructive. We could not afford to wait for events, even if Americans were already becoming intensely preoccupied with internal affairs and the nation's economic problems. An informed consideration of future actions, however, is dependent upon an understanding of past experience and current realities. It is to those subjects that I now turn.

PART II

The All-Volunteer Total Force

CHAPTER VII
The Development of a "Total Force" Policy

"A total force concept will be applied in all aspects of planning, programming, manning, equipping and employing Guard and reserve forces."

—*Melvin R. Laird, secretary of defense,*
memorandum to the military services,
August 21, 1970

The summer of 1970 had not been an easy one for the Nixon administration. As a result of the 1968 election, the president faced a Congress heavily controlled by Democrats. Not since 1848, when Whig Zachary Taylor and a Democratic Congress were elected had a president in office for the first time confronted a Congress of the opposite party.[1] In the spring, the Senate had refused to confirm Nixon's nomination of Judge G. Harrold Carswell to the Supreme Court. In June, and over the ardent protests of his attorney general and the entire White House Congressional Liaison Staff, the president had signed into law legislation extending the 1965 act that had given the vote to approximately one million black citizens in the South. The cause of the intense internal debate was a surprise move in the Senate to attach to the legislation an unrelated provision that would extend the right to vote to eighteen-year-olds. With the country's young people threatening violence and revolution, other presidential advisors had warned of fire in the streets if the legislation was vetoed.[2]

Action that would ultimately prove successful, however, had begun on two other emotional issues—draft reform and the war in Vietnam. The need for reform was obvious. Between 1965 and 1968, more than 1,000 antiwar demonstrations had taken place in the country.[3] Many involved widely publicized burnings of draft cards. In 1966, *Newsweek*

137

had reported that for the first time since the Civil War, avoidance of military service in times of armed conflict had become socially acceptable.[4]

The problem was worse in the field. In the previous two years, a series of disturbing reports on drug use, racial incidents, and poor morale among American troops in Vietnam had reached the Pentagon. Available data suggested that at least twenty-five percent of all U.S. soldiers had used drugs.

Particularly disturbing were the reports of failed discipline and the disintegration of unit cohesion. Soldiers in the war zone were refusing to fight, deserting, and even rebelling against their officers. More than 350 officers were assaulted by their own troops in the three years after the Tet offensive, a figure that far exceeded that of similar incidents during World War II.[5] Between 1969 and 1971, army investigators recorded 800 instances of hand grenade attacks by American soldiers in Vietnam against unpopular leaders. The practice of "fragging" had left forty-five officers and noncommissioned officers dead.[6] In the opinion of many, by the end of the 1960s the ability of the armed forces to meet the nation's worldwide security requirements was at its lowest point in the history of the republic.[7]

In the 1950s and 1960s, each incumbent administration, Democrat and Republican, had favored the retention of the draft. By 1968, however, candidate Nixon had changed his mind. Conceding that for many years since World War II he had believed that "even in peacetime, only through the draft could we get enough servicemen to defend our nation," he now asserted that "once our involvement in the Vietnam War is behind us, we will move toward an all-volunteer force."[8] While a formal announcement that the draft would be ended would not be made until 1971, the new president was already committed.

Nixon's conviction that the draft could and should be ended apparently rested on three foundations, one demographic, one social and economic, and one political.[9] A practical, demographic fact was that the baby-boom generation would mature during the 1970s. A large pool of young people would be available from which a volunteer force could be recruited. The social-economic factor related to the inequities in the way the draft system was working. A random lottery had replaced draft-board decisions, but draft exemptions and a perceived economic burden on those selected made it appear "unfair" after the fact. Finally, there were obvious political benefits to a clean break with the draft as soon as possible after the end of an unpopular war.[10]

In March 1969, the Gates Commission, chaired by the then secretary of defense, had been appointed to study the costs and practicability of an all-volunteer force. Not surprisingly, given the realities, the commission circumvented the philosophical question of duty, i.e., each citizen's responsibility to his country, and reported in February 1970 that compensation could successfully replace compulsion as the vehicle for the manning of the armed forces.

In the presidential campaign of 1968, Nixon had said that he had secret plans "to end the war with honor." There is substantial doubt that any such blueprint existed,[11] but he clearly intended to reduce casualties by withdrawing American ground forces.[12] To blunt the economic impact of the war, he promised to curb government spending and even experimented with wage and price controls.[13] He preferred to stabilize defense spending by about seven percent of the GNP, but as the country continued to turn against the war, Congress cut the defense budget.

The turn to an all-volunteer force would, of course, significantly increase manpower costs at a time when inflation and mismanagement were already causing the costs of new weapons systems to skyrocket. If manpower and modernization costs were permitted to increase within an overall declining defense budget, the obvious sacrificial lamb would be the operations and maintenance accounts. Ships would spend less time at sea; aircraft would fly less; fewer exercises would be engaged in; fewer munitions would be fired in training—and readiness would inevitably suffer.

As a result of a major change in national strategy, however, the force-planning ground rules were also changed. Instead of the "two-and-a-half war" that had—at least in theory—guided force planners prior to Vietnam, the Nixon administration adopted a "one-and-a-half war" strategy that required only such peacetime general purpose forces as were necessary for simultaneously fighting an all-out conventional war with a major power in *either* Asia or Europe (one war) and a limited war, e.g., providing assistance against non-Chinese threats in Asia (half of a war).[14]

It was in these circumstances that Secretary of Defense Melvin Laird, a former congressman from Wisconsin and long-time member of the House Armed Services Committee, issued an August 21, 1970, memorandum to each of the military services that first articulated in express terms a Total Force approach to the design of military forces. The fiscal concerns that lay behind the new approach were obvious.

> Within the Department of Defense, . . . economies will require reductions in over-all strengths and capabilities of the active forces, and increased reliance on the combat and combat support units of the Guard and Reserves.

> Emphasis will be given to the concurrent consideration of the Total Forces, active and reserve, to determine the most advantageous mix to support national strategy and meet the threat. A total force concept will be applied in all aspects of planning, programming, manning, equipping and employing Guard and Reserve forces.[15]

The same candor characterized Laird's reports to Congress on the total force concept. A few months later he observed that "lower sustaining costs of non-active duty [i.e., reserve] forces . . . allows more force units to be provided for the same costs as an all-active force structure, or the same number of force units to be maintained at lesser costs."[16] For this and other reasons, the concept was welcomed by a Congress already concerned about the rapidly deteriorating state of the armed forces.

The Laird memorandum was widely perceived as the Magna Charta of the contemporary reserve forces.[17] On its face, it seemed to justify the high expectations of reserve leaders. It expanded the overall mission of reserve forces to include activation for crises other than general war: "Guard and reserve units and individuals of the Selected Reserve will be prepared to be the initial and primary source

of augmentation of the active forces in any future emergency requiring a rapid and substantial expansion of the active forces."[18] It
was also intended to give the reserves the experience necessary to
fulfill their expanded role. The military services were directed to provide and maintain combat standard equipment for Guard and reserve units in the necessary quantities for the purpose of increasing
"the readiness, reliability and timely responsiveness of the combat
and combat support units of the Guard and reserve and individuals
of the reserve."[19]

Perhaps the most important but least understood provision of the
Laird memorandum was that which, if followed to the letter, would
alter the force planning process in significant ways. Now all forces,
active and reserve, were to be considered to determine "the most ad-
vantageous mix to support national strategy and meet the threat."[20]
Little could anyone know then how this sound general principle
would be misunderstood and often ignored during the next almost
quarter of a century, and how often Congress would prevent its effective implementation when it was followed by the Department of
Defense.

By 1973, the all-volunteer force was quickly becoming a reality. The
last general draft call was issued in December 1972, and the last in-
duction took place in June 1973.[21] As the move toward Total Force
planning continued, the strength of the active forces began to predictably wane. In 1968, active forces numbered 3,547,000.[22] By 1973
their numbers had been reduced to 2,252,000.[23]

Two years after Laird issued his August 21, 1970, memorandum,
his successor, James R. Schlesinger, issued new direction that formalized the Total Force idea. In a memorandum to the secretaries
of the military departments and others on August 23, 1973,
Schlesinger stated that "Total Force is no longer a 'concept.' It is now
the Total Force Policy which integrates the Active, Guard and Reserve
forces into a homogeneous whole."[24] As forthright as the policy statement sounded, some analysts would later conclude that it was more
of a "political gesture to bolster the sagging morale of the Reserve
community than a strong conviction of the new secretary."[25]

By 1975, the theoretical basis of the new Total Force Policy was well
established. The implementation of the policy, however, had run into

major obstacles. The policy assumed that as active force reductions came into effect, the planned increased reliance on reserve forces would be accompanied by increases in reserve manpower. In fact, reserve strength began to decline.

Prior to 1973, large numbers of draft-eligible men sought to join reserve and National Guard units. Many did so in order to pursue graduate studies or other civilian career interests while satisfying their military obligation. During my tenure on the naval ROTC faculty at Dartmouth College, there were many occasions on which I counseled students on the various reserve service options. Almost without exception the students did not want their military obligations to place them in a competitive disadvantage within the civilian career patterns they were about to enter. Draft-age men also understood implicitly that it was very unlikely that reserve forces would be mobilized en masse to fight in Vietnam.[26] One study concluded that during this period, the draft motivated approximately eighty percent of the enlistments in the Air National Guard and Air Force Reserve.[27]

When the nation ended its involvement in Vietnam and the draft ended, reserve recruiting and retention problems began to increase. As a result of the disappearance of the war and draft pressures, long lines of young men were no longer waiting to join a reserve unit. Public perceptions of the armed forces didn't help. A 1973 Harris poll revealed that Americans ranked the military only above sanitation workers in relative order of respect. Beginning in 1974, large numbers of individuals who had joined the reserves during the Vietnam buildup also began to complete their military obligation. As a consequence, reserve manpower strength began a decline that continued through 1980.[28]

Other factors were also inhibiting the implementation of the new Total Force Policy. While the integration of the Air Force Reserve and Air National Guard with the active air force was proceeding reasonably well, new problems were being encountered in the army and navy.

The navy, tradition-bound and never aggressively inclined toward the use of reservists, continued to believe that its forward deployment obligations required a force mix heavily in favor of the active navy. It was not an entirely unreasonable position. In the 1960s and 1970s, the size, capabilities, and sphere of operations of the Soviet Union's fleet were greatly expanding. As a result, the Soviet navy was in a position to threaten sea lanes and navigational choke points through which a very high percentage of the free world's trade had to pass. As a maritime nation that imports a very high percentage of its strategic materials by ship, the United States could hardly ignore such a critically important development. Control of the seas is fundamental to our security.

At the same time as the Soviet naval expansion, rapid reductions had been made in both the navy's sea control forces (i.e., the combined capabilities of naval air, surface, and submarine forces which could be used to defeat an enemy at sea) and its power projection forces (those that could be applied to overseas land areas, e.g., amphibious lift for marine units, aircraft from carriers, and sea lift and other combat logistics for all of the military services). The combined effect of the two developments was serious. In a meeting with President Nixon on August 18, 1970—only two days before Laird signed his Total Force memorandum—the Chief of Naval Operations had expressed the judgment that we had only a fifty-five percent probability of prevailing in a conventional war at sea with the Soviet Union.[29]

There were other important considerations as well. As part of the nation's general effort to deter war, and for purposes of crisis management and diplomacy, navy and Marine Corps forces were deployed globally in peacetime much as they would have been in wartime, even if at only one-third of the tempo expected in wartime operations.[30] Six-month deployments were routine for most ships, and only fifty percent of a ship's time was spent in its home port. There was also disagreement about the navy's mobilization requirement. Between 1972 and 1978, various Defense Department or navy studies calculated the requirement at somewhere between 92,000 and 117,000 reservists.[31]

All in all, it was difficult to see how a significantly greater number of missions could be assigned to part-time naval reservists, but there was also little doubt that the regular navy had an almost institutional resistance to innovative uses of the Naval Reserve.[32]

The situation was even more complex within the army, the service with the largest number of reservists. Two developments were particularly significant: a major restructuring of active army forces, and initially flawed assumptions about the early deployability of large National Guard and reserve units.

In the early 1970s, the army was in the process of reducing its active force to thirteen divisions of 800,000 troops. Contingency plans then in effect assumed that certain high-priority National Guard and reserve divisions would achieve sufficiently high standards of combat readiness that they could be deployed almost as rapidly as active army divisions.[33]

In 1974, however, the Army Chief of Staff, Gen. Creighton Abrams, announced plans to field sixteen combat-ready divisions by the end of fiscal year 1978, with no increase in either the overall number of soldiers—which had dropped to 784,000 because of recruiting problems—or the currently approved level of funding.[34] According to some analysts, the change was based partly on the view that the assumptions underlying the thirteen-division force, especially assumptions about the reserve deployability in the earliest stages of a crisis, were flawed.[35] Secretary of Defense Schlesinger said as much in 1975, only two years after he had formalized the Total Force Policy. After advising Congress that in the changeover to the all-volunteer force the nation had gone too far in reducing the number of active ground forces, he concluded in frustration that "during the past decade, the costs of the Army National Guard forces have nearly tripled, and they now have received substantial quantities of modern equipment. Yet despite repeated efforts to increase their readiness, even the highest priority Army reserve brigades do not become available for deployment as early as we would like."[36]

Even while the army was backing away from its previous assumptions about reserve deployability and moving toward a larger but leaner structure, Abrams was pursuing plans to integrate active and reserve forces in an unprecedented way. When he served as Vice Chief of Staff during the buildup for Vietnam, Abrams had had to deal with the problems that resulted from President Johnson's refusal to mobilize reserve forces. According to his biographer, Abrams deliberately built into the sixteen-division structure a reliance on reserves that ensured that no president would be able to send the army into war in the future without activating reserve forces.[37]

One mechanism by which Abrams hoped to achieve both an additional three divisions and greater use of reserve units was a new "roundout" concept.[38] Four divisions, including the three new divisions, would be composed of two active brigades and one National Guard or reserve brigade that would round out each division. The total number of reserve divisions would not change.

Another mechanism was the transfer of additional combat support and combat service support missions to the army's reserve components. For some time Congress had expressed concern about the ratio between the army's combat and support forces in Europe, the so-called tooth-to-tail ratio. To meet this concern and in order to man the three new active divisions, the army converted many active support billets to combat positions and turned the vacated support responsibilities over to the reserve components.[39]

The primary impact of the army restructuring, therefore, was felt by its reserve support units, especially combat service support units. Many support units were no longer to be held "in reserve" in the traditional sense for postmobilization training. They were now expected to be ready to deploy to Europe almost immediately. With the exception of those brigades and battalions designated as roundout units, National Guard combat divisions were, in the opinion of two analysts, "relegated to the more realistic role of late-deploying reinforcements."[40]

Throughout the remainder of the 1970s, considerable rhetoric continued to be devoted to discussions of the merits of the Total Force Policy, but the effective integration of the active and reserve components was still very much an illusion. The policy was endorsed by the Carter administration, but as recently as two years earlier, the Defense Manpower Commission had candidly concluded:

The Total Force Policy is still far from a reality, and the expectations of it may have been overstated. To assume that many National Guard or Reserve units will be operationally ready for deployment overseas 30 to 90 days after mobilization is not realistic; a more practical readiness time for most units would be from 120 to 180 days. There are some anomalies and some great differences among and within the Services as to the conditions of their Reserve components, and their support, readiness and what can realistically be expected of them.[41]

Major problems continued to defy quick resolution: lack of equipment for reserve units, the difficulty of obtaining necessary training for individual reservists, and continued doubts among active force personnel about both the quality of reserve forces and the willingness of political leaders to use them.

When the Reagan administration assumed power in 1981, there was little doubt that change was coming. Concerned about what was perceived to be unchecked Soviet expansionism and a "window of vulnerability" caused by the recent growth of Soviet military capability, Reagan had promised a rapid buildup of U.S. military strength during his 1980 campaign. The implications of such a buildup for the reserve components was never in doubt. The new secretary of defense, Caspar Weinberger, lost little time in affirming his own belief in the Total Force Policy. The reserve components were to be "full partners with their active counterparts in [the new] administration."[42] The following year Weinberger informed the Congress of the Interallied Confederation of Reserve Officers that: "We can no longer consider reserve forces as merely forces in reserve. . . . Instead, they have to be an integral part of the total force, both within the United States and within NATO. They have to be, and in fact are, a blending of the professionalism of the full-time soldier with the professionalism of the citizen-soldier. Only in that way can we achieve the military strength that is necessary to defend our freedom."[43]

Far more important than the continued rhetorical support was the step taken by Weinberger on June 21, 1982. In a memorandum to the military services, he established what would become known as the "first to fight, first to equip" policy. Having concluded that "early deploying and employing Guard and reserve units must have the equipment to perform their mission," he asserted that "active and reserve units deploying at the same time should have equal claim on modern equipment inventories."[44] Henceforth, "units that fight first [would] be equipped first, regardless of component."[45]

The new policy did not come too soon. During the decade of the

1970s, the amount that the nation invested in defense had declined by twenty percent—after inflation. By fiscal year 1974, defense outlays were less than thirty percent of the federal budget compared to over forty-five percent only ten years earlier.[46] When the Reagan administration assumed office, the figure had dropped to less than twenty-five percent. The impact had been felt among all of the armed forces, but relatively speaking, reservists had been hit hardest because they started with less.

The new equipment policy combined with significant increases in congressionally approved defense budget authority during the period 1980 to 1985 permitted procurement of new equipment and an increased flow of combat-serviceable equipment from the active components. The two developments would eventually contribute substantially to the rapid improvement in the quality of the reserve forces that took place in the second Reagan and Bush administrations. In 1988, I informed the Congress that if the reserve forces were mobilized, they would be able to field approximately eighty percent of their required equipment in terms of dollar value.[47] By early 1992, I was able to report that the figure had risen to over ninety percent.[48]

Clearly the most remarkable change in the development of the Total Force Policy in the 1980s, however, involved the men and women in uniform. Few areas of defense policy were in greater need of immediate attention than manpower.

After initial success, the all-volunteer system for the manning of the armed forces was no longer working by the late 1970s. In a meeting with President Carter at Camp David in November 1979, and again in testimony to Congress in the spring of 1980, the army Chief of Staff had declared that the nation had a "hollow army."[49] In May 1980, the Chief of Naval Operations had referred to a "hemorrhage of talent" and a shortfall of navy petty officers in excess of 20,000. Privately, his subordinates were telling him that as many as half the people in the navy were on drugs.[50] Many of the best company and field grade officers were leaving military service as the nation continued to feel the demoralizing effects of the Vietnam War. The willingness of young males to join the armed forces had continued to decline, and only about sixty percent of the enlisted ranks were high school graduates. Increasing concern was also being expressed about

an overrepresentation of minorities in the force and the utilization of women. A series of incidents had even raised questions
about whether the existing force could perform essential military
missions.[51]

These manpower problems were not limited to the active forces.
The total strength of the Selected Reserve had fallen from over
896,000 in fiscal year 1975 to less than 869,000 in fiscal year 1980.
Recruiting challenges were greater for the reserve components because of geographical restraints that limited the makeup of reserve
units to the part-time citizen warriors who lived nearby.

Suddenly, and almost tangibly, things began to change. A number of symbolic acts by President Reagan had an electrifying effect
on both the morale of the armed forces and the nation's sense of
pride in its warriors. Almost overnight it once again became an honor
to wear the country's uniform.

Perhaps the best remembered of Reagan's gestures involved the
presentation of the Medal of Honor to retired army MSgt. Roy P. Benavidez in a Pentagon ceremony on February 24, 1981. Because the
acts for which the award was to be given had taken place in Vietnam
and the Carter administration had been reluctant to engage in public reminders of that war, protocol officials in the Pentagon were un-
sure whether to schedule a ceremony for the presentation. The new
secretary of defense, Caspar Weinberger, later described what happened: ". . . with all flags flying and a huge crowd assembled in the
Pentagon's inner court, the president of the United States, for the
first time in the history of the award, read the citation himself and
then placed the light blue collar, with its myriad white stars, the
Medal of Honor below, around the neck of Sergeant Benavidez."[52]

A series of new manpower policies and certain external factors
also had an important impact on the turnaround. High unemployment rates among young people and the increasing size of the recruit-age population were among the external factors, but there is
little doubt that other factors were more important.[53] A series of pay
raises restored military compensation to competitive levels. Resources for recruiting people into the Selected Reserve, including
advertising and targeted enlistment cash bonuses, continued to increase substantially. As draft-induced volunteers completed their

obligation, reserve recruiters relearned skills that had been lost during the period of the draft.[54]

Another important factor was the adoption of a new G.I. Bill. The World War II era G.I. Bill had provided educational benefits to veterans. In contrast, the Cold War G.I. Bill, which had lapsed in 1976, had offered educational benefits to personnel who had not served in wartime and it had demonstrable merit as an enlistment incentive.[55] The Carter administration had offered a program that was much less lucrative to recruits. By the early 1980s, the House Armed Services Military Personnel and Compensation Subcommittee strongly favored a new G.I. Bill. The Reagan administration had come into office favorably disposed toward a new program, but because of budgetary pressures, it preferred to rely on the projected pay increases to stem recruitment and retention problems.

The administration eventually agreed to implement a new G.I. Bill beginning July 1, 1985. The reserve part of the program was aptly referred to as the "Montgomery G.I. Bill" in honor of Congressman G. V. Montgomery, who was in great part responsible for it. Administration of the Montgomery G.I. Bill was vested jointly in the Department of Defense and the Veterans Administration, and it very soon became a valuable recruiting and retention tool for the Selected Reserve. The program was aimed at young high school graduates interested in continuing their education. Benefits were payable to participants for as long as thirty-six months of education so long as they satisfactorily met their monthly reserve training requirements. Participation in the program required an obligated term of reserve service of at least six years, but the program showed steady growth from its inception. By the time of my first testimony before the Subcommittee on Military Personnel and Compensation of the House Armed Services Committee in March 1988, I was able to note that over thirty-two percent of those eligible for the program were already participating in it.[56]

The first four years of the 1980s witnessed substantial growth in the reserve components. Between fiscal year 1980 and fiscal year 1984, the strength of the Selected Reserve for all of the military services increased by 177,200, or twenty percent, compared to a growth rate of 4.8 percent for the active components. The Individual Ready

Reserve (IRR) was also growing. The IRR and its National Guard counterpart, the Inactive National Guard, are a pool of pretrained manpower consisting primarily of individuals who previously served on active duty or in the Selected Reserve and who have some period of their military service obligation remaining. Most members of the IRR do not train on a regular basis like members of the Selected Reserve, but they are the principal source of trained individuals to fill wartime shortages in active and reserve units, and to replace combat casualties during the first 120 days of a full mobilization. After declining to a low point of only 334,000 in June 1978, the strength of the IRR had risen to 406,000 at the end of fiscal year 1983.[57]

The number of full-time support reservists was also increasing. Assigned to assist Selected Reserve units in administration, training, logistics and recruiting/retention, full-time support personnel were being increasingly recognized as a "force multiplier," enabling reserve units to take maximum advantage of their limited training time. By fiscal year 1986, the number of full-time support personnel in all of the reserve components had reached 160,347.[58]

The policy objective that lay behind the rapid growth was simple: cost savings. Weinberger's manpower advisor in the first Reagan administration put the matter this way:

> The goal is to choose the least costly form of manpower to perform each function within the DoD, subject to accomplishing the tasks at an acceptable level of proficiency.

> Over the first term of the Reagan administration, that form of defense manpower which is generally considered to be the least costly—selected reserves—increased the most, while that form which is generally considered to be the most expensive—active military—expanded the least.[59]

As the number of reservists continued to increase, the dramatic changes in the active/reserve "mix" of the armed forces were becoming more visible. When the Bush administration assumed office in 1989, the number of active component personnel had increased from 2,040,000 to 2,133,000—an increase of less than five percent—

between fiscal years 1980 and 1989. But the number of selected reservists alone had increased from 869,000 to 1,171,000—an increase of thirty-five percent—during the same period.[60]

The changes in force mix had different implications for each of the military services. The Marine Corps Reserve increased by almost seventeen percent between 1981 and 1989. By the end of the decade, fifty percent of the Marine Corps's force reconnaissance companies, forty percent of its tank battalions, thirty-three percent of its heavy artillery batteries, and one fourth of its infantry battalions were in the Marine Corps Reserve.[61]

The number of selected reservists in the navy increased by fifty-five percent between 1981 and 1989. All of the navy's U.S.–based logistic airlift squadrons, light attack helicopter squadrons, and combat search and rescue squadrons, over ninety-five percent of its control of shipping personnel, ninety-three percent of its cargo handling battalions, eighty-two percent of its ocean minesweepers, and sixty-five percent of its mobile construction battalions were in the Naval Reserve.[62]

The Air Force Reserve and the Air National Guard increased by thirty-two percent and almost eighteen percent respectively between 1981 and 1989. The integration of the air reserve components with the active air force was, in fact, a model for the other services. Most Air National Guard and Air Force Reserve units were aligned with their wartime "gaining commands" and trained with them on a regular basis in peacetime. In 1989, the Air Force Reserve and the Air National Guard provided a combined ninety-two percent of the U.S.–based strategic interceptor forces, fifty-nine percent of its tactical airlift and fifty-five percent of its tactical air support capability, a third of its tactical fighters, forty-six percent of its tactical reconnaissance, and almost thirty percent of its special operations capability.[63]

Because of its size and the nature of its wartime missions, the changes in force mix were felt most keenly within the army. At the end of 1987, more than half of the army's total combat forces and seventy-nine percent of its aggregate combat support and combat service support was in its reserve components.[64] By 1989—only a year before Desert Shield—a third of its eighteen active divisions included a roundout brigade and three other divisions included roundout battalions.

Despite obvious improvement in the early years of the decade in numbers and equipment, combat readiness remained a serious concern for both active and reserve forces. In 1984, the first Reagan administration could claim that the United States could fight an intensive war for up to thirty days, but it was estimated that several more years of buildup would be necessary before a major war effort could be sustained for as long as ninety days.[65]

As the buildup continued, there was also increasing recognition that while the nation's citizen warriors were being asked to assume unprecedented peacetime responsibilities in order to perform their increasingly important wartime missions, there were limits to what could be asked of them. In his January 1987 statement of the national security strategy, President Reagan injected this note of caution:

> On the manpower side, the Total Force Policy established in the early 1970s, places increased responsibilities on the reserve component of the U.S. forces. Today, fully fifty percent of the combat units for land warfare are in reserve components. Reserve units perform important missions and support functions on a daily basis. Their priority for manning, training, and equipment modernization is not based on their peacetime status as forces "in reserve," but on the basis of their direct integration into the nation's operational plans and missions. In many cases, the sequence of deployment in the event of conflict would place reserve component units side by side and sometimes ahead of active duty forces.
>
> To maximize the cost effectiveness of the Total Force Policy, we must continue to balance the combat and support elements of our active and reserve force structure, their costs, and attendant levels of risk. While there are specific mission areas in which the role of reserve components can be expanded, we must exercise care to avoid making demands on our personnel that would fundamentally alter the nature of service in the reserves.[66]

Nine months later, I informed the Senate in my confirmation hearing that my highest priority would be the improvement of the combat readiness of the reserve components.[67] I was already concerned about what appeared to me to be a tendency within the Department of Defense to assign reservists greater responsibilities without commensurate increases in resources. It is one thing to increase the numbers of reservists and to assign them new and increasingly demanding missions. It is something else to attract the right kinds of reservists, to assign them realistic and the most appropriate missions, and to ensure that they receive the kind of training and the other "tools" that will make them capable of performing those missions.

While measurable improvement had been made recently in units of the Selected Reserve, serious problems remained. At the commencement of 1987, some thirty percent of the Selected Reserve units were still rated not ready for combat. The primary factors limiting their readiness and overall capabilities were shortages of both modern operational equipment and fully trained manpower. Many of the readiness problems were the result of factors that are unique to reserve units and individual reservists. Fortunately, as Congress continued to "dedicate" appropriations for the procurement of reserve equipment only, and as additional equipment was "redistributed" from the active forces, equipment-related factors were becoming proportionately less of an obstacle.

Problems relating to the recruitment, training, and retention of personnel in certain skill areas remained. Shortages of skilled personnel in reserve medical units were particularly bad. That problem was already being characterized as a "war stopper." One study concluded that an additional 7,100 physicians, 31,000 nurses, and 3,000 enlisted health specialists were required to provide adequate care of the estimated casualties that would flow from a major conflict with the Warsaw Pact forces.[68]

Several initiatives were undertaken in a frontal attack on these remaining problems. First, a renewed emphasis was placed on the training of reserve leaders. In his Pulitzer Prize–winning memoir of the First World War, Gen. John J. "Blackjack" Pershing, the commander in chief of the American Expeditionary Forces, had written:

Without efficient leadership, the finest of troops may suffer defeat by inferior forces skillfully led.

In our Regular Army in time of peace, the system of promotion by seniority, instead of by selection, deprives many capable and energetic officers of the opportunity to command the larger units. . . . The same comment applies with equal or greater force to our National Guard, in which politics adds another factor, often adverse to efficiency to the higher grades.[69]

Fairly or unfairly, the same perception was held by too many almost six decades later. The art of war had become substantially more complex in that time. I was determined to do something about it.

Much greater attention was paid to the improvement of reserve training generally. Training courses were reconfigured to meet reserve component needs. Contract training with local colleges and vocational technical institutes was authorized. Greater use of battlefield simulators and interactive video systems was made at reserve centers and National Guard armories. Regional training sites were established so that units from different states could pool training resources. Reserve leaders were instructed to minimize administrative functions during weekend drills in order to concentrate on training.

Increased emphasis was also placed on combined arms, joint service, and overseas training. In 1980, 400 National Guard and reserve units had trained in countries other than the United States. In 1988, 3,536 reserve units, or cells, trained overseas. More than 82,000 reservists trained at locations in Germany, the Middle East, Norway, Korea, Central America, and elsewhere.[70]

The army began to rotate reserve heavy equipment maintenance companies to its equipment maintenance center in Kaiserslautern, Germany, to solve theater maintenance backlogs; the navy began to use selected reservists at its shore intermediate maintenance activities to provide intermediate level maintenance on ships in the Naval Reserve force; the National Guard sent guardsmen to its aviation classification repair activity depot in Brussels, Belgium; the Air Reserve components developed regional training centers similar to the army's.

Innovative improvements in training techniques and technology was the objective, but the use of common sense went far. Since the reserve components of the military services pursued separate training programs, I ensured that an army general officer who served as one of my deputies chaired a departmentwide committee for the regular exchange of information of training problems encountered by each reserve component, and how those problems were being resolved. I also assigned him to a special army task force charged with the preparation of an army reserve component training development action plan. I fought with success for the resources that were used to fund the implementation of the plan. I also made sure that training developments and innovations were a priority subject of my regular meetings with the chiefs of each of the reserve components.

Training was not the only focus of our attention. Several other actions were also taken. In an effort to obtain a more effective integration of the active and reserve forces, for example, I issued instructions that the DoD "first to fight, first to equip" policy was now to be interpreted as "first to fight, first to resource." The priority of equipment and training resources for active and reserve units was to be realigned to conform to the relative priorities of their wartime missions.

A new program to measure the readiness and availability of the members of the Individual Ready Reserve was also expanded. For years, the IRR had been little more than a paper organization. The current addresses of many of its members were unknown and no one really knew how many would show up in the event of a mobilization. Significant numbers of eligible IRR personnel were now being "screened," i.e., required to perform at least one day of active duty each year to permit evaluation of their retention of military skills, to determine what training would be needed to bring them to acceptable readiness levels, to confirm their location and general availability for mobilization, and to remind them of their remaining military obligation.

Because the active forces were continuing to deal with readiness problems of their own, I became increasingly convinced that we should look at both active and reserve readiness problems on a continuing basis and in a Total Force context. I thus recommended to

Secretary of Defense Frank Carlucci in 1988 that a conventional forces readiness committee be formed and chaired jointly by the two assistant secretaries of defense who were responsible for all active and reserve forces. He readily agreed, and the committee soon began work.

Mobilization procedures were also improved. Combat-ready reserve forces can contribute effectively to the nation's overall military power only if effective and reliable procedures are in place for transitioning those forces from a peacetime inactive status to a wartime active-duty status. As a practical matter, the mobilization of reserve units and individuals is a very complex process. Several different types of mobilization are possible, depending upon the nature and scope of the crisis at hand. Sound planning is essential to success. Flexibility, reliable methods for the notification of reservists of their orders to active duty, and the integration of mobilization execution actions with overall crisis management operations are some of the factors upon which the planning must be based.[71] On May 10, 1989, I published a detailed mobilization guide that defined relevant policies and described specific procedures for the mobilization of the Selected Reserve, the IRR, and the Standby Reserve.[72]

As readiness indicators continued to improve, I became convinced that a subtle but important new factor had begun to influence the quality of the reserve forces. Like the merging patterns of ripples on a quiet pond, the synergistic combination of serious wartime missions and peacetime responsibilities, new and challenging training opportunities, modern equipment, and what I liked to refer to as the "adventure element" began to attract to the reserve components people of unprecedented ability. As reservists began to be perceived as part of the "first team," the rewards of reserve service began to increase and outweigh the sacrifices inherent in that service.

Experienced military personnel completing their active service obligation began to seek reserve positions.[73] By 1988, almost fifty-nine percent of the reserve enlistees had prior military service. The quality of new recruits improved. More than ninety-two percent of the non-prior-service enlistees had a high school education or equivalent, and more than ninety-five percent of them tested in the three highest categories of the Armed Forces Qualification Test.[74] Retention was becoming less of a problem. Experienced reservists were no longer leaving military service at earlier rates, and many were joining the active forces. Competition for command and senior enlisted positions increased. The performance of reserve units in training exercises was noticeably better. A "can-do" attitude was increasingly evident in the ranks of reserve units I visited all over the world.

As the decade of the 1980s came to a close, the implementation in practice of the original theory of the Total Force Policy was thus rapidly improving. The improvement in the combat readiness of most reserve units was indisputable. Senator John Glenn, the chairman of the Senate Armed Services Subcommittee on Manpower and Personnel and a constructive critic of several Defense Department policies, agreed. At a June 9, 1989, hearing of the subcommittee, he informed me and the uniformed leaders of the reserve components that we could all be justly proud of the National Guard and reserve forces. "They are undoubtedly the best in the world. And you are to be congratulated for that."[75] I was under no illusion, however, that all serious challenges had been conquered.

I was now serving in the new Bush administration and under my third secretary of defense. My brief work with Cap Weinberger and the longer service with Frank Carlucci had been enormously rewarding. I had not expected to be asked to serve in the Bush administration since the new president had expressed a desire for a complete turnover of senior officials, a request which I considered healthy and which I supported.

When Dick Cheney, the new secretary of defense, informed me that he wished to recommend my continued service to President Bush, I had no idea of the demands that would be made on the nation's reservists during the next four years. I did suspect, however, that my rather unusual longevity was due in part to my habit of giving frank advice to the secretaries I served. I had never had a misplaced desire to be a blind cheerleader for everything that related to the reserve components. In my testimony at the June 1989 hearing, therefore, I asserted that while major gains had been achieved in the capability and readiness of the reserve forces, "Much remains to be done."[76]

One major problem remained. Despite the new reliance in theory on reservists for wartime missions; despite the clearly improving capabilities of each of the reserve components; and despite changes in the law in 1976 which made it easier for U.S. presidents to activate reservists for operational needs short of all-out war, no president had ever exercised the authority. Not a single reserve unit had been involuntarily called up and tested under the operational stresses of a real crisis. As recently as the summer of 1987, when minesweeping capability was needed in the Persian Gulf, the naval reservists who normally manned the minesweepers had been left behind. Strong conventional wisdom continued to hold that political restraints would prevent the use of the nation's citizen warriors in all but the most dire situations.

Little could anyone predict just how wrong the conventional wisdom was and how soon the first test would come.

CHAPTER VIII
First Steps in a New Era

"We are entering a new era: The defense strategy and military structure needed to ensure peace can and must be different."

—*President George Bush,*
Aspen, Colorado, August 2, 1990

It was expected that the hearing that morning of June 9, 1989, would be routine. I would appear with the uniformed leaders of the reserve components before the Senate Armed Services Committee's Subcommittee on Manpower and Personnel. My testimony would be in support of the first defense budget proposal of President Bush. We were only six months into the new administration, but as one of two assistant secretary holdovers from the Reagan administration, I was familiar with the issues likely to be discussed.

I knew that I would arrive at the hearing a few minutes late. I had an early morning breakfast meeting with Sen. Sam Nunn and others in his office. The discussion would center on the new role of the armed forces in what the inflated political rhetoric of the day was already referring to as the "drug war." Bill Bennett, the administration's new "drug czar" would be there, along with several senators, and the military commanders in chief of the Southern Command and the Special Operations Command. I had only recently been asked by the new secretary of defense, Dick Cheney, to assume double duty as the head of the new Pentagon Office of Drug Enforcement Policy and Support. It was important that I be at the meeting.

Meanwhile, the hearing had started on time. If I had been present to hear the opening remarks by the chairman, Senator Glenn, I could have predicted his comments at the conclusion of the hearing. He noted that in the sixteen years that the Total Force Policy had been in effect, no singular authoritative study of the policy had been conducted. While everyone in the Defense Department seemed to have some responsibility for it, no single official had "the whole on this assignment of missions to different services and the missions between the regulars and the reserves."[1] Concluding that an assessment of the Total Force active/reserve mix was overdue, he indicated that he would try to force one, by including language to that effect in the Defense Authorization Bill for fiscal year 1990. Although somewhat surprised, I welcomed the development. Anything that focused light on the procedures employed by the military services to assign missions to active or reserve units seemed desirable. A new study might even stimulate fresh approaches to force planning within each service.

Few people who attended the June 9 hearing had any idea just how soon, and how fundamentally, events taking place elsewhere would affect decisions on the future size and shape of American military forces. In a speech the following month, Deputy Secretary of State Lawrence Eagleburger would reflect with some nostalgia that for all its risks and uncertainties, "the Cold War was characterized by a remarkably stable and predictable set of relationships among the great powers."[2] That predictability had not required much in the way of imagination and innovation in the planning of military force structure and force mix.

The first breezes of the later storm winds of change, however, could already be felt. Gorbachev's perestroika and glasnost were subjects of intense public speculation and discussion. Only a month earlier he had informed Secretary of State James Baker in Moscow that reductions in the size of the Soviet armed forces were a crucial part of perestroika. He had added that those reductions would be easier for Soviet military leaders to accept if they were matched by the Americans.[3]

On May 12, the new president had declared in a commencement speech that it was time to move beyond a foreign policy of containment to "a new policy for the 1990s—one that recognizes the full scope of the change taking place around the world."[4] At a NATO summit at the end of May, Bush had proposed the completion of significant mutual conventional force reductions in Europe by 1992 or 1993.

As the fall of 1989 turned to winter, both the worldwide political changes and our own movement toward force reductions were gaining momentum. On August 25, the Solidarity movement gained power in Poland, becoming the eastern bloc's first non-Communist government. On November 9, the East German government opened the Berlin Wall.[5] The demolition of the wall began the next day.

The pace of the political changes inevitably resulted in some uncertainty in the West about how to respond. Despite previous rhetoric in support of German unification, for example, some NATO allies were now apprehensive about the idea. Different views about the priority that still needed to be given to defense spending were also emerging. On November 20, Cheney informed his senior political staff that given the national mood, the changes in Europe, and the pressures of the budget deficit, we would have to change the culture of the Pentagon's budget planning and prepare a "more realistic" budget for each year of the five-year planning cycle. Only four days later, Prime Minister Thatcher had argued to the president at Camp David that defense spending should not be cut because there would always remain the unknown threat which must be guarded against.[6]

On December 17, the proposed defense budget for fiscal year 1991 was submitted to the president. It called for $295 billion in spending authority, a reduction of $22 billion from the plan the president had approved only the previous April.[7] The "blue top" Pentagon news release that later announced the budget request described it as one that represented the first steps in responding to changes in Eastern Europe and the Soviet Union, as well as tighter budget constraints.[8] It identified as a budget priority the continuation of efforts "to stress mobilization preparedness by adequately supporting reserve forces." It did not, however, involve any change in the defense strategy. Calling it "the worst possible time to contemplate changes in defense strategy," Cheney asserted broadly that for decades we had had a "bipartisan strategy of strong partnerships with our allies and flexible response" and that adjustments to that strategy were all that was necessary.[9]

In the small hours of December 20, and less than three days after we had submitted the proposed budget to the White House, 26,000 American troops stormed military and civilian targets in Panama as

Operation Just Cause began. On December 25 the Romanian Stalinist dictator, Nicolae Ceausescu, and his wife were executed in one of the bloodiest of the European upheavals. On December 29, Václav Havel, the playwright and former leading opponent of communism in Czechoslovakia, was elected his country's president. At eight fifty P.M. on January 3, 1990, former Panamanian dictator General Manuel Antonio Noriega walked to the iron gate of the Vatican Embassy in Panama City and surrendered himself to American soldiers.

On its face, Section 1101 of the National Defense Authorization Act for fiscal year 1990 seemed straightforward enough. The secretary of defense was to convene a study group to study the effectiveness of the total force policy, the force structure of the active and reserve components, and the assignment of missions within and between the two components. The study group was directed to consider several specific issues, including the "optimal structure of military forces required to meet the threat. . . ." The group was then to make recommendations to the secretary for the improvement of those policies and practices. An interim report of the study was due to Congress no later than September 15, 1990. The final report was due by December 31.

The apparently achromatic words of Section 1101 masked several brewing political problems. I knew from conversations with individual members of the Senate and House that Congress did not speak with one voice on the question of what the study was supposed to accomplish. Some hoped for a recommendation of a force structure and force mix that had a rational, quantitative, and almost mechanistic basis; that was totally free of political bias and almost free of value judgments; and that would, as a result of its obvious merit, be able to command broad congressional support. Others were merely searching for an intellectual framework that would provide cover as they worked toward a force structure/mix that met the needs of their personal political agendas.

Complex decisions on the design of a nation's armed forces, however, inevitably involve judgment. No analytical process can eliminate that. There is no mathematical formula that will guarantee a perfect size, shape, or mix of military forces if only the information upon which the formula is based is correct. The exercise of judgment in making the Total Force Policy Study Group's recommendations to the secretary of defense would necessarily require choices among competing interests.

There were additional obstacles. Faced with budget reductions for the foreseeable future, each military service could be expected to pull out all stops to obtain the largest possible slice of a much smaller pie. And as a result of the new authority given the chairman of the Joint Chiefs of Staff by the Goldwater-Nichols legislation, the Joint Staff was already pursuing its own agenda with aggressiveness.

Other problems had the potential to be even more serious. As a matter of policy and practice, instituted by Cap Weinberger, fundamental policy decisions on the size and shape of the armed forces as well as other major decisions regarding the allocation of the department's resources had been made by the secretary of defense within the framework of the department's planning, programming, and budgeting system (PPBS). The PPBS provided a formal analytical framework for the conduct of biennial reviews of force structure and force mix. Cost-benefit analyses and vigorous debate among members of the Defense Planning and Resources Board (DPRB)[10] were established and effective mechanisms for evaluating alternatives. The DPRB also focused on a range of factors affecting overall military capability that was much broader than force structure and force mix.

I was concerned that if the recommendation of the DPRB and the Total Force Policy Study Group should differ markedly and the secretary and the president should reject the latter's advice, serious institutional and partisan problems could arise between an executive branch of government under a new Republican president and a legislative branch in which both houses of Congress were controlled by Democrats. Moreover, it was unclear how any change in our national security strategy or military strategy might affect the work of the study group. The rapidity of political change in Europe was likely to force a substantial change in our strategy relatively soon, notwithstanding Cheney's recent comments to the contrary.[11]

Despite my concern about these and other similar matters, I was generally enthusiastic about the study. From two years of experience in DRB/DPRB and other policy meetings, I knew that far too many internal force structure/mix decisions were being made without reference to an overarching manpower policy that was itself traceable to a clear military strategy. The idea of centralized policy formulation by the secretary of defense and decentralized implementation by the military services was sound, but in the absence of a clear strategy and clear planning principles, and as reduced defense budgets became more likely, too much lip service was being paid to the Total Force Policy. Force planners within each service needed to engage in a more rigorous arm's-length analysis of future military requirements and realistic manpower options. Perhaps the study would push the Department of Defense in that direction.

I was personally very comfortable with the anticipated clash of policy ideas and the resolution of policy disputes on the basis of evidence and merit. Prior to joining the government, I had earned my living in courtrooms around the country doing similar work. I recognized, of course, that the work of the study group would be performed in a much different forum. The rules of procedure would be considerably less certain. The judges would include every political and military leader who disagreed with the conclusions of the study. Much was at stake, and we could expect fierce opposition to whatever we did.

In a December 26, 1989, memorandum to senior Defense officials setting out the charter for the establishment of a study group, Cheney declared that the study was a high priority of the department. Chris Jehn, the assistant secretary of defense for force management and personnel and the official nominally responsible for Total Force oversight, was appointed the chairman of the group. I was appointed vice chairman. The twenty-four-member study group was to include four other assistant secretaries of defense, the senior manpower officials of each military service, the department's general counsel, and active and reserve, flag and general officers. The study group would be supported by a thirty-member civilian and military staff.

Work began promptly and the first of some twenty formal meetings was held on February 2 with Cheney and Colin Powell in attendance. Over the course of the next several weeks, three colloquia were hosted to obtain the opinions and recommendations of outside defense experts, members of Congress, former senior civilian and military officials, the commanders in chief of the operational commands, and representatives of important public or private policy groups.[12] The work of the study group was supplemented by technical conferences that focused on costing methodologies and related matters.

From the beginning, Chris Jehn and I reminded Congress that the work of the Total Force Policy Study Group would be treated as but one part of the overall budgeting and programming activities of the Department of Defense. We stated clearly that the defense budget which the president submitted to Congress in January 1991 would reflect only those recommendations of the study group that were approved by the secretary of defense. Few people were listening. With building political pressure in Congress to reduce military spending drastically and to use the resulting "peace dividends" for domestic projects, congressional leaders were eagerly looking for an intellectual rationale to justify the reductions.

In Europe and elsewhere, political upheaval was continuing. On February 26, Daniel Ortega and his Sandinista National Liberation Front were defeated in a stunning election in Nicaragua. On March 11, the Lithuanian parliament declared independence from the Soviets. Gorbachev denounced the move as "illegitimate and invalid." On March 18, the first free elections were held in East Germany. On May 4, the Latvian Parliament declared independence.

By early May, the work of the study group was well along. It was becoming increasingly clear, however, that the level of misunderstanding of the Total Force Policy within the Department of Defense and the reluctance to implement it in a way that would permit the policy to reach its full potential was greater than anyone had realized. I knew that the level of misunderstanding within the Congress was even greater. Much of the confusion was simply the result of the absence of detailed written policy direction. The vacuum encouraged different interpretations of the policy among officials with varying and often competing agendas and responsibilities. Some of the confusion resulted from a lack of enforcement and from the unwillingness of dissidents to apply the policy in good faith.

Unanimity among study group members on almost any issue was going to be impossible. Even a clear consensus on the group's ultimate recommendations was unlikely. The representatives of the various constituent groups were simply incapable of viewing contentious issues other than through the prisms of their own objectives and experience. Bold, innovative ideas would not be forthcoming. The group's conclusions were certain to go no further than the lowest common denominator of agreement. I decided to lay down some markers.

A critical series of meetings of the DPRB was scheduled to commence on May 14 to review the program objective memoranda (POMs) of the military services.[13] Perhaps the programming and budgeting process and the work of the study group could be influenced and channeled by a preemptive shot across the bow of the Total Force debate.

In preparation for my scheduled testimony before the Senate Armed Services Committee on May 10, I prepared a thirty-eight-page written statement that would be submitted to the committee in advance for the record. Pentagon rules required policy statements by senior officials to be screened and cleared in advance to ensure policy constancy. Because they presented new and relatively provocative ideas, I was certain that two sections of the statement would draw fire from several quarters within the department. To my great surprise, they did not.[14]

The first section, entitled "Understanding the Total Force Policy," was designed to limit the scope of the Total Force debate. I hoped to dispel some of the more extreme arguments being made for and against the idea of greater reliance upon the reserve components. I noted that the Total Force Policy was never intended to make active, career soldiers and reserve soldiers fungible items or mirror images of each other, and that it was unrealistic to try to make every Reserve unit the absolute equal in terms of readiness and capability of the best active units. Rather, I asserted, the objective is to integrate the capabilities and strengths of active and reserve units in the most cost-effective manner, i.e., one that provides the most military capability and flexibility possible within the limitations of the budget.

I tried to lay to rest any illusion that the Total Force Policy required across-the-board cuts in the active forces or increased reliance on all reserve units. A balanced analysis, I argued, must start with a focus on *particular missions.* Some missions, which require a high surge of activity in wartime or in other times of crisis but comparatively low activity in peacetime, are obviously ideal for reservists. Others, such as those which require long periods of deployment in peacetime, are unsuitable. Yet others might be reasonably assigned to either active or reserve units.

I also attempted to make it clear that expectations for the results of the Total Force Policy study were unreasonably high. All force structure and force mix questions could not be answered so quickly. The world geopolitical situation was simply too fluid and dynamic for that. It would first be necessary to establish a new vision of the future and a coherent military strategy for implementing that vision.

I was hopeful, however, that certain "neutral" planning principles might be developed for future use. I proposed several. The one that would later attract the most attention was simple and rather obvious:

> If significant cost savings can be achieved by a transfer of force structure to a reserve component (for the performance of a particular mission), a working presumption should be established that the transfer should be made. The presumption can then be rebutted by the demonstration of a sound military reason why the transfer should not be made.[15]

This "rebuttable presumption" principle, as well as other force mix planning principles I suggested, was soon eclipsed by the introduction of a new concept: "Base Force."

The first session of the DPRB meetings scheduled for the week of May 14, 1990, started promptly on Monday morning at eight A.M. in Room 3E-928, Secretary Cheney's small conference room. Each of the military services was prepared to present its POM for review. The civilian officials present had been warned by Cheney at a senior staff meeting the previous week that the result of the work had to be something "more significant than a mouse" or we could expect to be hammered on the Hill. Because of the importance of the meetings and the fact that the customary defense planning guidance (DPG) was long overdue, there was greater than normal interest in the presentations expected of Paul Wolfowitz, the undersecretary of defense for policy and the official responsible for the DPG.[16]

As the threat of armed conflict with forces of the Warsaw Pact continued to decline, speculation had been mounting—especially within a Congress eager to shift resources from defense to domestic programs—that the number of active forces would be reduced substantially and that the less expensive reserve components would assume even greater responsibilities. In a March 22 letter signed by fifty senators who formed an ad hoc group called the "national guard caucus," Cheney had been urged to freeze the reserve force structure until the future role of the reserve components could be determined. In his second floor speech on the defense budgets on March 29, Sen. Sam Nunn had declared that since we had entered a "period of increased warning time and fiscal austerity, we must conduct a fundamental reexamination of the use of reserves in the military services."[17]

In his March 1990 *Report on the National Security Strategy of the United States,* President Bush had also encouraged the idea. After noting that the reserve forces are generally less expensive to maintain than their active counterparts, the strategy report declared that "as we adjust force structures, retaining reserve units is one alternative for reducing costs while still hedging against uncertainties. It is an alternative we must thoroughly explore, especially as we better understand the amount of warning we can expect for a major conflict."[18] Colin Powell, whose enormous capabilities were increasingly apparent, and who now had several months of experience as the new chairman of the Joint Chiefs of Staff, had further fueled the speculation in a recent interview. He had called for an in-depth review of personnel levels, military strategy, and operational doctrine—down to the wording of each field manual—that could result in a force size reduction of as much as twenty to twenty-five percent.[19]

I was frankly less interested in the absolute numbers of the ultimate active/reserve mix of forces than I was in the rigor and quality of the analysis that would be used to evaluate force mix options and guide decisions. If we critically challenged our own assumptions and applied our force planning methodologies in an even-handed, "honest broker" manner, our decisions were likely to be "the right thing to do." I was also confident that our ability to sell to Congress our own judgment of the most appropriate size and shape of the armed forces of the future would to a great degree be determined by the perception that our recommendations were informed, balanced, well reasoned, and not based on "false intellectualism."[20]

It was immediately obvious that Wolfowitz and Powell had been working energetically and quietly to develop a coordinated approach, not only on the kinds of broad strategic issues that normally appeared in the defense planning guidance, but also on military manpower issues that by tradition and practice had been the prerogative of the military departments. Subtly but definitely, Powell was asserting his new authority under the Goldwater-Nichols legislation.[21] He was also shrewdly injecting himself into security policy matters historically decided by the secretary of state and the secretary of defense and, in the process, confirming his growing reputation as a highly competent "political general."[22]

Assuming a fundamentally different threat environment as a result of an expected greater warning time of a conflict in Europe, Powell and Wolfowitz rejected any major shift from active to reserve forces and suggested substantial cuts in both. Asserting that geopolitical changes were already taking place more rapidly than our ability to adjust the structure of our forces, they argued that we should not base our force planning on specific threats, but rather that we should develop flexible, capability-based forces that could be rapidly deployed to any of a number of "generic" major regional contingencies and be capable of fighting two of them "nearly simultaneously." Since they would no longer be required for a global war in Europe, reserve forces, especially reserve ground forces, could be consigned to a limited reenforcement role and would not be involved in crisis response unless military force was required in two different regions of the world. Many reserve units would be nothing more than cadre or skeletal, equipment-holding units. In the event of an unexpected global confrontation, large numbers of active and reserve troops could be "reconstituted."

Powell and Wolfowitz then laid out a broad blueprint for a "Base Force," defined to be that force structure below which the nation could not go "if we are to retain superpower status."[23] The Base Force, they argued, required large numbers of forward-deployed troops in Europe and South Korea to establish a credible American "presence" in those areas of potential conflict. It also required mobility forces that could be deployed to contingency areas. In round numbers, their proposed force would include twelve active and eight army guard/reserve divisions; 450 navy ships, including twelve aircraft carriers; three active Marine Corps division/wing teams; sixteen active and twelve reserve air force tactical fighter wings and modernized airlift capability in the air force; and undefined numbers of special operations forces. The number of active personnel would be reduced from 2.1 million to 1.6 million and the number of guardsmen/reservists from 1.56 million to 898,000.

In an apparent effort to limit internal debate on the proposal, Powell suggested that the DPRB adopt the Base Force proposal and give "guidance" along this line to Chris Jehn and to me in connection with the Total Force Policy study. While the suggestion went nowhere, it reminded me with some amusement of my first formal meeting with Powell the previous year. Having only recently left the White House as President Reagan's national security advisor, then Lieutenant General Powell was awaiting promotion and assignment as the commander in chief of the army's Forces Command, FORSCOM, where he would control both active and reserve army units and prepare them for war. He had requested a "courtesy call" with me. Although all my previous military experience had involved the navy, and although I had served as assistant secretary for less than two years and had never previously worked in Washington, this master of Washington's political wars sat in my office solemnly taking notes on my pearls of wisdom involving army force structure issues. Much had happened since that first meeting.

I didn't doubt the sincerity of the Base Force proposal or the amount of effort that went into its preparation. It at least had a rationale. But I remained skeptical. So did others, including Cheney. The amount of military capability required to retain "superpower" status was an awfully fuzzy standard. The proposal was also based upon what I thought to be a rather optimistic view of the future. It assumed, for example, that the Conventional Forces in Europe

(CFE) Treaty would be entered into and that as a consequence, Soviet conventional forces would be reduced by fifty percent as soon as 1994. In the absence of one or more specific threats against which the recommendation could be gauged, it would probably be difficult to defend. Reasonable judgments could and would vary widely on what kind of and how much military capability was required for threats that were increasingly difficult to define. The proposal also lacked a principled rationale for the magnitude of the recommended cuts in the reserve forces.

As the DPRB meetings continued through the first week and the military services presented their programmatic responses to the inevitably smaller defense budgets, Cheney declared that no part of the budget was immune from cuts, and that everything was on the table. I was hopeful that at least one of the military services would suggest a new way of looking at the tension between our security needs and our likely resources. Their presentations, however, troubled me in several ways.

First, it was difficult to see just how the program proposals related to the changing threat environment. Various of the suggested cuts in force structure lacked persuasive logic and appeared to be nothing more than a response to new fiscal constraints. It was important, as Sen. Sam Nunn would later say, that we not go into the future with nothing more than a smaller version of our Cold War forces. Cheney shared this concern and at one time declared with some frustration that he needed to "understand the dynamics of why we're doing what we're doing in light of the reduced threat, earlier warning times, etc." There also seemed to be even greater than usual reluctance to search for new uses of the less expensive reserve components.

A second concern, which may have explained the first, was the fact that many of the participants in the DPRB discussions appeared to have an undifferentiated view of reservists, as if all National Guard and reserve units were of equal quality and importance. There was no obvious understanding of the opportunities that certain types of reserve units presented. At one point in the presentation of the navy's POM, I became involved in a particularly heated discussion with Secretary of the Navy Larry Garrett and the highly competent chief of naval operations, Adm. Carl Trost, over the navy's lack of imagination in the use of reservists aboard the gas-turbine-powered guided missile frigates of the Perry class, and the older Knox class frigates. At another point, Cheney had to bluntly ask one service chief, "How should we use reserves in FY 1997 versus FY 1989?" On yet another occasion, he found it necessary to ask, "What's the philosophy on the use of your reserve component?"

The service recommendations also wandered at times outside the limits of political reality. I had no doubt that we should develop a force structure/mix based upon the best professional military judgment available, and not upon politics. But since Congress would have the last word, we were wasting time discussing certain proposals that were of doubtful merit in the first place, and that had no prospect of becoming law. While it could be argued that Powell's Base Force proposal reflected too much sensitivity to the politics of force planning, the risk that Congress would reject out of hand any recommendations that failed to meet threshold tests of political credibility was real. In such circumstances, we could expect legislative mandates far less to our liking.

Something needed to be done to sharpen the force mix debate. Despite the consensus in the DPRB that the threat of a major war was much less than it had been a year earlier; that constrained defense budgets would be a fact of life for the short and intermediate term; that reserve forces were less expensive than active forces; and that we now had the most capable reserve forces in the peacetime history of the nation, the proposed Base Force and the service POMs would contract, not expand, reliance on the reserve components. The logic advanced for doing so was not persuasive to me.

On the morning of May 16, I sent a memorandum to Don Atwood, the deputy secretary, recommending that I make a special presentation to the DPRB on the historical use and current capabilities of each of the seven reserve components. The recommendation was instantly accepted.[24] I hoped that the presentation could be made within the next few days, and I prepared accordingly. It was not to be.

As May turned into June and July, intense work continued within both the DPRB and the Total Force Policy Study Group. The issues debated ranged from strategic mobility to medical readiness. The work of the study group was not performed in isolation within the Pentagon. Informal consultations with Congress on the progress of the work were continuing, and from time to time the work was the subject of inquiry at formal hearings. On June 22, a member of the National Security Council staff also called my office from the White House to request a paper on the ways in which reserve forces could be used "as tools of American security and policy objectives."

On July 6, in a "London declaration," President Bush and fifteen other NATO leaders approved a new political and military strategy in response to the sweeping changes in Europe. Under the new doctrine, NATO would "field smaller and restructured active forces" and rely more heavily on reserve units. Four days later, Chris Jehn and I were asked to come to the White House to discuss the study of the Total Force Policy with a senior member of the National Security Council staff. During the course of the meeting, we learned that Cheney, Powell, and Wolfowitz had met recently and privately with the president and Brent Scowcroft, his national security advisor, to discuss significant cuts in the force structure. The meeting had not appeared on the president's published schedule. This suggested, of course, that Cheney and the president were nearing a decision on the future size if not the shape of the armed forces, a decision that would be made outside the glare of attention usually given to DPRB deliberations.

On the morning of Monday, July 16, the DPRB finally turned its full attention to the reserve components. Each member of the Joint Chiefs of Staff was again present in Cheney's small conference room. The civilian officials present included Cheney, Atwood, the service secretaries, the two under secretaries of defense, and some of the assistant secretaries.

I opened my presentation by making two points. First, that each reserve component was different and had unique capabilities and weaknesses. Second, that while I did not advocate any across-the-board shifting of missions to reserve forces, the services had to recognize that cost savings and other opportunities were available through the selective use of certain kinds of reserve units for certain kinds of specific missions—if they were willing to leave the "business as usual" approach to force planning. In that context, I referred to the president's recent statement of the national security strategy and its emphasis on exploring the alternative of greater reliance upon reserve units.

At the risk of offending everyone present, I also felt it necessary to refer to an elemental fact sometimes forgotten within the most senior circles of the Pentagon. Nowhere, I noted, could the terms "Department of Defense" or "Joint Chiefs of Staff" be found within the text of the United States Constitution. Conspicuously prominent in Article I, Section 8 of the Constitution, however, is the following provision:

> The Congress shall have power to . . . provide for the common defense . . . [and] . . . To raise and support armies . . . To maintain a Navy . . . To provide for organizing, arming and disciplining the militia, and for governing such part of them as may be employed in the service of the United States. . . .

For the entire morning, the military leadership of the United States focused exclusively on the nation's citizen warriors. We discussed the legislative, executive policy, and operational history of each reserve component; how each had been used in the nation's armed conflicts; the kinds of peacetime missions each was currently performing and the wartime missions each was currently assigned; the readiness condition of each component; the kinds of missions that offered new opportunities for the use of reserve units; the factors that limited greater reliance on certain other kinds of reserve forces; the relative costs of each component; the factors that had contributed to what Colin Powell characterized as the "massive improvements" in the quality of the reserve components since 1980; the implementation to date of the Total Force Policy; and the effect of each military service's POM on its reserve component.

Many of the questions asked and comments made would soon have far more relevancy than the participants realized at the time. Cheney asked me to confirm that the nation had not called on the reserves, except on a volunteer basis, since 1968. That question was immediately followed with another: "What is the level of expectation of a call-up on the part of reservists?" Secretary of the Air Force Don Rice observed that we couldn't commence a deployment of any size without using the air reserve components for airlift missions. The commandant of the Marine Corps, Gen. Al Gray, made favorable comments about the mobilization readiness condition of the Marine Corps Reserve.

As I stood at the podium responding to questions and listening to the comments of others, I was delighted with the vigor and quality of the give-and-take. I doubted that such a comprehensive discussion of all of the reserve components had ever taken place with participants of this level of authority. The discussion ranged from broad topics like the use of reservists in Panama seven months earlier, to the percentage of officers in each component who had prior active duty experience. The review was certainly timely. That same day, the Soviet Union withdrew its objection to a united Germany remaining in NATO and it further agreed to withdraw 360,000 Soviet troops from East Germany within three to four years.

The DPRB discussion of the reserve components was resumed the next morning. Chris Jehn and I presented a major issue paper that focused on the future active/reserve mix of forces. We presented five force structure options, including the POM submissions, the Base Force alternative, and three additional alternatives that contained increasing degrees of reliance upon reserve elements. We addressed the capabilities and relative costs of each of the force mix alternatives. Once again the presentation was punctuated with vigorous debate on the cost and likely effectiveness of each alternative. Whatever direction the force structure/mix debate took, I could at least be confident that Cheney's eventual recommendation to the president on the most appropriate mix of forces would be an informed one. It would also need to be politically persuasive. On July 31, the House Armed Services Committee approved a defense budget for fiscal year 1991 that was $25 billion less than the president had requested six months earlier.

The complexities of dealing with the rapidly changing global security environment and designing armed forces for an ambiguous future did not, of course, slow work taking place in the Pentagon in many other areas of national security. Negotiations were continuing on the Conventional Armed Forces in Europe (CFE) and Strategic Arms Reductions Talks (START). Work was also under way on the Strategic Defense Initiative (SDI), the recommendations of the July 1989 Defense Management Report, and in many other critical areas.

A less conventional new mission for the Department of Defense was requiring a great deal of attention and large amounts of my personal time. The mission had significant manpower and other resource implications. A year had now passed since I had been asked by Cheney to accept a major task unrelated to my work as the assistant secretary for reserve affairs—the leadership of the new counterdrug mission of the department.

Title XI of the fiscal year 1989 National Defense Authorization Act gave the Defense Department major new counterdrug responsibilities. First, the department was directed to serve as the single lead agency of the federal government for the "detection and monitoring of the aerial and maritime transit of illegal drugs into the United States." Second, the legislation required that the secretary of defense integrate into an "effective communications network" the "command, control, communications and technical intelligence assets of the United States that are dedicated to the interdiction of illegal drugs." Finally, the act provided for an enhanced role for the National Guard, under the direction of state governors, to support state drug interdiction and law enforcement operations.

The counterdrug missions had not been welcomed by many civilian or uniformed military leaders.[25] Part of the general objection was the result of a January 1988 Rand Corporation study.[26] The study had concluded that the military services should not be the primary drug interdiction agencies and that a major increase in military support was unlikely to significantly increase the efficacy of drug interdiction.[27] There was also concern that the uncontrolled (by the Pentagon) use by state governors of part-time National Guard personnel for the new mission would greatly exacerbate readiness problems associated with federal missions. Some military leaders also worried about the danger of exposing troops to bribes and the other corrupting influences of the drug trade. On a broader plane, there was general nervousness about the assignment of a new, complex mission, when the defense budget was already being drastically cut.

By the summer of 1990, however, the department's implementation of the new mission was well underway. The previous December, the president had announced his first National Drug Control Strategy.[28] Thirteen days later, Cheney had declared that because the illicit traffic of drugs posed a direct threat to the sovereignty and security of the country, the detection and countering of the production, trafficking, and use of illegal drugs would henceforth be a "high priority national security mission" of the Department of Defense.[29] In a Pentagon press conference on March 9, 1990, I had announced the counterdrug plans of the commanders in chief of certain of the unified and specified commands. In May and June the subject of the new mission was incorporated into the deliberations of the DPRB and war gaming of the counterdrug campaign began.

Plans were also being laid for an aggressive series of detection and monitoring activities in international waters and air space off the coast of South America.[30] The idea was to greatly increase the number of navy ships and airborne early warning and intercepter aircraft in the area for a period of time in an effort to significantly interrupt drug-trafficking patterns and to establish a database for the conduct of future counterdrug operations. On June 13, I explained the proposed "enhanced interdiction operation" in a meeting of the National Security Council deputies at the White House. Sixteen days later, the president approved the operation. The final coordination of the several federal departments and agencies involved took place on July 30 in the Norfolk, Virginia, command center of Adm. Bud Edney, the commander in chief of the Atlantic Command and one of the most impressive military professionals I have ever met. On August 1, I joined Cheney in the "tank," the Joint Chiefs of Staff conference room, for a final operational briefing.[31] An hour later I went to the White House Situation Room to brief Vice President Quayle, who was preparing to leave on a trip to Colombia, Bolivia, and Peru. The operation would commence on August 15.

The plan was to have the president deliver a major address in Aspen, Colorado, on the occasion of the fortieth anniversary of the Aspen Institute. In his remarks, the president would outline in broad terms his decision the previous day on a military force structure for the future,[32] a structure designed for regional contingencies rather than global conflict. Details would follow in January when he submitted his proposed defense budget for fiscal year 1992 to Congress. The plan also called for Cheney and Powell to simultaneously brief the concept to the chairmen and ranking members of congressional committees. Press briefings and additional speeches would follow, all designed to lay the groundwork for the debate that would inevitably follow the president's proposal. The president's initial speech was scheduled for August 2. The plan did not anticipate that on the same day, Iraq would invade Kuwait.

Had it not conflicted with headlines describing the invasion, the president's Aspen speech would have received much greater attention. Declaring that by 1995 the nation's security needs could be met by an active force twenty-five percent smaller than the one then in existence, he noted that in the restructured forces, reserves would be important, but in new ways. "The need to be prepared for a massive, short-term mobilization has diminished. We can now adjust the size, structure, and readiness of our reserve forces, to help us deal with the more likely challenges we will face."

The dynamics of the force structure debate, however, had suddenly, if only temporarily, changed. The front-page article in the August 6 edition of the *Los Angeles Times* described the change: "In a single stroke, Saddam Hussein's foray of tanks and troops has blunted the momentum in Congress toward making deep cuts in the American military establishment and has redrawn the debate about the shape and size of the nation's future military forces."[33] Unfortunately, the potential for political conflict on force structure/mix issues remained. Even while the work of the DPRB and the Total Force Policy Study Group was continuing, the Defense Authorization Act that became effective in October ordered a twenty-two-percent reduction in active forces over a five-year period. Without waiting for the administration's recommendation, Congress had already made major force cuts and effectively mandated a shift to a reinforcement strategy more heavily dependent upon reserve forces, and away from a strategy of forward deployment that required larger numbers of active units.

The remaining months of 1990 were tinged with double irony. As we worked to shape and reduce the size of the force that would be included in the president's January defense budget and made plans to bring troops home from Europe, we were simultaneously building a large military force in Saudi Arabia. Twenty days after his Aspen speech, the president authorized the first involuntary call-up of reserve forces for a foreign crisis since 1968. By the end of the year, 325,000 active and reserve military personnel were already in the Middle East and more were on the way. And, as the administration worked to design a post–Cold War military structure, there were haunting reminders that despite a continuing series of positive developments, some Cold War concerns could not be quickly erased.

Some of the news was good, very good. On October 3, East and West Germany were officially united as the Federal Republic of Germany. On November 9, 1990, the Soviet Union signed a nonaggression pact with Germany. On November 19, the U.S. president and Gorbachev signed the CFE Treaty in Paris.[34] The Soviets had already committed to a total withdrawal of their military units from Czechoslovakia and Hungary in 1991 and from the eastern areas of Germany in 1994.

At the same time, some news was discouraging. There were ominous signs of the increased strength of conservative and reactionary forces in Moscow. The first steps of a Soviet crackdown in the Baltic republics of Latvia, Lithuania, and Estonia were taken.[35] And after delivering a warning of a new dictatorship in the Soviet Union, Eduard Shevardnadze resigned as its foreign minister on December 20.

In September and October, the administration and Congress engaged in intense negotiations on a deficit-reduction package. The eventual agreement locked in reductions in defense expenditures for a five-year period. Budget issues and the imminent prospect of a major armed conflict thousands of miles away were now occupying most of the attention of senior Pentagon officials. On November 8, the president announced that he was sending an additional 200,000 U.S. troops to the Persian Gulf to give the coalition an "offensive military option."[36] On November 29, the United Nations Security Council passed a resolution authorizing member states to use "all necessary means . . . to restore international peace and security" in the Gulf area. Iraq was given a deadline of January 15 to comply with previous U.N. resolutions, including those requiring it to withdraw from Kuwait.

Under the circumstances, and until matters cleared, we were not interested in expanding the current responsibilities of the Department of Defense. The "drug war" was a case in point. Because of our success to date, Bill Bennett and other representatives of the White House Office of National Drug Control Policy had repeatedly suggested that the armed forces take even more of a lead role in counterdrug enforcement. On November 16, I presented their latest proposal to Cheney and recommended that at least for the time being, it be rejected. Colin Powell agreed. The idea died instantly.

It was now clear that the military services would not be advancing bold new force structure/mix alternatives to that included in the Base Force plan,[37] even though resentment among the services over the new influence of Powell and the Joint Staff in the budget planning process was also increasing. Part of the resentment had a parochial basis since future missions and funding were at stake, but there was little doubt that the Joint Staff had briskly, sometimes crudely, and often with arrogance, asserted the new authority of the chairman and closely guarded the details of the Base Force proposal. Unfortunately, the quality of the Joint Staff's work in several manpower areas was not high. This added to the tension. Cheney seemed wary of the intramural rivalries and strongly inclined to accept Powell's recommendations.

Meanwhile, skirmishes were continuing within the Total Force Policy Study Group. Some of the group's participants were still hoping that the final report of its work would reflect the results of votes by the participants on various force structure and force mix options. During the early months of the study, I, too, had contemplated the possibility of some form of voting mechanism. Secretary Cheney could then consider the recommendations of the study group in the context of the DPRB deliberations and select the best elements of each. Deputy Secretary Don Atwood didn't like that idea at all. A warm, likable former senior executive with General Motors Corporation, Don was apparently offended by the potential for confusion that such a process offered. He did not want the study group's views to compete with decisions that Cheney was making as part of the department's regular planning, programming, and budgeting process. I was not greatly troubled by this development since alternative force mix options had been presented during the meetings of the DPRB.

As 1990 came to a close, work was completed on both the study of the Total Force Policy and the Base Force plan. The final report of the Total Force Policy Study Group was submitted on December 31, 1990.[38] While much of it had the collective support of all the participants in the study, Chris Jehn and I made no effort to suggest that every member agreed with every point in it. The final report was not intended to answer with finality the many complex issues which the study group had addressed. It could not have. Events were moving too rapidly.

Unfortunately, the report did not meet my own hopes. It was not worthy of the subject. It did not clearly define neutral planning principles to guide future decisions on force mix. It didn't clarify which kinds of regional crises should be met with active and volunteer reserve forces, and which kind would presumably require an involuntary call-up.

Still, the work of the study group had much to offer. It was the first broad-based effort in the Pentagon to rethink the underlying premises of the Total Force Policy and their application to a totally new threat environment. It required civilian and military force planners to analyze each service's force planning process and the relative costs of different types of active and reserve units. It helped to educate the Pentagon leadership on the capabilities and weaknesses of each of the reserve components just as the nation was about to enter a major war. All in all, the study of the Total Force Policy had been a useful endeavor—with short-term benefits.

Under the Base Force plan that was now formally submitted to the White House as part of the recommended defense budget, the total force was to be managed differently. Active and reserve units previously assigned missions based on the threat of a short-notice global conflict would be eliminated. It was assumed that they could be reconstituted in the event of a resurgent global threat. Land forces would be smaller, more versatile, deployable, and mobile. Increased emphasis would be placed upon flexible, sea-based power projection forces, namely, carrier battle groups and amphibious groups with embarked marines. Strategic mobility forces would be better suited to non-European needs and designed to discharge cargo in less-developed ports.

Active forces would continue to provide the primary capabilities for day-to-day operations, and provide most of the combat and support units needed for the initial response to regional crises. Certain of the reserve components would assume broader responsibilities, e.g., for the entire continental air defense mission. The extent to which reserve forces would be used in the initial stages of the response to a regional contingency would depend upon its nature and size, the skills and experience required to meet it, the speed with which the response had to be made, the availability of forces already in the area, and other factors.

The Base Force plan was far from perfect. It was clearly a transitional concept. I still believed that with little risk, the administration could have shifted even greater responsibility to certain types of high-quality and less-expensive reserve forces. But the plan adopted was reasonable and one that I could comfortably defend in congressional hearings—which were expected to be heated.

One writer would later accuse Colin Powell of pushing through the most significant changes in our military establishment since the 1940s "without guidance from above."[39] Powell's own staff historian would conclude that instead of responding to guidance from the president and secretary of defense, "Powell successfully shaped that guidance."[40] There can be no doubt that Powell employed the full authority and resources of his position to aggressively promote his own views. But such comments reflect a misunderstanding of the dynamics of the DPRB process as it was used in 1990 and of the personalities involved.

Whatever else might be said about the Base Force proposal, it was the subject of substantial analysis and criticism by other senior Pentagon officials. President Bush was undoubtedly focused primarily on events in the Middle East, but he had highly developed foreign policy skills and considerably more foreign policy experience than most presidents. Brent Scrowcroft, his national security advisor, had previously served in that position and was a retired lieutenant general.

And while it might have been difficult for a secretary of defense with no personal military experience to reject the strong recommendations of the president's senior military advisor who had himself served as national security advisor to the previous president, Cheney was smart, tough, and had no problem making decisions. If an alternative strategic view had been advocated by Wolfowitz, and if another force structure plan in support of that view (and which was clearly superior to the Base Force proposal) had been presented, it might well have commanded the support of the secretary and, ultimately, the approval of the president.

At the beginning of 1990, American armed forces had been engaged in Operation Just Cause in Panama. As the year ended, American forces were engaged in Operation Desert Shield. Almost a quarter of a million reservists had been mobilized in one of the largest and most successful deployments of military power in our nation's history. During the course of the year, rapid and historic changes had taken place in the strategic environment and the Department of Defense had undertaken major new counterdrug responsibilities. Working through it all, a path had been developed to guide the nation's first steps toward a secure future. It remained to be seen whether the path would be followed.

CHAPTER IX
Defining Our National Interests—and Ensuring the Power to Defend Them

"It is not worthy for a great State to fight for a cause which has nothing to do with its own interests."

—Otto von Bismarck, 1850

"It is not given to the cleverest and most calculating of mortals to know with certainty what is their interest. Yet, it is given to quite a lot of simple folk to know every day what is their duty."

—Winston S. Churchill,
world broadcast, August 31, 1943

"War is a pretty rough and dirty game. But politics—by gum!"

—Field Marshal the Viscount Montgomery
of Alamein, Memoirs

═══════════════

As America approaches the beginning of the twenty-first century, there is less consensus on our role in the world and on the use of American military power, including the use of the nation's citizen warriors, than at any time since the period prior to World War II. National leaders don't even agree on the amount of consensus that exists.

Three days after the 1992 presidential election, Colin Powell addressed the Chicago Council on Foreign Relations and asserted that the reason national security issues weren't debated during the campaign was that "there is a remarkable degree of consensus across the American political spectrum about our role in the world." Leaving aside the fact that candidate Bill Clinton did not want to debate issues on which President Bush was clearly more skilled and more experienced, Powell was simply wrong. Only a year later, Paul Nitze, one of the deans of the national security establishment, stated a much more widely shared view: "There is less consensus today among Americans about the direction of U.S. foreign policy and security policy than there was at the end of World War II."[1] One scholar even argues that one of the few propositions on which a consensus exists is that American foreign policy is in disarray.[2] Before it can determine what circumstances will require measures such as the mobilization of reservists, of course, America must first determine fundamental questions about what interests are worth fighting for in an emerging international order which is already more complex than that which existed when the bugle sounded in Desert Shield and Desert Storm.

Much has been written in recent years about the conflicting American attitudes toward foreign policy and the role that the nation should now assume on the world stage. These attitudes have everything to do with decisions regarding size and shape of the nation's armed forces. Contrary to the assertions of some, however, the end of the Cold War has not given the American people the chance to make an unhurried decision about their degree of involvement around the world.[3] Events are moving too rapidly.

Along the broad spectrum of public opinion there are, of course, several strategic world views.[4] They often defy categorization along traditional partisan or ideological lines. Many people hold to aspects of more than one and consider some elements of each much more important than others. One view of America—as an idealistic evangelist or missionary—holds that our country's system of government, values, unique moral standing, and military and economic strength impose upon it an obligation to crusade around the world for these characteristics and for our professed standards of public policy. Adherents of this view, which are often referred to as the school of democratic internationalism, believe that the most effective way to further U.S. objectives is to promote and protect economic reforms and democratic practices and institutions around the world.[5] They are sometimes tempted to "remedy every wrong and stabilize every dislocation."[6]

A second view, basically minimalism or self-righteous isolationism with an idealistic bent, is that "America serves its values best by perfecting democracy at home, thereby acting as a beacon for the rest of mankind."[7] Convinced that much of the cost of U.S. foreign engagement is an unnecessary drain on U.S. resources and talents, it has been said that proponents of this idea of "strategic independence" counsel a deliberate withdrawal from many overseas security commitments, a redirection of resources toward domestic renewal, and the development of a narrow, nonideological definition of U.S. national interests.[8] One critic of U.S. national security policy has described the "fundamentals" of this world view as: "The primacy of domestic affairs; the dissociation and depreciation of power and diplomacy; utopianism; aversion to violence; distrust of large standing military forces; and impatience."[9]

A third, or "realist," view of American security interests is that our country must be careful not to overextend itself and that our security is best guaranteed by a stable balance of power among nations in regions that are important to our well-being, e.g., Europe, East Asia, and the Persian Gulf, rather than by our own superior virtue. Proponents of this strategy often seek to capitalize on and perpetuate America's status as the sole remaining superpower, and they tend to take a triagelike view of the long list of claims on U.S. attention and resources.[10] It has been said that, operationally, this means maintaining the military strength to act alone if necessary or, better yet, in ad hoc U.S.–led coalitions and remembering that dealing with interstate aggression is what U.S. military forces do best.[11] One distinguished advocate of this view asserts that America's ability to employ power to shape the rest of the world has, in fact, decreased, that in the future America will need partners to preserve equilibrium in several areas of the world, and that these partners cannot always be chosen on the basis of moral considerations alone.[12] Another asserts that the most fundamental security interest of the United States is to achieve and maintain a "pluralist system of world public order, based on a balance of power and regulated by law."[13]

These conflicting views as well as other attitudes continue to be reflected in national debate. In the 1992 presidential election, American voters reconfirmed their preoccupation with domestic battles rather than international issues. That preoccupation is still apparent as this book goes to press during the presidential election year of 1996.[14] While the public understands that America has a unique leadership role in world affairs, the day-to-day operational meaning of leadership is much more ambiguous than in the days of the Cold War. Americans generally believe that the United States should intervene abroad only in coalitions with allies or with the United Nations.[15]

Public opinion on international issues is, of course, greatly dependent upon the presence or absence of vigorous presidential leadership, especially now that the Cold War balance of power can no longer be relied upon as a frame of reference.[16] During the first years of his presidency, Bill Clinton seemed unwilling and incapable of asserting U.S. leadership abroad, to the embarrassment of both leaders of his own party and professional diplomats. Reflecting upon continued policy failures in Bosnia, one leader of his own political party accused Clinton of "acting like he's one more bit player in a multinational scenario" instead of playing the role of "leader of the free world."[17] Foreign service officers had concluded that his foreign policies were "so ill defined, or so prone to sudden flip-flops, that they collectively [were] known within the bureaucracy as 'the lurch'" and that where policy was spelled out, it often reflected "a quasi-isolationist shrinking from leadership . . ."[18] One writer was later more charitable, observing simply that the administration had "chosen to defer" the matter of developing an overarching, rigorous, and explicitly documented U.S. national security strategy and associated foreign policy.[19]

After what were described as "dismal" results of U.S. diplomacy that were "not . . . flattering to America's image as a world leader," the Clinton administration reexamined its expectations for U.S. foreign policy in the spring of 1994.[20] A year later its foreign policy was still being described as involving "frequent gaps between rhetoric and behavior, policy changes or even reversals, undue sensitivity to domestic political considerations . . . an unwillingness to speak out regularly to the American people about foreign policy . . .[and] a lack of clarity and consistency."[21] The lack of leadership was reflected in prevailing American attitudes about the appropriate level of defense spending.[22]

President Clinton's own frustration at his lack of clear foreign and national security strategies was evident in a speech delivered on October 6, 1995. Arguing that the world is now too complex for comprehensive strategies, he reached for a computer metaphor: "There seems to be no mainframe explanation for the PC world in which we are living."[23] As the nation worked its way through the election year of 1996, his lack of success was being heavily criticized, even by former partisan supporters. His former assistant secretary of defense criticized the administration's policy vacuum and lack of effective leadership in Sino-American relations.[24] Democrat Sen. Bill Bradley characterized Clinton's policy in Bosnia as a "prime example of the reigning ad hocism" in the administration.[25] The administration's policy of "strategic ambiguity" in connection with China's military threats to Taiwan was universally ridiculed. One leading newspaper severely criticized the president's "Don't ask, don't tell" philosophy of world leadership and concluded that "the Clinton foreign policy consists primarily of trying to push problems beyond [the] November [elections]."[26]

The two American presidents with the most foreign policy experience in recent decades have left no doubt about their own beliefs that the nation must not only be actively engaged in world affairs, it must lead them. Speaking at an Air Force Academy graduation shortly after the conclusion of the Persian Gulf War, President Bush was unequivocal: "Many here and abroad wondered whether America still possessed the strength and will to bear the burden of world leadership. My fellow Americans, we do, and we will."[27]

In a farewell address at West Point almost two years later, he was even more direct. Acknowledging that there is no support abroad or at home for us to be the world's policeman, he nevertheless concluded that "it is the role of the United States to marshal its moral and material resources to promote a democratic peace. It is our responsibility—it is our opportunity—to lead. There is no one else."[28] In a manuscript completed in 1994 only days before his final illness, former President Richard Nixon was equally clear: "Americans do not know how to be second. They only know how to be the best. After World War II the U.S. became the leader of the free world by acclamation. No other option was even conceivable. We should be just as resistant to playing a secondary role now."[29]

However clear the need for American leadership in world affairs may be to some recent presidents, the translation of that need into domestic political support cannot be assumed.[30] One of President Bush's former senior foreign policy advisors believes that "no president—not the previous one [Bush] nor the current one [Clinton]—has made a compelling case for how the lives of Americans are intertwined with and affected by what goes on in the world."[31]

Seldom in our history have Americans been able to agree on and articulate a coherent definition of our national security requirements. It has been rightly observed that this failure is a serious obstacle to rational sustained policy making and it means that we often act on the basis of instinct rather than strength. It should thus come as no great surprise that within a national community of such varying viewpoints, America has struggled to define its national interests, especially those for which it is willing to fight.[32]

Probably the best-known criteria in recent years for the use of military force abroad were postulated in 1984 by then Secretary of Defense Caspar Weinberger. In remarks to the National Press Club, he outlined six tests: (1) Do the circumstances involve vital American interests? (2) Is there a clear intention of winning (measured in part by a willingness to use whatever military force is necessary to succeed)? (3) Are the political and military objectives clearly defined? (4) Is there a continuing reassessment and reevaluation of the need for military force after it has been applied (i.e., in case the objectives change)? (5) Do the American people and Congress support the effort? (6) Is military force being used only as a last resort?[33] Former Secretary of State Al Haig, Weinberger's cabinet colleague in the first Reagan administration and a former military commander of NATO, disagrees with Weinberger's formulation. In his view, the U.S. should "never telegraph in advance when we will use military force."[34] By 1995, Frank Carlucci, Weinberger's former deputy and successor as secretary of defense, was also of the view that military power could be used for limited purposes (i.e., where a "vital" interest is not at stake) even if there is an absence of strong public support currently, so long as the objectives are clearly defined and there is strong national leadership.[35]

President Bush recognized the futility of a quest for a set of hard and fast rules to govern the use of military force, but he urged consideration of certain principles to inform decision makers. In his view, and assuming that a vital or at least an important American interest is at stake, using military force makes sense "where the stakes warrant, where and when force can be effective, where its application can be limited in scope and time, and where the political benefits justify the potential costs and sacrifice."[36] Colin Powell, his chairman of the Joint Chiefs of Staff and a former military assistant to Cap Weinberger, emphasized Weinberger's second element—decisive force.

In its first years, the Clinton administration was much more inclined to treat military force as a "sharp tool of diplomacy, rather than a blunt instrument of controlled violence."[37] As a result, it lowered the threshold for the use of force. After initially following what has been called a "left-isolationistic agenda with humanitarian interests and multilateralism setting the tone"[38] and suffering the tragic failure of policy in Somalia in 1993, the administration veered sharply closer to the Weinberger doctrine, but it still adopted a lower standard for the use of military force. On May 6, 1994, President Clinton signed Presidential Directive (PDD) 25 in which he outlined his administration's approach to "peace operations." The PDD did not require that a "vital" American interest be at stake before force is used. Rather, the test to be applied is whether military participation "advances U.S. interests."

Four months after he signed the PDD, Clinton ordered the use of significant military force in the invasion of the small island of Haiti. A year later, Vice President Al Gore argued that only an "essential" national interest must be at stake before military force is employed and that even then "we have to be flexible" in understanding what is an essential interest.[39] Secretary of Defense William Perry went further. He urged the use of force in situations where *no* important American security interest is at stake, so long as we have a "deep humanitarian concern."[40] The application of this principle has nowhere been more clear than in President Clinton's November 1995 decision to send approximately 20,000 American troops to Bosnia.

Because Americans are slow to anger in international matters, when we have acted it has historically been only after substantial provocation. When action is taken, it is usually with a vengeance. Almost a half century ago Churchill noted this trait: "There are no people in the world who are so slow to develop hostile feelings against a foreign country as Americans and no people who, once estranged, are more difficult to win back."[41]

Historically, when Americans decide to fight it is in pursuit of a cause or a great national purpose. This characteristic is not uniquely American, of course. It was Napoleon who observed that in war the moral is to the material as three to one. But it is particularly important in our heritage. Civil War general William Tecumseh Sherman, described by the great British soldier-historian B. H. Liddell Hart as "the world's first modern 'Man of War,'" saw clearly that the fighting power of a democracy depends more on the strength of the people's will than on the strength of its armies.[42]

President Nixon put the matter this way: "America is a reluctant great power. We are fundamentally isolationists and become engaged in the cut-and-thrust of world politics only if we perceive a great idealistic cause hanging in the balance."[43] We are willing to spend American blood, treasure, and honor to advance moral principles—sometimes even abstract principles—but we are reluctant to go to war for narrow, selfish interests, no matter how concrete or well-defined they may be.[44] Speaking of the U.S. involvement in the Bosnia operation in 1996, a prominent British military historian curtly observed: "This kind of thing is not really America's cup of tea, is it?"[45]

This lesson has not been lost on American political leaders who have committed American military power as part of national efforts to "remember" the *Maine* and Pearl Harbor, to resist the Soviet Union's "evil empire," to war against an Iraqi tyrant characterized as the moral equivalent of Adolf Hitler, and to replace a military regime in Haiti characterized as "the most brutal, the most violent regime anywhere in our hemisphere."[46] Even Lincoln relied upon this national characteristic. Convinced that the fighting spirit of the North would quickly wane and that European sympathy for the South would increase unless a new moral force was injected into the Union cause, he decided to free the slaves. Only a month before he issued the preliminary Emancipation Proclamation, however, he wrote a letter to Horace Greeley, the abolitionist editor of the *New York Tribune,* in which he declared that "my paramount object in this struggle *is* to save the Union, and is *not* either to save or destroy Slavery."[47]

* * *

In the absence of clear consensus on our national interests and international responsibilities it is, perhaps, inevitable that even less agreement has been reached on the quantum of military power necessary to protect those interests. Only two months into his term as the new Speaker of the House of Representatives, Newt Gingrich argued that the U.S. should be strong enough militarily "to defeat any plausible combination of opponents."[48] This criterion is reminiscent of the two-power standard for British naval strength that was established by the British Naval Defence Act of 1889, i.e., that the Royal Navy would always have to be superior to the fleets of the two next-strongest naval powers. The Speaker, however, was even more direct: "We intend to dominate air, space and sea against anybody and have a mobilizable ground force capable of winning within a reasonable length of time. Period."[49]

Others believe, however, that since the end of the Cold War, the issues to which military force is even relevant have diminished, and that in the absence of an overriding ideological or strategic threat, the relative military power of the United States will inevitably decline as a result of domestic pressure to shift resources to other priorities.[50] One long-time student of U.S. defense policies and the author of a recent analysis of future U.S. military needs asserts that most Americans don't object to having a strong military or to paying for it when necessary. But, he concludes, "without a palpable and plausible threat, maintaining a sizable and consistent level of defense spending will remain among the most elusive of national objectives."[51] Recent opinion surveys support this view.[52]

Some observers argue that the demographic character of modern, post-industrial societies, especially the fact of smaller families and the movement toward more democratic control of foreign policy decisions, have neutralized the ability of our leaders to threaten and resort to the use of military force at all. Ordinary people, they assert, are no longer willing to rely on foreign policy professionals and feel entitled to a larger share in decisions that might send them out to die.[53] Some believe that America is increasingly shaped by an "ethical system that is commercial, individualistic, libertarian, and hedonistic" and at the other end of the spectrum from the classical republics of Greece and Rome with their great respect for the power, leadership, and glory of their states and the sacrifices these require. Modern states, in their view, especially the United States, have surely demonstrated "a powerful aversion to the casualties that are sometimes inevitable in the preservation of peace and civility."[54]

A former member of President Bush's National Security Council staff has concluded that "Desert Storm taught the American people, wrongly, that vital interests could be defended with a handful of casualties in a video-game war."[55] Shortly after the conclusion of Desert Storm, Gen. Maurice Schmitt, then chief of staff of France's armed forces, visited a foreign general to talk about the war. "It will never be the same," Schmitt is reported to have said. "No army in a democracy can fight a war again without the fear of looking ridiculous unless it wins in a week or less using smart bombs and suffering almost no casualties."[56] One analyst argues that the "Vietnam syndrome has been replaced by the Gulf War syndrome: total intolerance of casualties."[57]

It has been suggested that in the current absence of threatening great powers it may be possible to conduct armed interventions in circumstances that do not involve vital national interests, if modest objectives and casualty avoidance are the set goals.[58] One conclusion would seem obvious, however, for at least the near term. In an age of global computer networks, handheld digital video cameras, and instant TV images of body bags and grieving relatives, public pressures to stop military action may become irresistible before national leaders have had a chance to develop thoughtful positions or react to developments.[59] Only an exceptionally determined leader skilled in the art of political leadership will be able to overcome the increasingly widespread refusal of democracies to tolerate even modest numbers of combat casualties, whatever national interest is at stake.[60]

Nevertheless, students of the twists and turns of history continue to remind us that war has been a persistent part of the human experience and has not diminished with civilization or democracy;[61] that military strength is always relative and international balances of power can *never* be still;[62] that the preservation of peace requires active effort, planning, the expenditure of resources and sacrifice—just as war does;[63] and that in the end, even the most conciliatory foreign policy of states who wish to preserve the peace will be impotent unless it is backed by credible force, i.e., by the preponderance of power and the will to accept the burdens and responsibilities required to achieve peace.[64]

Theodore Roosevelt subscribed to this view, but at the end of his presidency, seventy-five years before the end of the Cold War, he worried that the country at large did not: "I suppose that [the] United States will always be unready for war, and in consequence will always be exposed to great expense, and to the possibility of the gravest calamity, when the Nation goes to war. This is no new thing. Americans learn only from catastrophes and not from experience."[65] It remains to be seen whether the current generation of Americans is prepared to accept the burdens and sacrifices necessary to the preservation of peace in an unstable world in which modern weapons can give even small states the power to unleash forces of vast human suffering.

To say that for the foreseeable future America will face a variety of real and potential threats to its security is to state the obvious. Defining the relative importance of those threats is another matter. An armed invasion by a foreign military power on the coast of California or Maryland would have the certainty of a high priority, but there is no serious possibility of such a threat. One thing is clear. Within a brief period of time, responsible and informed people can reach very different conclusions about the most significant current and future threats.

In the summer of 1993, one distinguished scholar wrote that the fundamental source of conflict in the post–Cold War era will be cultural and that the principal conflicts of global politics will occur between groups of different civilizations.[66] Only a few months later Secretary of State Warren Christopher announced the six priorities of American foreign policy to be "economic security," reform in Russia, a new framework for NATO, trade relations with the Far East, Middle Eastern affairs, and nuclear proliferation.[67] Four days later, the secretary general of the United Nations laid out a view of global security that was pointedly different. Ethnic conflict was characterized as posing the great danger to world security.[68] Not long thereafter, the national security advisor to President Clinton broadly defined America's main security challenge as the containment of the "backlash" states of Iran, Iraq, Libya, North Korea, and Cuba."[69] Only weeks later the secretary of defense declared that the two "really big national security problems" which the nation faced at that time were Russia and Korea.[70] More recently, students of security policy have expressed concern about other specific security problems, including China's increasing ability to project military power far beyond its shores, the transitional threats of international terrorism and organized crime, and the proliferation of weapons of mass destruction.

It has also been effectively argued that it is unlikely that America will face a coalescing or unifying threat in the foreseeable future and that this condition of strategic uncertainty and ambiguity requires both a shift from a threat-specific basis for defining national security to other criteria and a rigorous analysis of the assumptions underlying what level of military capability is deemed necessary. According to this view, the only basis for decisions on the amount of military capability required is judgment and experience.[71]

Whatever short-term security needs America may have, its friends have no doubt about the importance of America remaining the world's dominant power. Contemplating an unstable world one hundred years from now in which there are more than half a dozen "great powers," each with its own clients, and all "engaged willy-nilly in perpetual diplomatic maneuvers to ensure that their relative positions improve," one close friend, former British prime minister Margaret Thatcher, has expressed strong views about the key to the avoidance of war: a dominant America, surrounded by allies which, in their own long-term interest, generally follow its lead.[72]

In these circumstances, and when U.S. foreign policy in the post–Cold War period is still evolving and domestic support for foreign endeavors is arguably "contradictory, weak and growing weaker,"[73] debate is inevitable on the questions of how much military power is necessary to protect those national interests for which we are prepared to use force, what form that power should take, and how much of it should be placed in the reserve components. On these questions, the debate was heated during the final two years of the Bush presidency.

* * *

Even as American armed forces were making final preparations to commence offensive combat operations against Iraq in Desert Storm, American political leaders were warring over the issue of the future active/reserve mix of the armed forces. On December 3, 1990, only days before President Bush was to submit to Congress his defense budget for fiscal year 1992, Congressman Jack Murtha, chairman of the House Appropriation Committee's defense subcommittee, sent a warning to Secretary of Defense Dick Cheney. Murtha reminded Cheney that the 1991 Defense Appropriations Act forbade the expenditure of any funds to reduce reserve personnel strength. He went on to assert that during a period of decreasing defense budgets, it made sense to put more, not less, force structure into the reserve components.

Over the ensuing weeks and months, the debate intensified. Unfortunately, it also became more confusing as several of the participants failed to articulate their positions with precision and others focused on headlines. A case in point was a news article that carried the headline: "Cheney Would Reduce Reserve Combat Role."[74] In an interview, Cheney had expressed the view that in light of our Desert Shield/Desert Storm experience, the army's "roundout" concept should be abandoned and the army's rapid deployment divisions should be composed entirely of active forces. Leaving aside the fact that his conclusion was premature and, in my opinion, wrong—at least with respect to smaller than brigade-size units—the headline suggested a lack of confidence in all reserve combat units of all the military services, rather than in certain brigades of the Army National Guard. The headline caused considerable scrambling within the Pentagon to set the record straight. It simply did not accurately reflect Cheney's views. In fact, in an interview the following day, Cheney emphasized that he regarded the recently concluded Gulf War as a vindication of the Total Force Policy.[75] Predictably, however, several members of Congress expressed great unhappiness with his remarks.

Throughout the spring and summer of 1991, reservists who had been activated for Desert Shield/Desert Storm continued to return home. Meanwhile, the administration continued to plead its case for the Base Force. My own advocacy primarily involved hearings before Congress, with interviews and an occasional speaking engagement. Cheney conducted his advocacy primarily in speeches and television interviews. In a July 16 speech he laid out the essence of the administration's proposal in language that—to use a phrase that the then commandant of the Marine Corps, Gen. Al Gray, liked to employ— would be fully understood by the guys at the 7-Eleven store:

> The way we're structured in the military today is that we've got Guard and reserve units that provide the combat support and service support for the active duty combat units. . . . If we're going to cut a third of the active army, then I don't need as many reserve units to provide the combat support for those active units. . . . We've got Guard and reserve units that no longer have a mission.
> But I'm told by Congress, . . . that I can't get rid of one single guardsman or reservist. . . .
> If I cannot cut the National Guard and reserve, the army alone is going to be short $11 billion over the next five years.[76]

Two days later, the commander in chief of Army Forces Command corroborated this argument. General Ed Burba, the highly decorated and highly respected officer who had responsibility for the readiness and post–Desert Storm demobilization of the Army National Guard and reserve units, went straight to the point in a letter to Cheney: "[W]e now know more about the proper AC/RC mix than ever before." But, he added, "despite our energetic efforts to educate the Congress, I fear we are on an azimuth which protects excess RC force structure at the cost of diverting funds from the AC and RC training, maintenance, personnel and infrastructure resources we need to maintain the readiness standards required by our contemporary contingency environment."[77]

By August it was clear to me that we were getting nowhere with Congress. To get the debate unstuck, I recommended that Colin Powell and other uniformed leaders assume a more visible role in explaining to Congress the "war-fighting" rationale upon which the president's proposed reductions in the reserve components were based. I further recommended that Pentagon leaders advocate no more than three themes in support of those reductions: first, that we couldn't afford to pay for unnecessary readiness; second, that a proper balance had to be maintained between combat and support forces; and finally, that we should not have a force structure that requires the nation to involuntarily activate a significant number of reservists for every contingency, no matter how limited in scope or time. The recommendations were generally followed.

Just as the shrillness of the debate appeared to be reaching its highest pitch, another foreign development sent tremors through the defense establishment. On August 18, a group of Soviet hard-liners initiated a coup attempt against Gorbachev. Three days passed before he was able to return to Moscow and reassume control. His tenure as the head of a Soviet government was to be short-lived. On December 1, Ukraine voted to secede from the Soviet Union. Seven days later, Russian president Boris Yeltsin declared the formation of the new Commonwealth of Independent States. On Christmas Day, Gorbachev resigned and the Soviet Union ceased to exist.

In late August, the nation's governors weighed in to the force mix debate. Whatever the degree of their interest in the nation's larger security problems, they could be counted on to yell loudly about their individual problems. Forgetting that only ten years earlier the National Guard had several thousand fewer soldiers and airmen, the governors went on record at the National Governor's Conference as totally opposed to any reduction in National Guard troop strength.[78] The overall situation was summarized by the *Kansas City Star:* "With lots of pride and billions of federal dollars at stake, no state wants to take the hit."[79]

In such circumstances, important facts were often ignored. On the afternoon of Sunday, September 22, I sat next to Colin Powell at ceremonies for the dedication of the new National Guard Memorial Building. We discussed the responses he would give two days later to written questions posed by the Senate Armed Services Committee in connection with his confirmation for a second term as chairman of the Joint Chiefs of Staff. His frustration was evident, but the answers he later submitted were straightforward. He stated unequivocally that there was "no diminishment in the role or relative size of the reserve components" in the Base Force proposal.[80] He also noted that the reserve proportion of the Total Force had increased since 1980 from thirty percent to thirty-six percent and that the proposal called for it to remain at thirty-six percent through fiscal year 1997.[81] Few people were listening.

On November 19, 1991—the very day that the last reserve unit mobilized for Desert Storm returned home, the House Armed Services Committee completed action on the fiscal year 1992 Defense Authorization Bill. In a memorandum to "National Guard and reserve supporters" the following day, Les Aspin, the committee chairman, could not resist the opportunity to inject a note of partisanship. Boasting that the House bill "[r]ejected the administration's plan to eliminate hundreds of thousands of Guard and Reserve personnel and force structure over five years,"[82] Aspin and the committee offered no alternative force structure, no alternative force mix, no alternative military strategy, and no vision for the future. Instead, they prohibited significant reductions in the reserve components and directed another study.

Section 402 of the National Defense Authorization Act for fiscal years 1992 and 1993 was clear. The secretary of defense was to submit to Congress a report containing an assessment of a wide range of alternatives relating to the structure and mix of active and reserve forces "appropriate for carrying out assigned missions in the mid to late 1990s." The report was to include a study conducted by a federally funded research and development center that was "independent of the military departments." It was also to include an evaluation by the secretary and the chairman of the Joint Chiefs of Staff of "the independent analysis, assumptions, findings, and recommendations of the study group." The group conducting the study was to be assisted by a panel of experts. The recommendations of the study group were to be transmitted to Congress no later than December 15, 1992. The secretary's and the chairman's evaluation was due on February 15, 1993—twenty-six days after the inauguration of the president whom Americans would elect on November 3.

After brief discussion by a small group of senior Pentagon officials, Rand was selected to conduct the study. At my suggestion, the adjutant general of the state of Washington was selected to join five retired (and former regular or career) admirals and generals on the panel of experts. I wanted it to be apparent to the National Guard leaders who served as adjutants general of the fifty states and four U.S. territories that the unique "domestic interests" of the individual states were considered fully and fairly by the panel.

Just as the Rand study was getting under way, four important and related developments took place almost simultaneously. First, the president submitted to Congress his defense budget for fiscal year 1993. The budget request called for a reduction of 530,000 in the active forces by fiscal year 1995, twenty-five percent below the 1987 peak of 2,174,000 personnel. It also recommended reductions in reserve personnel, but to a level only twenty percent below the 1987 peak. Several congressional critics promptly called for larger overall reductions, but Cheney held firm, arguing that "we don't think we ought to change [force structure plans] every six months or twelve months, based upon developments either on Capitol Hill or overseas."[83]

Second, Colin Powell published a document entitled *The National Military Strategy, 1992*. It was described as a vehicle to implement the president's new regionally focused defense strategy. It immediately raised the suspicion of congressional opponents who were expecting a large "peace dividend" from the defense budget since it stated that the decline of the Soviet threat had "fundamentally changed the concept of threat analysis as a basis for force structuring" and that "the real threat we now face is the threat of the unknown, the uncertain."

The document went on to declare that forward presence forces (i.e., those deployed throughout the world to demonstrate U.S. commitment, to enhance regional stability, etc.) would be drawn predominantly from the active component of all of the military services. For regional crises, U.S. forces would be drawn "in large part" from the active components with "essential support" from the reserve components. If a crisis became larger or more protracted, the reserve components would be increasingly relied upon.

Lines of political battle were established by the two remaining developments. In a February 1992 paper, the National Guard Association of the United States and the Adjutants General Association of the United States (the latter consisting of the National Guard leaders of the individual states) proposed a force structure much different from that included in the president's budget.[84] The same month, Les Aspin also proposed several force structure options.[85] The chances for agreement with Congress had now all but vanished. In concluding that the intensity of the active-versus-reserve debate would only increase, a senior congressional staffer stated the obvious: "If you cut the Guard, you close armories and cut jobs in your own backyard. That's tough for Congress to do. The future active/reserve mix is the $64 million question."[86]

The National Guard Association proposal called for ten Army National Guard divisions instead of the six recommended by the president. It also recommended the retention of 160,000 additional Army Reserve component (National Guard and reserve) personnel and almost 35,000 fewer active personnel.

The Aspin alternative that seemed to be his favorite, or at least which soon received the most attention, was referred to as "option C." That alternative would have required much greater reliance on reserve forces by necessity since it called for the active forces to be reduced to nine army divisions (compared to the twelve proposed by the administration), ten air force tactical fighter wings (compared to fifteen), 360 navy ships (compared to 450), and 1.4 million personnel (compared to 1.6 million). It did not, however, provide the means for training reserve forces quickly enough to be used in an unexpected emergency. Had it been implemented, it would have failed to generate a decisive force for the first contingency, and the forces provided for a second contingency would have become available so slowly that there would have been significant delay in providing a force adequate for either deterrence or defense.[87]

The major problem with Aspin's proposal, however, was the artificial methodology employed to create it. The force level it recommended was calculated by comparing the power of "potential regional aggressors" (e.g., China, North Korea, Cuba, Libya, Iran, Syria, and post–Gulf War Iraq) to the military power of Iraq before the Persian Gulf War. The latter measure was referred to as a "Desert Storm equivalent." China, for example, rated a factor of 1.4, i.e., the proposal arbitrarily assumed that in order to defeat China in a conventional conflict, the U.S. would have to have 1.4 times the military power required to defeat Iraq in Desert Storm. The proposal clearly involved the kind of formalistic, mathematical approach to force building that proved so unsuccessful during the McNamara years, when Aspin had served in the Pentagon as a young analyst. It soon received much criticism. During congressional testimony on March 20, for example, Powell argued that its methodology was unsound, its strategy unwise, and the forces and capabilities it proposed unbalanced.[88] The air force Chief of Staff publicly dismissed the proposal as unrealistic.

By March 1992, the ongoing force mix debate was taking predictable turns and the rapid change in the international security environment was continuing to occupy the rapt attention of political leaders. On March 22, German chancellor Helmut Kohl emerged from an informal weekend of talks with President Bush at Camp David to declare that "the destiny of the world" was being decided on the foreign policy front. Four days later the noise level and contentiousness of the force-mix debate increased considerably after a Pentagon news conference that hit like a bombshell.

In an effort to take the initiative in the political debate, to deal with the realities of the declining defense budget, and to demonstrate that congressional opposition to cuts in the reserve components was based more on pork-barrel politics than on any coherent military strategy, Cheney and Powell announced plans to reduce or inactivate 830 National Guard and reserve units during the next two years. Nearly eighty percent of the Guard and reserve units to be inactivated had wartime missions in support of active units, also being eliminated, that were assigned to the defense of Europe in the event of a major attack from the Warsaw Pact, which by that time was already defunct.[89] Most of the reductions would come from the army's reserve components.

The decisions as to which reserve units to cut had not been casually made. I had worked with all the services for weeks to ensure that the reductions related to current thinking on war-fighting needs, to recruiting realities—and that they were as fair as possible to each reserve component and to each state.[90]

Cheney opened his case at the news conference with the argument that "Congress cannot have it both ways. They cannot tell us we have to cut the defense budget and then object every time we move to cut the defense budget."[91] He then framed the issue as a simple choice between a lean, ready force and one that was not needed: "If we have to pay for Guard and reserve units that no longer have a mission, . . . then something else has to give."[92] He went on, "If we don't cut the reserve component strength enough, we end up having to cut . . . operations and maintenance, and that affects training, and that affects readiness. . . ."[93] Finally, he added, "We're not a social welfare agency, we're not an employment agency, and we're not an agency that's operated on the basis of what makes sense back home."[94]

The move was courageous—and politically risky. It was an election year. The reductions would be made in all fifty states, the District of Columbia, and Puerto Rico. Many of the cutbacks would take place in states that already had economic and unemployment problems. The states likely to be hit the hardest included California, New York, and New Jersey, all of which had hefty electoral strength.

The public reactions to the plan were predictable. The president of the National Guard Association solemnly proclaimed that the reductions would "break" the National Guard.[95] The Reserve Officers Association called the reductions "premature" and urged Congress not to permit any reductions until the "independent force-mix assessment" (i.e., the Rand study) was completed the following year.[96] Fifty-four senators, all members of a loosely organized "Senate National Guard caucus" opposed any reductions. Congressman "Sonny" Montgomery argued that the Pentagon was making a mistake: "National Guard and reserves have a big economic impact on local communities," he asserted. "A 150-person armory brings $2 million into the local economy."[97] Even though it noted that the cuts would affect New England disproportionately, the *Boston Globe* gave, perhaps, the most candid assessment of the political reality: "Congressmen, for their part, love the reserves, which represent home-district jobs worth about $6,000 per slot each year—in other words, votes."[98]

The less vocal opposition to the plan to cut the reserve components was more complex. Some of it was based on the simplistic and wrong notion that because reserve units are less expensive units, active units should always be cut before reserve units. Some of it had to do with congressional interest in restraining the president's freedom to use only active forces to police international hot spots. Some of the opposition was plainly partisan as Democrats sought to use the planned cuts to their advantage in an election year. Some of it found its source in the historical American distrust of a large standing army and in the romanticized vision of a vigilant militia of citizen warriors. Some of it was the result of understandable community pride. Much of it had to do with the desire of state governors to continue their reliance on federal largess—rather than on politically difficult-to-obtain state funds—to guarantee the availability of National Guard troops for domestic emergencies and other state missions.

In the noise and dust of the debate, few people recognized or were interested in the fact that if the cuts proposed by Cheney were carried out, the National Guard would still have 10,000 more troops in 1997—years after the end of the Cold War—than it had in 1977, and eighteen percent more than it had in 1980. Few would have predicted that only a year later the Clinton administration's own "bottom-up review" of military force structure would recommend almost three fewer Army Guard/reserve divisions and five fewer reserve fighter wings for the air force, or that as soon as 1995 the administration would be considering an even smaller force structure in order to pay for needed modernization of various weapons systems. Fewer still would have predicted that only three years later, a long-awaited report of the Commission on Roles and Missions of the Armed Forces—a commission mandated by a Democrat Congress and chaired by President Clinton's own soon-to-be-confirmed deputy secretary of defense—would declare that "the army has eight National Guard combat divisions with approximately 110,000 [troops] that . . . are not needed for the current national security strategy."[99] It was the classic Washington power struggle. Several of the arguments advanced on each side of the debate were reasonable, but the combatants were talking past each other to various constituencies.

Ironically, only days after announcing the planned reserve cuts, Cheney quietly approved a measure that would make it significantly easier to use reserve forces in crisis situations. On April 8, I met with the secretary to recommend a legislative change to Title 10 of the U.S. Code, the primary legal authority upon which we had relied in Desert Shield/Desert Storm to activate reservists. After studying the matter for months, I had become convinced that activation of certain selected reservists in the early stages of a crisis, especially those assigned time-sensitive missions such as airlift, cargo handling, port security, and medical evacuation, was essential to the flexibility required for rapid deployment and expansion of our fighting power. To that end, I recommended that we seek an amendment to the law that would authorize the president to order members and units of the Selected Reserve and certain members of the Individual Ready Reserve to active duty for 180 days (with a possible extension of an additional 180 days) rather than the 90 days currently permitted. I further recommended an amendment that would authorize the president to delegate to the secretary of defense authority to activate as many as 25,000 ready reservists. The secretary quickly approved the recommendations.[100]

Concerned that too much posturing and avoidable misunderstanding was obscuring the true nature of the president's force structure and force mix recommendations, I went straight to the point in my testimony before several congressional panels that were considering the recommended cuts. I explained our intent to continue to place major reliance upon reserve forces. I noted Colin Powell's agreement that as the size of the Total Force was reduced, we would move certain units or functions into the reserves to avoid the costs associated with keeping them in the active force structure. I warned again, however, that care had to be taken to avoid a requirement to involuntarily activate large numbers of reservists to active duty in the initial stages of every contingency: "If we presume upon the time—time normally devoted to their civilian occupations or education—of our citizen-soldiers for every minor skirmish or trouble spot, we may ultimately face retention problems involving precisely the same high quality reserve personnel that we need most."[101]

Over the course of the next several weeks, events demonstrated why reserve force reductions could now be made. They also demonstrated the continuing importance of the reserve components. The weekend of May 9 was the setting for a demonstration of each. In Saturday ceremonies marking the forty-seventh anniversary of the Nazi surrender, the command band of the Air Force Reserve, accompanied by a color guard carrying the national ensign and the flags of each of the United States Armed Forces, marched proudly into Moscow's Red Square—the heart of the former "evil empire" itself—playing the "Stars and Stripes Forever." The next day Governor Pete Wilson of California announced that 10,000 national guardsmen activated after the Rodney King jury verdict to quell rioting would have to remain on the streets of Los Angeles indefinitely.

As the spring of 1992 turned to summer and then fall, and as Americans began to focus on the upcoming presidential election, changes in the security environment continued. So did the political struggle over the kind of armed forces the nation needed to respond to the new environment.

On June 17, Russian president Boris Yeltsin addressed a joint session of Congress to declare that communism had collapsed in his country and that he would not permit it to rise again. He also announced a new agreement with President Bush to slash each country's strategic offensive arsenal by seventy percent. Two hours before the speech, I talked briefly to Col. Gen. Dimitri A. Volkogonov, historian, former chief of Soviet military's psychological warfare department, and Yeltsin's closest military advisor. The general was interested in a future meeting to discuss the creation of a part-time Russian reserve force as the size of the Russian army was reduced.[102]

Meanwhile, new proposals for the use of our own reserve components continued to be raised in Congress. Senator Nunn proposed the use of the armed forces, especially the reserve components, to address domestic problems such as urban decay, unemployment, racism, drugs, and even poverty and poor nutrition. Senator Stevens proposed a rotation plan in which one-third of the U.S. forces in Europe would be reserve component personnel serving for brief tours of duty. Senator John McCain and Rep. Dave McCurdy co-chaired a study that recommended a National Guard–sponsored residential training camp for teenage dropouts.

As Election Day approached, the heated rhetoric of the force mix debate showed few signs of waning. It was becoming increasingly clear, however, that substantive progress on the reshaping of the armed forces could not be made until at least the Rand study was completed and a new mandate was received from the people. The last shouts of the debate were made by the two presidential candidates.

On the morning of September 15, President Bush addressed a conference of the National Guard Association in Salt Lake City. He appealed for support, but he pulled no punches. After reaffirming his commitment to the Total Force concept and declaring that the maintenance of strong, capable reserve forces would remain "essential to our military strategy," he injected the same note of reality that I had advanced in earlier congressional testimony. "We recognize," he said, "the need to be sensitive to the demands placed on individual national guardsmen, reservists, and really . . . their families. As true citizen soldiers, our guardsmen must devote time to their families, civilian occupations, or education. If we intrude upon you for every trouble, we may find it hard to keep the very best soldiers that characterize the Guard today."[103] He added: "The new National Guard will be smaller—just as our active forces are being reduced. Anyone who tells you different is simply not leveling with you."[104]

Four hours later, his opponent attempted to convey a much different message. Addressing a military audience after being attacked for months for his avoidance of military service during the Vietnam War, Arkansas Gov. Bill Clinton was selling hard to those in attendance. Giving no hint of his view of the role of America in the new world or of any strategy to implement that role, he repeatedly but vaguely promised "a stronger role for the Guard and the reserve than is called for in the present Bush force plan."[105] Conceding that the National Guard would not be exempt from future cuts, he nevertheless promised that the reductions would retain the "traditional combat orientation" and "historic combat role" of the National Guard.[106] If he knew, he did not explain what he meant. Four years later, his own administration would preside over a plan for a sweeping conversion of eleven Army National Guard combat brigades and one scout unit from combat missions to support responsibilities.[107]

Eleven days before the election, the president signed into law the National Defense Authorization Act for fiscal year 1993. In doing so, he noted that the law would assign new domestic civil functions of government to the armed forces, including such matters as local school funding, community medical care, and the training of children. However laudable, those functions, he said, were "not . . . appropriate roles for the military." He directed the secretary of defense to implement the provisions in a manner that would do the least damage possible "to the traditional role of the military" and to propose remedial legislation where that was not possible.[108]

On November 3, America elected a new president. Work by the Bush administration on the design of the armed forces of the future came to an effective stop the next day. A new administration would now have the responsibility of defining the nation's security interests and maintaining military strength sufficient to defend those interests. The task of cutting reserve units made unnecessary by the historical changes in our strategic requirements had not been accomplished. Years later, Dick Cheney and Colin Powell would describe the political obstacles that this task presented in almost identical words.[109]

The end of my own participation in the debate reminded me of an incident that had taken place four years earlier. As I was leaving the office of then Secretary of Defense Frank Carlucci after briefing him on a reserve readiness issue, he observed with some amusement that I had one of the toughest political jobs in Washington. When I inquired into his reasoning, he explained that I had to help develop and then sell to each of six reserve components the president's policy on the force structure, budget, and the like for each component. "Then," he said, "you have to help sell it to each of the military departments and the Joint Staff." "Finally," he added, "you have to persuade each of the authorizing and appropriating committees in the Congress, as well as any other committee that thinks it has jurisdiction over the issue." By the end of 1992 I had little reason to disagree with his observation.

It remained only for the leadership of the Department of Defense to comply with the statutory obligation to evaluate the conclusions of the Rand force structure/mix study. On December 15, the Department of Defense transmitted the Rand report to Congress. The Christmas holidays, emotional feelings associated with the impending change in administrations, and the reality that the evaluation of the Rand study was not due to Congress until a month after the new administration had assumed power all worked to deflate the energy and interest of several civilians in the Pentagon who had been so actively involved in the force structure/mix battles of the past.[110] On December 23, I offered a detailed evaluation of the alternatives presented in the Rand report. It met with little enthusiasm. The intervention of a new humanitarian crisis in Somalia and the fact that the administration's policy position was well established and well known almost inevitably resulted in technical but insubstantial compliance with the statutory obligation.

So it was that one of the most remarkable periods in American military history came to a close. In the brief span of three years, the Cold War had been won; democracy had been restored in Panama; almost a quarter of a million reservists had been mobilized for an armed conflict for the first time since the draft ended two decades earlier; the international security environment had changed rapidly and dramatically; major studies of future American military requirements had been conducted; and a major war had been fought with unprecedented success in an area 8,000 miles from American shores.

Now complex challenges new to most living Americans had to be addressed. The nation's tradition of bipartisan and predictable foreign and military policies would be severely tested as we struggled to define our role and responsibilities in the post–Cold War world and to identify those national security interests which duty requires us to defend, even with the use of military force. The design of the armed forces of the future would depend on the resolution of these fundamental and threshold questions. The security of the nation would rest on the answers.

Chapter X
Remembering Fundamentals

"All wars should be governed by certain principles. . . . War should only be undertaken with forces proportional to the obstacles to be overcome."

—Napoleon

"Through all this welter of change . . . your mission remains fixed, determined, inviolable—it is to win our wars. . . . All other public purposes, . . . all other public needs . . . will find others for their accomplishment; but you are the ones who are trained to fight; yours is the profession of arms."

—General of the Army Douglas MacArthur,
speech at West Point, May 12, 1962

As America enters the last few years of what has been aptly described as the most violent century in the history of the world and staggers toward its new post–Cold War role, its reserve forces are being given orders for missions that have become more demanding and more ambiguous daily. Their readiness to perform those missions is being adversely affected by factors that are, for the most part, avoidable.

Sweeping cuts in the defense budget in recent years have kept the military services off balance.[1] The failure of the Clinton administration to adopt clear, competent, and principled national security and force planning policies has caused a loss of credibility abroad and a loss of confidence at home.[2] Unwise political interference in the force drawdown and turbulence caused by endless reorganizations and far too frequent changes in mission assignments have greatly exacerbated the situation. It has been clear for some time that the nation is no longer capable of performing two global power projection missions of the kind that was required in Desert Storm. Ironically, at a time when they are being called upon to perform peacetime operational missions previously performed by active forces, national guardsmen and reservists are also being asked to assume responsibilities for domestic social programs and other missions that have little to do with serious national security problems.

Increased use of reserve forces when serious crises threaten the nation's security, and increased reliance even in peacetime on selected reservists who have special skills, who volunteer for additional assignments, and who are assigned wartime missions which, if they require postmobilization training, do not have to be performed in the early stages of a conflict, is both sound policy and politically inevitable. Common prudence dictates that we continue our efforts to find innovative, new ways to take advantage of the remarkable talent and experience that exists in the reserve components, especially for the performance of certain missions.[3]

Reservists currently make up more than half of the airlift crews and eighty-five percent of the sealift personnel that are needed to move troops and equipment in either wartime or peacetime operations. Reserve medical and other specialists are also essential to a wide range of operations. Efforts by the reserve components to move beyond a traditional wartime backup role and to provide peacetime support to active units are thus desirable. The Naval Reserve and Air Reserve components have made particularly impressive progress in this direction.[4]

Where reservists can be *effectively* trained for their combat missions by participation in activities that have collateral benefits, those activities should obviously be fully explored. For years I pursued such opportunities with the commanders in chief of the unified commands. Considerable success was achieved in training reserves for military missions by engaging them in a wide range of training activities.[5]

National leaders should also have quicker access to the reserve components in times of armed conflict, when contingency operations are required,[6] or when the nation otherwise faces a truly serious national crisis. This is one of the major themes of this book and I have strongly advocated greater flexibility in this regard. My 1992 recommendations regarding the president's statutory call-up authority, however, were made in the context of the recently completed Persian Gulf War and for the purpose of ensuring early access to reservists in time of war or major emergency, not with the idea of using them for public needs that can be met by others.[7] The Clinton administration subsequently resubmitted my proposal, but in August 1994 it was rejected by Congress.[8] By then, much had changed.

Policies that place greater reliance on reservists must, however, have limits. In recent years, it has become fashionable for political leaders, military lobbyists, and some uniformed leaders to attempt to apply the rhetoric of military strategy and certain military resources, including the reserve components, to social and foreign problems that end up in the political "too hard" box and have little or nothing to do with serious threats to the nation's security. What started as a well-meaning if shortsighted bipartisan attempt by some to prevent further raids on the defense budget by making the armed forces appear more relevant to what was hoped to be a tranquil new world order[9] has evolved into broader and, in many cases, unwise policies.

This trend was first highlighted in the Clinton administration's much publicized 1993 "bottom-up review" of strategy, force structure, and other aspects of the nation's military strength. The administration there advanced what it characterized as an "era of new dangers" to our national security. The purported new dangers were described as falling into four broad categories, including the "danger" of failing to build a strong U.S. economy and the "threat" to democratization and reform in the former Warsaw Pact countries.[10]

As part of its reaction to the purported new dangers, the administration adopted an ambiguous new doctrine of "assertive multilateralism" soon after it entered office. Under that doctrine, American troops would regularly participate in United Nations and other international military actions to handle "threats" to democracy and human rights even in domestic political contexts. Until a congressional and public opinion backlash brought about a rethinking of the issue, there was even a broad commitment to place United States forces under the command of foreign officers.[11] The policy continues to be severely criticized, even by foreign leaders.[12]

One scholar has attributed the criticism of the administration's foreign policy to the agenda Clinton embraced in the 1992 election campaign. According to this view, Clinton's "strategy in the game of political poker he played with Bush was to see all bets the incumbent had placed and then raise him."[13] The result was that there was "scarcely any item on the wish-list of contemporary American internationalism—preventing aggression, stopping nuclear proliferation, vigorously promoting human rights and democracy, redressing the humanitarian disasters that normally attend civil wars—where Clinton promised a more modest U.S. role."[14]

The same philosophy and political motivation appeared to govern the administration's national security efforts well into the election year of 1996. The secretary of state proclaimed a broad new definition of national security. Now environmentalism would rank with preserving the peace as a top administration priority.[15] After declaring that the encouragement of free market economies and the training of new governments in the basics of democracy were now military assignments,[16] the secretary of defense outlined a vague new "preventive defense" strategy.[17] President Clinton even called for an amendment to the 1878 Posse Comitatus Act that bars military personnel from engaging in domestic, civilian law enforcement.[18] The administration's actions inevitably came under fire.[19]

So pervasive has the idea of using military forces for purposes other than fighting and winning the nation's wars become, that an entire chapter of a recent army doctrinal statement is devoted to "operations other than war."[20] On the express assumption that nations must use "all the resources at their disposal to pursue national objectives" (and apparently, the implicit assumption that all national objectives have equal or at least some claim to the nation's military resources), the doctrine characterizes as "typical" a broad menu of peacetime operations. They include disaster relief, humanitarian assistance, support to domestic civil authorities, treaty verification, noncombatant evacuation operations, security and advisory assistance, arms control, nation assistance, and shows of force as well as the more predictable peacekeeping operations, counterdrug operations, and noncombat support for insurgencies and counterinsurgencies (e.g., logistical and training support).[21]

Similarly, the 1995 *National Military Strategy,* prepared by the Joint Chiefs of Staff, formally added "peacetime engagement" to the mission list that included defending the U.S., nuclear deterrence, and fighting and winning two near-simultaneous regional conflicts. Not surprisingly, the idea was also picked up in the 1995 report of the Commission on Roles and Missions of the Armed Forces. Chaired by a former member of the Carter administration who became President Clinton's choice as deputy defense secretary shortly before its report was released, the commission recommended that what it called "peace operations" be given higher priority by the Department of Defense and that "extensive use" of military reservists be made, especially in law enforcement operations and in the "constabulary training" of foreign personnel.[22]

In 1996 the trend continued. In what appeared to be the beginning of a move away from the "two major regional conflicts" standard of the Bush administration's Base Force and the Clinton administration's "bottom-up review," the chairman of the Joint Chiefs of Staff published *Joint Vision 2010,* a concept paper that described his vision of the armed forces' future. In introducing the paper, he argued that America cannot leave peacekeeping to others: "We will, in years to come, be faced here and there in very selected cases with getting involved . . . in [the] Bosnias of tomorrow."[23]

The increasing and almost instinctive tendency to use military personnel for purposes other than armed conflict or in situations where demonstrably important American security interests are not at stake has affected reservists as well as active personnel. Indeed, since the end of Desert Storm, national guardsmen and reservists have been used in such wide-ranging activities as flying relief supplies into Bosnia-Herzegovina and protecting United Nations relief convoys there by enforcing "no-fly" zones; quelling riots in the streets of Los Angeles; aiding victims of natural disasters, e.g., Hurricane Andrew in Florida; fighting crime in housing developments in Puerto Rico; supporting counterdrug operations in all fifty states and the Caribbean; and providing first humanitarian relief and then much broader assistance in Somalia.

A reserve call-up was even given consideration in August 1994, when the Clinton administration suddenly found itself overwhelmed by a Cuban refugee problem made worse by its own handling of the situation and another new policy driven by domestic political considerations.[24] And, in September 1994, at a time when an ABC News poll found seventy-three percent of the American people opposed to an invasion of Haiti and to American nation-building efforts there, when a substantial majority of Congress saw no important U.S. interest involved, and when there was not even a "fig leaf" claim of some emergency that required unilateral presidential action, President Clinton signed an executive order authorizing the involuntary activation of as many as 1,600 reservists for precisely that purpose. The following month authority was given to activate an additional 4,100.

By the summer of 1995, a battalion of volunteers from the army's reserve components was participating in an unprecedented six-month deployment to Egypt's Sinai Peninsula for a peacekeeping mission;[25] approximately 200 navy, marine, and army reservists were on a three-month deployment to Albania; and a Pentagon quality-of-life task force had floated the idea of using reserve units to relieve active units during the reservists' annual active duty for training.

After a meeting with U.S. commanders in Europe in October 1994 to discuss the stressful operating tempo caused by the administration's new "peacetime engagement" policies, the secretary of defense also announced plans to use reservists in many peacetime operating missions, including overseas activities, previously performed by regular forces.[26] He specifically advocated involuntary call-ups of reservists for prolonged peacekeeping and humanitarian operations.[27] The first major exercise of this policy took place in early December 1995, when it was announced that approximately 4,000 reservists were being activated for the peacekeeping mission in Bosnia.

The reasons that policy makers reach for reservists are simple. Peacekeeping, humanitarian assistance, and similar operations depend heavily on military capabilities that require strategic and tactical airlift, civil affairs, medical, engineering, military police, transportation, and similar skills. Most of these capabilities reside in the reserve components.

Some reserve leaders have encouraged wider across-the-board use of reserve forces because of the opportunities that such use presents to minimize the budget cuts within the reserve components.[28] This type of narrow, "special interest" pleading is not defensible. Many opportunities exist for greater reliance upon reservists, but those opportunities are often lost by predictably adverse reactions to what appear to be and sometimes are nothing more than parochial attempts to protect turf or resources.

A particularly serious problem arises when civilian leaders urge greater use of reservists as cheap and handy solutions to domestic social problems they are unable to solve, or merely because they see short-term political benefits in doing so. A mayor of Washington, D.C., asked the president to authorize the use of the National Guard for routine police work such as answering 911 calls, transporting prisoners, and directing traffic during roadblocks.[29] A U.S. senator proposed sending National Guard troops to patrol the border with Mexico in an effort to fight illegal immigration.[30] In 1993 over $58 million was distributed by the Defense Department in two dozen states so that national guardsmen could provide medical care in inner cities and rural areas and establish educational programs to train high school dropouts and improve science and math education in inner-city schools. At the same time, a defense official announced plans to use reserve personnel to build recreation centers and engage in other efforts to keep high school dropouts from turning to welfare.[31]

From its first days, the Clinton administration aggressively attempted to assign reservists to an even greater range of domestic social problems. Officials at the Pentagon denied that the military was being turned into a social welfare agency, but they proudly announced plans to have reservists repair housing, restore the environment, build a pier for fishing vessels in an economically depressed fishing community, dig wells, and survey the safety of dams, airport runways, and other parts of the domestic infrastructure.[32] In an almost comical and certainly tortured stretch of logic, one administration official loudly called for reservists to be actively involved in "defending America at home" by attacking "low literacy levels, high unemployment rates, increasing numbers of high school dropouts, unavailability of health care, rising crime, and drug abuse."[33] Declaring that "we have fewer active forces, fewer overseas forces, and more work to do than ever before but fewer people to do the work,"[34] the same official even threatened reservists with force structure cuts and the loss of missions if they resisted the administration's desire to use reservists in such "operations other than war."[35] It ultimately became necessary for Congress to pass legislation aimed at limiting such policies.[36]

It is worth noting that many of the political appointees who are most aggressive in their recommendations on the use of military power and who are most vocal in the exhortations to the men and women in the front lines of reserve service about the need to address domestic social problems and participate in foreign situations where vital, or at least important, American interests are not at stake, have themselves never served in a military uniform.[37] Many have never handled significant responsibility in a market economy. Many have spent most or all of their careers in government, academia, and think tanks, or as lobbyists for military associations based in Washington, D.C. Few have actually attempted in recent years to balance part-time reserve duties with the conflicting demands of civilian careers in private industry and family obligations.

This does not mean that personal military service and business and/or professional experience outside of government are a guarantor of good national security policy making. It strongly suggests, however, that as a consequence of this development, policies and practices directly affecting reservists and untempered by the realities of personal experience are being adopted far too easily. Reservists are not fungible items that can be mindlessly used for problems unrelated to the purposes for which they joined the armed forces in the first place.

By the end of 1994 the gap between military missions unrelated to America's important security interests and the willingness of individual reservists to make ever-increasing personal sacrifices in order to carry out those missions was widening.[38] The Noncommissioned Officers Association had recognized a growing problem of "mission creep" and had warned that more frequent call-ups for missions that fall short of true national emergencies would "profoundly impact, not only reservists, but their families, employers, and self-employed members as well."[39] The chief of the Air Force Reserve, noting that the increased pace of recent peacetime operations was causing friction in families and growing resentment among civilian employers, had just declared that "we have not been articulate about how close we are to the breaking point."[40]

The intensive deployment of U.S. forces was also beginning to clash with financial, training, and readiness realities. Despite the conclusion of the General Accounting Office that the defense budget was already $150 billion short of the amount needed to fund the strategy contemplated by the administration's so-called "bottom-up review," Congress had failed to act on the Pentagon's request for supplemental appropriations for operations in Rwanda, off the coast of Haiti, and at Guantanamo Bay, Cuba, where thousands of refugees were based.[41] As a result, the military services were being forced to absorb the costs of the operations from budgets normally used for training.

For the first time ever, the navy had to cancel training and drills for thousands of naval reservists after being forced to apply training funds to operations involving the interdiction of refugees in the Caribbean and the extraction of U.S. troops from Somalia.[42] A special Pentagon task force on readiness had found "pockets of unreadiness" resulting from budget cuts and new demands and had just warned that "unless the Department of Defense and Congress focus on readiness, the armed forces could slip back into a 'hollow' status."[43] The chairman of the Joint Chiefs of Staff had expressed fear that "we're becoming mesmerized by operations other than war,"[44] and he and the Army Chief of Staff found it necessary to state publicly and on separate occasions that the ultimate purpose of the armed forces is to fight and win the nation's wars.[45] Even the secretary of defense felt compelled to observe that "we are an army, not a Salvation Army."[46]

Still, this evidence did not faze all administration policy makers. One Pentagon official claimed to be "conscious" of the problem,[47] but the administration's senior reserve official disparaged as a "Cold War relic" the idea that reservists be involuntarily activated only in time of war or emergency.[48]

By the fall of 1995, and even before the administration announced plans to send approximately 20,000 troops to Bosnia to enforce a cease-fire there, the results of its aggressive use of the armed forces in new circumstances and the continuing reduction in the size of the force structure were becoming even more clear. A heavy toll was being taken on military personnel and their families, including reserve personnel. According to a report to the secretary of defense from an advisory group that interviewed more than 3,000 men and women, many officers and enlisted personnel were reaching burnout.[49] The problem had improved very little for reservists by 1996.[50] Despite the downsizing of both active and reserve forces, the number of deployments had increased fivefold since the end of the Cold War. The percentage of people deployed away from their home station at any one time in 1995 was twice what it was in 1991, the year of Desert Storm.[51] The consequences were inevitable: weaker job performance, an inclination for the more qualified personnel to leave military service, and enormous stress on families.[52]

Many citizen warriors do, of course, volunteer for duty assignments in addition to their regular training for armed conflict. Even for an operation as unpopular as that in Haiti, there were several hundred reserve volunteers. Unfortunately, the military skills of the volunteers often do not match those that are needed. Since reservists normally train as units, the performance of groups of individual volunteers can also be uncertain. And despite the strong patriotism that runs through reserve ranks, it is very difficult for force planners to confidently assume in advance the availability of sufficient numbers of reserve volunteers with the proper skills for future contingencies, which are themselves increasingly unpredictable.

The *involuntary* activation of citizen warriors, however, for activities that do not involve important American security interests, that have no urgency, and that in many cases have limited training value is an ironic perversion of an important premise upon which the Total Force concept was originally based. According to his biographer, former Army Chief of Staff Creighton Abrams intentionally integrated reservists deeply into the modern army's force structure for one reason: to make it very difficult, if not impossible, for a president to use any significant military force without calling up the reserves.[53] The implicit assumption in Abrams's approach to force planning was that increased reliance on reserve forces would act as a brake on future American presidents. No longer would they be able to pursue unwise foreign ventures that lack public support, especially when no important national security interests are involved.

The Clinton administration has demonstrated the weakness of the assumption. The September 1994 involuntary activation of reservists was for a Haitian operation that bore no serious relationship to any important American security interest, had no urgency, and was opposed by Congress and by the American people by a two to one margin. Similarly, the December 1995 decision to involuntarily activate thousands of reservists for a peacekeeping mission in Bosnia was made shortly after the House of Representatives had voted overwhelmingly against sending American ground troops there, and at a time when public opinion was running strongly against the operation.

Contrary to the views of some reserve leaders,[54] that kind of use of reservists, coupled with their expanded use in other domestic activities that have little or no positive effect upon their ability to help fight the nation's wars, will result eventually and predictably in significant declines in combat readiness and the quality of reserve units. One respected observer argues with force that peacekeeping and similar operations will actually corrupt the armed forces' reason for being.[55] At least one former secretary of defense believes that we have "lost sight of the basic fundamental fact of life that the military is a unique institution, there specifically for the purposes of defending the nation and going to war if need be."[56] There is no doubt that the war-fighting skills of ground units erode at battalion and higher levels of command during peacekeeping and related operations.[57]

This is not to say that "operations other than war" should never be engaged in, or that reservists should never be involuntarily activated for them, or that reserve volunteers should not contribute to routine peacetime operations. It is to say that the question of *why* we are using the armed forces at all in a particular operation should dominate any consideration of the use of reservists. While the nation must inevitably depend more upon its citizen warriors in the future, it is important that political leaders understand two fundamental points.

First, U.S. foreign and security policies must have a strategic foundation so that they are predictable, not just to adversaries and allies, but also to the American people. If the political ground is always shifting, the public will be unprepared and unsupportive when our security needs really require the activation of large numbers of reservists.

Government officials must also understand that if the American people have not been persuaded to pay for an active force structure large enough to carry out the number of "operations other than war" desired by a particular administration, the solution should not inevitably include involuntary activations of reservists. Rather, the number and scope of such operations should be reduced. In the alternative, more courageous and effective advocacy and leadership should be undertaken by political leaders so that Americans understand why the operations are in their best interest. Stated differently, if an activist foreign policy that requires frequent call-ups of reservists is to be pursued, strong and effective political leadership, especially presidential leadership, is essential. Such leadership was almost entirely absent in the Clinton administration.[58]

Some argue that the murky nature of missions in which the armed forces are deployed to foreign countries to deal with the shambles of failed political and economic systems will eventually undermine public support for the use of military force in situations where important American interests are unquestionably at stake.[59] While this is almost certainly true, the more immediate danger to the reserve components is reduced readiness for clear-cut crises that do pose a direct threat to our interests. Limited training time does not expand merely because the intentions upon which new peacetime missions are based are good.

For years the most serious readiness problem facing the reserves has been the mismatch between the military skills in which individual reservists have been trained and those which they need in order to perform their combat missions. Active soldiers can be moved to units where their current skills are required. Reserve soldiers are necessarily wedded to a unit near their civilian home. Limited training time and other factors such as turbulence caused by the frequent changes in mission assignments, reorganizations, new equipment,

geographical moves related to civilian employment, and the schedul-
ing of military training courses in formats and at times inconvenient
to reservists make it very difficult for them to keep their military occupational skills current.

To rationalize the use of funds already budgeted for reserve training for questionable peacetime operations, civilian officials in the
Pentagon argued in 1994 that training for assigned combat missions
should be a "by-product" of the performance of peacetime operations.[60] While this can be accomplished to a certain extent for a limited number of very experienced reservists who have certain military
skills, e.g., airlift crews, logisticians, and medical personnel, the argument is not generally true. Work is not the same thing as training.
Few peacetime operations by a tank driver or a fighter pilot can sub-
stitute for hard, realistic training for combat. Every minute spent ad-
ministering social welfare, or on operations that do not train reservists directly for their combat missions, must be suspect.

Like any other skill or culture, combat skills and the warrior culture can be lost through inattention. It has been recently argued that
the cultural challenge for military organizations is increasingly going to be the maintenance of a warrior spirit and the intuitive understanding of war that goes with it, even when their leaders are not,
in large part, warriors themselves.[61] Military professionals understand
that readiness for combat must always be first in priority.[62]

Plans for more peacetime operations for reservists also ignore an
important fact of reserve service. Reservists are highly imbued with
a "can-do" attitude and they generally enjoy operational challenges.
In the absence of a clear crisis that commands broad national support, however, their civilian employers and families are much less enthusiastic about their prolonged absences from home.[63] Ultimately,
retention must be affected.

The dangers are real. If the United States continues to operate in
a strategy vacuum, if the armed forces are diverted from the fundamental mission of war fighting, if we continue to presume upon the
patriotism and limited time of our part-time citizen warriors by using them as a cheap labor pool for public needs that do not involve
serious threats to the nation's security, a day of reckoning will slowly
but surely arrive. At some point, the high-quality reservists whose

skills and experience make them the seedcorn for future combat leadership will reluctantly but inevitably conclude that they simply don't have enough time to remain in the armed forces and to adequately fulfill commitments to their civilian careers, to their families, and to educational and other private needs. Reservists who serve for the opportunity to engage in old-fashioned soldiering and to develop warrior skills of immediate use when the nation's safety is threatened will leave as much of the adventure, patriotic, and other features of reserve service that make the sacrifices worthwhile begin to disappear.[64] The quality of the reserve components will deteriorate. Our ability to protect national interests that are unequivocally "vital" will become seriously affected.

Should that situation occur, future historians will never understand how it was that the victor of the Cold War and Desert Storm permitted the dismantling of a Total Force described by President Bush in 1991 as "the finest fighting force this nation has ever known in its history"—a Total Force that had been built so carefully, and at such great cost and effort.

These results are not inevitable. In the absence of a new global rival like the former Soviet Union or some other factor that stimulates a clear national consensus on our foreign and security policies, it will continue to be difficult in the short term to determine with confidence the most "appropriate" mixture of active and reserve forces. After all, the process by which the size and shape of the armed forces is determined is inherently and inevitably a political process. Military need may be the ideal standard against which force structure/mix decisions are made, but the nature and urgency of perceived need depends upon who defines it.

The effort to reach consensus on this issue is made more difficult by important developments of recent vintage. First, we are currently involved in at least an evolution, and perhaps a revolution, in military affairs. Some believe that the inevitable change in our approach to force planning and to the conduct of armed conflict is revolutionary in nature, that contrary to conventional wisdom threats to our security will not necessarily increase, and that the attendant revolution in technology will permit much smaller military forces.[65]

Others, especially those experienced primarily in ground warfare, totally reject the idea of a "revolution in military affairs" to the extent
that that phrase means a radical upheaval in current military structure, organization, and doctrine.[66] Yet others argue that far-reaching
changes in military affairs have indeed begun, but that the changes
will have less to do with technology than with other aspects of
warfare, including a shift from "the age of the mass military manned
by short-service conscripts and equipped with the products of
high-volume military manufacturing," to armed forces manned by
high-quality volunteers who give long military service.[67]

Two other developments that are likely to impede early consensus on our military needs are more personality dependent. As America's use of nationwide conscription recedes into history and the
quality of its military officers continues to improve, increasing numbers of people with comparatively modest or no military experience
will gain positions of authority on matters relating to national security. As recently as 1977, some eighty percent of the members of the
U.S. House of Representatives and sixty-five percent of the Senate
were veterans. In 1991, during Desert Shield/Desert Storm, only
thirty-seven percent of the House members and fifty percent of the
Senate had served in uniform. By 1993, the nation was governed by
a newly elected president who had actually evaded military service.[68]
Of the eighty-six male members of Congress elected in 1994, only
ten were ever on active military duty.

Meanwhile, the voluntary nature of contemporary military service,
improvements in professional military education, and the nature of
the political appointment process have arguably created a growing
disparity between the quality of military leaders and many of their
civilian political appointee superiors. When combined with the uniformity of approach that often results from the efforts of the military services to select their best officers for joint duty assignments,
the result may be a coherence of perspective on national security
matters among military leaders that is absent among civilian defense
officials who serve in government for only brief periods.[69] These and
other developments are likely to make civil-military relations more
challenging and the ability to reach early consensus more difficult.[70]

Whatever the difficulties, decisions on the future size, shape, and missions of our active and reserve forces must be made soon. In the absence of a significant new threat, defense budgets are likely to continue to decline. A strong public rationale for military strength is thus essential. As one former congressional leader and secretary of defense has put it: "If you look at the '92 election, the '94 congressional election, and I think even the 1996 presidential election, there has been almost no discussion—this will be the third election cycle without it—of the U.S. role in the world from a security standpoint, our strategic requirements, what our military ought to be doing, or how big the defense budget ought to be."[71]

Any force planning process must, of course, begin with clear political strategy and policy guidance.[72] Until such guidance is given, there may be no satisfactory answers to the questions of how much military power is enough and what kind of power it should be.[73] Equally plausible arguments can be made for a variety of designs.

It is thus substantially beyond the scope of this book to recommend future strategy or policies. Certain fundamental principles do exist, however, that can be easily identified and successfully used within a planning framework for good active/reserve force mix decisions. They can also be successfully used for the recruitment, retention, and effective training of reservists.

Decisions on the most appropriate balance between active and reserve forces must be made within a common analytical frame of reference—a frame of reference that helps to eliminate unrepresentative anecdotal evidence and bias. This can be accomplished only by a methodology that allocates active and reserve manpower, equipment, and other resources solely on the basis of demonstrated *capability* to perform specific missions and objectives. I have long believed in this rather obvious approach to force planning. Indeed, in 1990 I stated to Congress that the entire focus of Total Force planning should be on the performance of particular missions and that what matters is capability, not which component (active or reserve) it comes from.[74]

This *mission-to-capability* framework will require a series of interrelated top-down decisions by force planners that link strategy with specific operational objectives and tasks. The idea is to organize and train reserve units upon the basis of mission requirements rather than attempting to satisfy mission requirements within given institutional structures and constraints.[75] If combined with certain "neutral" planning principles, the framework has the capacity to minimize, if not eliminate, force mix decisions that are the result of parochialism, lack of imagination, improper political pressure, and similar influences. It can also provide a tool to evaluate the utility of specific reserve units.

Some missions, for example those that require a high surge of activity in times of crisis but comparatively low activity at other times, are obviously ideal for reservists. Other missions, such as those that require long periods of forward deployment even in peacetime, are normally unsuitable. Yet other missions can be reasonably assigned to either active or reserve units, depending upon such factors as how soon they must be performed after a crisis or conflict develops, the particular characteristics of individual units, how often the mission must be performed in peacetime, among other factors. Assuming then that a *mission-to-capability* framework has been adopted, what fundamental concepts or planning principles—based upon experience—can be relied upon for future force-mix policy decisions?

I propose that future decisions on the number and use of America's citizen warriors be based upon the principles that follow. These principles are not all-inclusive nor are they absolute, either as truths or as general rules of future force planning practice. They are merely commonsense conclusions born of experience; they are prescriptive in nature; they are designed to cover presumptive situations; they define limits, positive and negative, within which policy, when those situations present themselves, ought to operate; they recognize that situations may arise to which they are not applicable. But, barring special circumstances, they should be applied, and whatever policy maker proposes to ignore them should be required to explain why the violation is unavoidable.[76]

1. The Total Force Policy can and must be adapted to future needs.

Operation Desert Storm conclusively proved the success of the policy. One incisive observer has described the success this way: "We have found in the total force a superb combination of federal or state governance; national or local representation; and professional or citizen-soldier competence, uniquely suited to America—a state, a nation, and a democracy—all of which reflect the diversity of a continent."[77] The task now is to find ways to adapt the policy to the very different challenges likely to be faced in the first decade of the twenty-first century.

2. The Total Force Policy of the future should not attempt to make active, career soldiers and reserve soldiers fungible items or mirror images of each other.

Given the limited training time of most part-time citizen warriors and constrained defense budgets, it is unrealistic to attempt to make all or even most reserve units the absolute equal of the best active units. The readiness and capability of many reserve units, however, do compare very favorably with those of active units and because of previous military or civilian experience, many reservists have individual capabilities and technical competence that exceed those of active soldiers. Some types of missions can thus be performed better by reserve units. The objective must be to integrate the capabilities and strengths of active and reserve units in the most cost-effective manner, i.e., in a manner that provides the most total military capability and flexibility possible within the limitations of the budget.

3. The myth that political leaders will not involuntarily activate reservists is dead.

If it ever could be, the previous conventional (military) wisdom that political leaders will not activate reservists short of global war must no longer be used as an excuse not to integrate reservists fully into the armed forces. The rapid, involuntary activation of reservists in Desert Shield/Desert Storm put that myth to rest. The participation of at least some reservists is now critical to the success of almost any sizable military operation. Consequently, war plans should not be based on the use of volunteers only, but rather on the use of whatever reserve units are needed.

4. New ways to integrate active and reserve units must be found.

Despite the remarkable development of the Total Force Policy to date, considerable distrust remains between the active and reserve components, especially at certain senior levels within the army. Many active soldiers focus too much on the operational shortcomings of some reserve units. Others are deeply frustrated by the political clout of senior reserve military officers and reserve associations who, they believe, are special-interest pleaders who do not always act in the best interest of the service or the nation at large.[78] Many reservists focus too much on the lack of understanding by active force leaders of the often unique strengths and needs of reserve units. Some continue to worry too much about real but often historical biases against reserve forces. Some reserve commanders also tend to have inflated views of the capabilities of the units they lead. These kinds of problems can and must be reduced, if not eliminated. A first step is to make both loyalty to the concept of integration and clear operational competence elements in the selection of active and reserve leaders.[79] Some active force leaders have recently demonstrated impressive leadership on this issue.[80]

5. The active, peacetime force should be as small as the military strategy permits.

In the absence of an immediate or at least a predictable global adversary or group of adversaries who pose a visible threat, most Americans prefer the cheapest defense that can fairly be characterized as prudent. Cost considerations alone make the merits of this principle self-evident.

6. A rebuttable presumption should be established that missions are to be assigned to reserve units.

Depending upon the nature of the mission being performed (e.g., airlift, ground combat, etc.), a reserve unit is usually one-quarter to two-thirds as costly as an active unit. Citizen warriors train an average of only thirty-nine to sixty days per year, they normally sleep and eat at home, and the infrastructure required for them is less. For cost reasons, and in order to provide defense "insurance," a starting presumption should be made that each military mission will be assigned to a reserve unit. The presumption should be subject to being rebutted, but only if force planners who challenge it can meet the burden of demonstrating on a cost-benefit, risk-reward basis that there are sound military reasons for assigning the mission to an active unit.

7. Factors other than capability and cost are relevant to force mix decisions.

While the capability to perform and the cost of performance are threshold criteria in deciding whether to assign a particular mission to an active or reserve unit, flexibility, the maintenance of a rotation base (e.g., sea/shore rotation, forward deployment/CONUS rotation, etc.), retention of the most qualified reserve personnel, the intensity of training requirements, and several other factors must also be considered.

8. Quick response units should come primarily from the active force structure.

The merit of this principle is also self-evident. The unpredictable nature of future crises requires fully trained, highly ready forces that can be immediately deployed. These forces should be drawn primarily, though not exclusively, from the active force structure. Strategic reserve forces should be drawn primarily from the reserve components.

9. Some early deploying missions can be assigned to reservists.

Certain reserve units, especially those that have military assignments requiring skills closely related to the civilian skills of their members and that thus require no postmobilization training—e.g., airlift crews and port handlers—can confidently be used during the earliest stages of most contingencies. Reservists in these units are thus misnamed because they do not constitute forces held in "reserve" in the traditional meaning of that term. For the most part, however, these early deploying missions should be assigned only to units of volunteers who have made special arrangements with their civilian employers and who commit in advance to be instantly available.

10. The time-phased deployment requirements of reservists should be tied to the most likely contingencies.

The availability, capability, and especially the overseas deployment schedule of specific types of reserve units for specific types of contingencies must be constantly evaluated. Abstract active/reserve mix ratios are meaningless unless they are applied to the mission requirements of specific conflicts or operations.

11. Reservists train as units and should normally be deployed as units.

Reservists in many units have trained together for years. The cohesion of these units, especially ground units, often compensates for limited training time. To the greatest extent possible, the unit integrity of such units should be maintained. The degree to which this principle should be applied, however, will usually vary inversely to the size of the unit under consideration.

12. Combat commanders must have access to individual skills.

Operational commanders should not be burdened with entire units that are unnecessary if minimum numbers of reservists with particular skills are needed. Sufficient numbers of reservists with critical skills should be maintained in a special status, available for prompt use.[81] This is especially true for members of the Individual Ready Reserve who have left active service recently or whose military skills have not decayed.[82]

13. Reservists should become accustomed to the ideas of ad hoc force composition and task organization.

The uncertainty and potential range of future contingency operations require the ability to tailor military forces with specific functional capabilities to particular missions and geographical areas as evolving events require, rather than to rely on the "all-purpose, balanced-unit force of traditional, industrial-age warplanning."[83] The adaptive joint task force package concept has demonstrated potential, and so long as the tactical integrity of their (small) units is preserved, reservists— especially those whose skills place them in high demand—must be prepared to be a part of its development.

14. Reserve combat units should be kept small and should train with active units as much as possible.

Combat missions as well as support missions can be assigned to reserve units. Indeed, the ability of reserve units to perform combat missions is limited almost entirely by their training time. Large units, however, e.g., large ground combat maneuver units, typically require substantially greater total training time than do smaller units. For this reason, the reluctance of active force leaders to accept and rely upon reserve units generally varies inversely to the size of the reserve unit in question. The idea of integrating smaller reserve units into larger (parent or gaining command) active units (e.g., the army's "round-out"/ "roundup" concepts) remains a good one despite recent criticism and can be used more extensively within the army and by the other military services. Reserve units should train with active units as much as possible. When reserve units become a synchronized part of the larger active organization, their potential combat effectiveness is greatly increased.

15. Turbulence must be severely reduced.

Stability is critical to reserve readiness. New missions, reorganizations, and new equipment often require individual reservists to obtain new military skills. While some reservists have military assignments that require the same range of skills used in their civilian occupations, most do not. It is possible to hold part-time reservists to the same standards of performance as full-time active soldiers only if the reservists are trained on fewer total tasks that do not constantly change.

16. Unique missions and equipment should be viewed with suspicion.

The performance of certain missions may require skills and experience found uniquely in reserve units, e.g., civil affairs. In most cases, however, the cost of uniqueness is unacceptably high. If a reserve unit is given a mission or equipment not found in the active forces, there may soon be no pipeline from which the unit can receive former active personnel trained to perform the mission, spare parts for the equipment needed for the mission, or doctrinal development.

17. Qualified reservists should not routinely be assigned "backfill" missions.

In Desert Storm, most Naval Reserve medical personnel who were activated were not sent to the theater of operations.[84] Rather, they were assigned to stateside medical facilities to "backfill" vacancies created by the departure of active personnel to the theater. Aside from the inefficiency involved (two personnel moves instead of one), the reservists were extremely frustrated by assignments to provide care for dependents and retirees, instead of being permitted to perform the combat missions for which they were fully qualified and for which they had trained and made sacrifices for several years. Unless there are clear military reasons for doing so, reservists should be assigned to the theater of future operations. In the alternative, they should be trained for backfill missions and not solely for service in a combat zone.

18. Reserve units must be given the tools to perform assigned missions.

A policy of "first to fight, first to equip" was adopted by the Department of Defense in 1982. That policy required that all units, regardless of component, be resourced for modern equipment according to the sequence in which they were required to be in place to perform their wartime missions. Planning for today's unpredictable contingency operations is more difficult than that which was required for a Soviet-based Cold War threat, but clear priorities must be established. Priority for all resources must be given to units scheduled for early deployment, whether active or reserve. It is morally indefensible to assign important missions to reserve units in order to achieve cost savings, and then fail to give those units the resources that permit successful performance.

19. High turnover in Congress will eventually dilute the institutional parochialism favoring reservists.

A majority of the members of the U.S. House of Representatives have been elected since 1990, i.e., at least a year after the fall of the Berlin Wall. Most of the newcomers have no military experience and no long-standing ties to the reserve forces. Many are fiscal conservatives who want to balance the budget and shift power and financial responsibility to the states. It can no longer be assumed that the reserve force structure freezes and equipment dedication policies mandated by Congress in the past will be a part of the future.[85] The standard by which reserve forces should and will increasingly be measured in Congress will be (1) demonstrated capability, (2) the availability of sufficient numbers of quality personnel, and (3) postmobilization training requirements—all versus cost.

20. Reserve units should not normally be used in peacetime operations that do not relate directly to the performance of their wartime missions.

Modern American citizen warriors are volunteers who must deal with increasingly complex military equipment and doctrine. Limited training time and civilian employment/family demands require that if readiness for combat is to be maintained, reservists not be used as a cheap manpower pool for public needs unrelated to the nation's security. Individual volunteers and national guardsmen acting in their "state" status should be the only regular exceptions to this rule. Moreover, reduced defense budgets require that needed modernization of aging weapons systems be paid for from within, i.e., through reduced funding for readiness or fewer missions of questionable importance. The latter is the better choice.

21. There are limits to the sacrifices that the families and employers of reservists are willing to make.

The time that American reservists devote to training exceeds that of reservists in every other country in the world. Every day spent by a reservist in training or other peacetime operations is a day away from family and civilian employer. In contrast to active forces, the conflict between family roles and military duty increases rather than diminishes as a reservist moves up the military career ladder.[86] Sacrifices are obviously an inherent part of reserve service, but while they are also required to make sacrifices, the families and employers of reservists do not receive the same level of satisfaction enjoyed by reservists themselves. If policy makers presume unfairly upon the high motivation of reservists, subtle but real pressures from reserve families and employers will eventually cause serious retention problems and, ultimately, recruiting problems.

22. Excessive activations of reservists for relatively unimportant contingencies will threaten public support for serious crises.

Strong empirical evidence suggests that as increasing numbers of reservists were mobilized in Operation Desert Shield, more and more Americans were "touched" by the crisis. As they became more interested in and informed about the nature of the crisis, they became more supportive of President Bush's policy. It does not follow, however, that partial mobilizations of reservists can or should become a tool to build public support for less important operations. If reservists are consistently and involuntarily activated for operations perceived to be routine, public support for serious crises will be more difficult to build.

23. The move toward substantially greater use of reservists is not supported by all reservists.

With rare exception, most senior reserve leaders and the reserve lobbying associations aggressively support wider use of reserve forces. Their views are given considerable attention. Much of their enthusiasm results from the traditional "can do" culture in the armed forces. Often, they stand to benefit from the larger budget and increased opportunities that would accompany such use.[87] They are also more likely to have already reached success in their civilian careers. Junior members of the reserve components are in the early or middle stages of civilian careers and are more likely to have young families with pressing needs. While they are typically very enthusiastic about their reserve duties, they have less time for association or other extracurricular activities, so their views on frequent activations are not as well known. They are, however, the leaders of the future and their views of reserve service must not be ignored or taken for granted.

24. Staggered or variable readiness must be weighed against its costs.

Current threats do not require and resource limitations do not permit all reserve units to be maintained at the highest states of readiness for every possible operational task. Units that are most likely to be deployed first for the most likely contingencies should be given priority in resources and attention. The readiness of some reserve units, however, may need to be kept higher than that which can be justified solely on the basis of strategy or threat evaluation. Nonmonetary and intangible factors such as morale can be quickly and adversely affected by the loss of a sense of importance. Those factors are often involved in decisions by highly qualified reservists to leave or remain in military service.

25. Family support programs must be improved.

Operations Desert Shield/Desert Storm demonstrated the importance of premobilization family preparedness and post-mobilization family support. Most reserve families do not live near military bases and lack the networking and support systems to which families of active soldiers are accustomed. In the absence of such support, there is little interaction between the spouses of reservists. Conflicts between a reservist's family obligations and military duty must be worked out within the family itself. Long periods of mobilization can thus cause irreparable injury to family relationships. Reserve families must

be made aware of the nature of their family member's reserve
service and of the support that is available to them.

26. Reservists should rarely, if ever, be placed directly under foreign command.

While Americans want U.S. allies to shoulder more of the
burden of peacekeeping and similar operations, they strongly
oppose efforts to place U.S. forces—even regular or active (career) forces—under foreign command.[88] There is almost certainly even less support for placing American reservists under
foreign command. The unique nature of the American citizen
warrior tradition compels the employment of American reservists in association with other American forces, except in the
most unusual circumstances.

27. There is a clear correlation between the amount of full-time support and reserve readiness.

While policy makers can debate the merits of the various
types of full-time support, there can be little doubt that the combat readiness of reserve units increases with the number of full-
time support personnel.[89] The sheer complexity of some modern high-tech equipment and weapons systems makes it difficult
for part-time reservists to remain fully ready. Skill degradation
can be very high in the absence of high-intensity training. Reserve units that are required to use such equipment should be
given proportionately higher numbers of full-time support personnel. As support personnel assume more of a reserve unit's
administrative, recruiting, instructing, and equipment maintenance responsibilities, more time can be devoted to effective
training.

28. Support must be available for nonfederal requirements.

Through the years, force planners have been insensitive to
the legitimate nonfederal requirements of the National Guard.
At the same time, the states have become too dependent upon
the federal government for the resources required to support
these requirements. Both tendencies must be changed.

29. Priority in reserve manning must be given to recent active service experience.

As force reductions continue, competition for reserve positions will increase. While reserve unit commanders should be sensitive to fairness and equity concerns in the selection of personnel for vacant positions, the high correlation between recent military service and performance and the savings in training costs that can be achieved require adoption of this principle.[90]

30. Reservists should be visible in Heartland America.

The presence of Army and Air National Guard units within each state enhances public support for the armed forces generally, as well as for those services. As bases are closed, it is becoming more difficult to maintain a visible reserve presence in all states. It is particularly difficult to maintain a Naval Reserve presence in the heartland states. This factor, along with the location of ships and squadrons to which units may be assigned, the tempo of likely operations, PERSTEMPO (i.e., amount of time away from home), demographic factors (e.g., the availability of a sufficient recruiting base to meet manpower needs), and related factors must be considered in deciding where to place reserve units and which reserve installations to close.

31. Force mix decisions should be made only by public officials who are accountable.

Consensus on complex and difficult issues is very desirable, but decisions on the size and active/reserve mix of the armed forces are too important to be left to outside commissions, consultants, or ad hoc groups that include unofficial organizations. The December 19, 1993, offsite agreement of the army's reserve components is an example. The secretary of defense left the force mix decision[91] to the army. The army left the decision to an "offsite" (arbitration) process which, in order to achieve agreement among the competing interest groups, including unofficial military associations, adopted the lowest common denominator of consensus. According to the General Accounting Office of Congress, the subsequent restructuring cost more than ten times the original estimate. Correct decisions on complex issues seldom attract universal appeal. Public officials—both civilian and military—should seek to understand public opinion, but they must not abdicate their responsibility of making such decisions themselves—solely on the merits of the issues involved.

32. Flexible training has definite advantages.

Traditional weekend drills minimize employer conflicts but are often inefficient because of the disproportionate time required for administrative matters. Depending upon the nature of a unit's combat mission and the availability of personnel, fewer but longer and more concentrated blocks of training time usually pay larger readiness dividends.

33. Promotions must be made on the basis of the most qualified persons who are eligible.

This principle would seem obvious, but there have been past instances where qualified—but not the most qualified—reservists have been promoted on the basis of seniority or even for quasi-political reasons. If active and reserve forces are to be fully integrated, such practices cannot be tolerated. Reserve promotions must be based solely on the basis of competence.[92]

34. The reduction of attrition must be a priority.

As increasing demands are placed on reservists, attrition pressures are likely to increase. The smaller reserve components cannot afford the costs associated with the training of new recruits to replace reservists who might be retained in the force. Old-fashioned leadership will be required at all levels if quality reserve forces are to be maintained.

35. Professional military education courses must be reconfigured to permit greater reserve participation.

The requirement that reservists meet the same standards of performance and career development as active force personnel is desirable, but it inevitably conflicts with the limited time available to reservists. Noncommissioned officers need to take military courses that are essential to a change in MOS and eligibility for promotion. Reserve officers must attend staff and war colleges and a variety of specialized courses. Reservists who have the most promise as future senior officers or noncommissioned officers often face conflicting time demands of a successful and fast-moving civilian career. Unless military career development courses are made more compatible with these demands, future reserve officers and NCOs are likely to come from a narrower range of civilian backgrounds and may, in fact, be generally less qualified than those in the reserve components today.

The thirty-five principles just described are likely to command sufficient support to at least serve as a starting point for an approach to Total Force planning around which a consensus may be built. They are useless unless civilian and military policy makers are fully informed, honest, and courageous; unless they are open-minded and innovative in their approach to the use of reserve forces; unless they are willing to put aside parochialism and prejudices for or against the use of reservists; and unless they are willing to consider such principles in the process of making force planning decisions that are in the clear interest of the nation because they are based on merit.

During this period of transition from the end of the Cold War to the first decade of the twenty-first century, a fundamental restructuring of the nation's military capability has begun. Additional restructuring is essential. Many contentious restructuring issues remain to be decided. Some necessarily had to await the judgment of the American people as they chose their new leaders in 1996.

Whatever decisions are ultimately made, it is clear that America's citizen warriors, sailors, marines, and airmen will continue to be a cornerstone upon which our security rests. They have demonstrated their immense value to the nation in blood upon a hundred battlefields for over two hundred years.

Their public service must not, however, be taken for granted. Reduced defense budgets and the absence of a clear global threat do not justify a mindless use of reservists for unimportant military missions or nonmilitary work that can be performed by others. When danger to the nation has passed, they must be permitted to lay aside the warrior and return to the citizen. Only if we are wise in our reliance upon our citizen warriors, can we be assured that in the future, as in the past, they will immediately respond to the war tocsin when new dangers arrive.

Epilogue

The most enduring story in the folklore upon which the concept of citizen soldier is based is that of Lucius Quinctius Cincinnatus, a fifth-century B.C. Roman hero. According to the traditional accounts of his career, which have almost certainly been embellished by legend, Cincinnatus was the proprietor of only four acres of ground. In 458 B.C., two warlike nations, the Aequi and the Volsci, combined forces and surrounded a Roman consular army that was trapped on Mount Algidus. Called from the plough and given dictatorial power to save the situation, Cincinnatus is said to have defeated the enemy in a single day and celebrated the triumph in Rome. Having saved the Roman army from annihilation, he voluntarily relinquished his power at the conclusion of the emergency and returned to his farm.[1]

The American ideal of citizen soldier has many roots. Only the most untutored have not read of the Minutemen of the Revolution. Many also remember reading the words of General George Washington in a letter he wrote to the New York legislature as he traveled north to assume command of the Continental Army: "When we assumed the Soldier, we did not lay aside the Citizen."

The canvas that lingers the longest in my mind's eye, however, is the famous painting by John Trumbull which hangs in the Capitol rotunda in Washington. It shows General Washington in the statehouse in Annapolis on the morning of December 23, 1783, only three months after the signing of the treaty formally ending the war and only a few weeks after British troops had left American soil.

Having successfully commanded the militia of the states and the continental troops (both of which he addressed as "my virtuous fellow Citizens in the field") through an arduous conflict which would give birth to a new nation, the general stood facing the representatives of congress to whom he had come to submit his resignation. His horse was waiting at the door to carry him to Mount Vernon by

Christmas Eve, and as far as he then knew, away from public service forever. It is reported that his hand shook as he spoke:

> Having now finished the work assigned me, I retire from the great theater of Action; and bidding an Affectionate farewell to this August body under whose orders I have so long acted, I here offer my Commission, and take my leave of all the employments of public life.[2]

In the last four years of the twentieth century it may be reasonably asked whether this citizen soldier ideal remains relevant to America's modern security needs. The question is not likely to be answered to the complete satisfaction of skeptics. Fair-minded military analysts will, of course, be quick to point to the undisputed capabilities of various National Guard and reserve units. I count myself among those who still believe that the capability and quality of the warrior is more important than the quality of the weapon, and that Patton was figuratively correct when he argued that "it is the gleam in the attacker's eye and not the glitter of the bayonet that breaks the line." While some defense leaders have asserted in recent days that combat readiness equals modern weapons plus people, I still subscribe to the ethos of John Paul Jones, which I learned as a plebe at the Naval Academy and which I quoted in my remarks after taking the oath of office as assistant secretary of defense: "Men mean more than guns in the rating of a ship." The quality of the modern American reservist is undeniably the best in the world.

The quality and capabilities of reserve units and individual reservists should not, however, be the central point in the ongoing national debate about the shape of the armed forces of the future. There will always be outstanding reservists and new opportunities to use them. No, the fulcrum upon which the importance of our citizen warriors rests primarily is the unique American system of civil-military relations. It has been said that any system of civil-military relations involves a complex equilibrium between the authority, influence on the one hand and ideology of the military and the authority, influence, and ideology of nonmilitary groups on the other.[3]

Almost forty years have now passed and the nation has endured severe cultural and political tensions since the same observer argued that within our system of civil-military relations, America can learn more from West Point and its values of loyalty, duty, restraint, and dedication than West Point can learn from America.[4] Many now believe that there is a growing gap between American society and the armed forces.[5]

And yet, the citizen warrior ideal is perhaps the most vivid modern example of practical and successful patriotism. I believe that the absence of mandatory military service for all Americans, the tenets of effective democracy, and a concern for proper balance in our civil-military relations will continue to require citizen volunteers who can assume the warrior in the interest of country, and return to their figurative ploughs when danger passes. Operations Desert Shield and Desert Storm demonstrated the relevancy of the ideal to the demands of the present. The task now is to apply it to the demands of the future.

EXECUTIVE ORDER
ORDERING THE SELECTED RESERVE OF THE
ARMED FORCES TO ACTIVE DUTY

By the authority vested in me as President by the Constitution and the laws of the United States of America, including sections 121 and 673b of title 10 of the United States Code, I hereby determine that it is necessary to augment the active armed forces of the United States for the effective conduct of operational missions in and around the Arabian Peninsula. Further, under the stated authority, I hereby authorize the Secretary of Defense, and the Secretary of Transportation with respect to the Coast Guard when the latter is not operation as a service in the Department of the Navy, to order to active duty units and individual members not assigned to units, of the Selected Reserve.

This order is intended only to improve the internal management of the executive branch, and is not intended to create any right or benefit, substantive or procedural, enforceable at law by a party against the United States, its agencies, its officers, or any person.

This order shall be published in the Federal Register and transmitted promptly to the Congress.

George Bush
THE WHITE HOUSE, August 22, 1990

NATIONAL DESERT STORM RESERVIST DAY, 1991
By the President of the United States of America
A Proclamation

On this occasion we gratefully salute the members of the National Guard and Reserve forces of the United States—dedicated and highly trained men and women who played a major role in the success of Operation Desert Shield/Desert Storm. Whether they served directly in the Persian Gulf or on military bases in the United States and elsewhere around the world, as members of our Nation's Total Force, these National Guardsmen and reservists made a vital contribution toward the liberation of Kuwait.

During the course of the war in the Persian Gulf, more than 228,000 members of the Ready Reserve were ordered to active duty. Thousands more volunteered in advance of being called to support the coalition effort. Members of the Army National Guard, the Army Reserve, the Naval Reserve, the Marine Corps Reserve, the Air National Guard, the Air Force Reserve, the Coast Guard Reserve—these men and women were trained and ready to do their jobs. As they have done for all conflicts since colonial times, guardsmen and reservists responded quickly to the call. They promptly assumed a variety of combat missions such as armor, artillery, tactical fighter, tactical reconnaissance and minesweeping. Their support missions included transportation, medical, airlift, service/supply, civil affairs, intelligence, military police, and communications.

When called to active duty members of the Ready Reserve were suddenly required to leave behind their families and their careers. As we thank our Desert Storm reservists for the many sacrifices that they have made of behalf of our country, it is fitting that we also honor their loved ones. They too have shown the extraordinary degree of patriotism and courage that we have come to expect of the Nation's military families.

National Guard and Reserve units worked in close cooperation with the Active Services to develop a broad-based family support network to assist these new military dependents.

The Nation's employers, educators and other institutions throughout the private sector have provided strong support and assistance to their reservist employees and students who were called to duty on short notice. The National committee for Employer Support of the Guard and Reserve, a 4,000-member network of business and civic leader volunteers, has put forth special efforts to help guardsmen and reservists, as well as their employers, to understand their job rights and responsibilities.

In recognition of their vital role in the liberation of Kuwait, the Congress, by Senate Joint Resolution 134, has designated May 22, 1991, as "National Desert Storm Reservists Day" and has authorized and requested the President to issue a proclamation in observance of this day.

NOW, THEREFORE, I, GEORGE BUSH, President of the United States of America, do hereby proclaim May 22, 1991, as National Desert Storm Reservists Day. I call upon all Americans to observe this day with appropriate ceremonies and activities in honor of the courageous men and women of the United States Ready Reserve.

IN WITNESS WHEREOF, I have hereunto set my hand this twenty-first day of May, in the year of our Lord nineteen hundred and ninety-one, and of the Independence of the United States of America the two hundred and fifteenth.

George Bush

Notes

Part I: Chapter I

1. George Bush, "Preface," *National Security Strategy of the United States,* March 1990, p. v.

2. George Bush, Address to the Aspen Institute, Aspen, Colorado, August 2, 1990.

3. *Perpich, et al. v. Department of Defense, et al.,* 496 U.S. 334, 110 S.Ct. 2418 (1990). In an opinion authored by Justice John Paul Stevens, the Court specifically upheld the authority of Congress to authorize the president to order members of the National Guard to active duty for purposes of training outside the United States during peacetime without either the consent of a state governor or the declaration of a national emergency. For a discussion of the political setting and the legal issues presented by the case, see pages 2420–2422 of the Court's opinion.

4. Mark Perry, *Four Stars* (Boston: Houghton Mifflin, 1989), p. 152.

5. In remarks to the Congress of the Interallied Confederation of Reserve Officers in August 1982, Secretary of Defense Caspar Weinberger succinctly summarized the goal of the policy:

> We can no longer consider reserve forces as merely forces in reserve. . . . Instead, they have to be an integral part of the total force, both within the United States and within NATO. They have to be, and in fact are, a blending of the professionalism of the full-time soldier with the professionalism of the citizen-soldier.

Edward J. Philbin, James L. Gould, "The Guard and Reserve: In Pursuit of Full Integration," *The Guard and Reserve in the Total Force* (Washington, D.C.: National Defense University Press, Bennie J. Wilson III, ed., 1985), p. 50.

6. Title 10, U.S. Code, Section 673b. The Selected Reserve consists of those units and individuals in the National Guard and fed-

eral reserve components designated by their respective military services and approved by the Joint Chiefs of Staff as so essential to initial wartime missions that they have priority over all other reserve forces. Title 10, U.S. Code, Section 268(c).

7. *A Report on the Navy's Total Force FY 90,* p. ii.

8. Hearings before the Committee on Armed Services, United States Senate, One Hundredth Congress, First Session, October 16, 1987.

9. *Ibid.*

10. Ninety-Fourth Congress, Second Session, Committee on International Resolutions, U.S. House of Representatives, *The War Powers Resolution* (Washington, D.C.: U.S. Government Printing Office, 1975), p. 1.

11. For an excellent discussion of the factors that had motivated Abrams's efforts, see Lewis Sorley, *Thunderbolt* (New York: Simon and Schuster, 1992), pp. 360–368.

12. U.S. News & World Report, *Triumph Without Victory: The History of the Persian Gulf War* (New York: Times Books, 1993), p. 69; Bob Woodward, *The Commanders* (New York: Simon and Schuster, 1991), pp. 248–250.

13. The theme of the remarks was that global shifts of power every twenty years or so have major effects on the nature of our defense planning. Under the circumstances, the remarks were not as dry as they might have been otherwise, and I was able to offer tangible evidence of my own interest in the women who serve in the Department of Defense by introducing my daughter, Ensign Kelly Duncan, who had graduated from the U.S. Naval Academy only two months earlier.

14. Stephen M. Duncan, Pentagon news briefing, December 15, 1987.

15. Stephen M. Duncan, Memorandum to the Secretary of Defense, August 8, 1990.

16. H. Norman Schwarzkopf, *It Doesn't Take a Hero* (New York: Bantam Books, 1992), pp. 285–291; U.S. News & World Report, *op. cit.,* pp. 29–30.

17. U.S. News & World Report, *op. cit.,* pp. 42–43, 86–87. Schwarzkopf, *op. cit.,* p. 323.

18. The absence of a TYPFDL was particularly irritating to me. At the end of the Reagan administration, I had requested information from the Joint Staff on the planned deployment sequence of reserve units that had been identified as essential to the execution of the early phases of each of our major war plans. Since I had responsibility for the readiness of all reserve units, it was critical that I know the readiness condition of early-deploying reserve units. If shifts in the allocation of resources or changes in policy were necessary to improve their readiness, I would know where to start.

The Joint Staff, however, had proved to be as much of a bureaucratic obstacle as any I encountered in the Pentagon. Civilian oversight on such matters was not welcome. Relying upon its own procedural rules that prohibited the release of such information to anyone other than the secretary and deputy secretary of defense, the Staff balked. Just as I was about to ask then Secretary of Defense Frank Carlucci to force a rule change, I obtained the information I needed from another source. If I had persisted with the Joint Staff, of course, I would have discovered just how unprepared some of the war plans and accompanying TYPFDLs were.

19. Michael R. Gordon, "U.S. May Call Up Some Reservists to Ease the Strain on the Military," *New York Times*, August 15, 1990, p. 1.

20. Powell's later description of the meeting reflects the continuing concern that most military leaders at the time had about the "politics" of a call-up decision. In his memoirs, Powell says that he informed the president that "a call-up means pulling people out of their jobs. It affects business. It means disrupting thousands of families. It's a major political decision." Colin L. Powell, *My American Journey* (New York: Random House, 1995), p. 470.

21. "The President at the Pentagon," *Washington Post*, August 16, 1990, p. 31.

22. Caspar Weinberger, *Fighting for Peace* (New York: Warner Books, Inc., 1990), p. 433.

23. Michael Howard, ed., *Soldiers and Governments* (London: Dyre & Spottiswoode, 1957), p. 19.

24. Winston S. Churchill, *Their Finest Hour* (Boston: Houghton Mifflin, 1949), p. 18.

25. In resolving such issues, it is not necessary for political lead-

ers to subscribe entirely to either of what has been described as the "two competing models of military professionalism: the apolitical warrior versus the soldier-statesman." Jerome Slater, "Military Officers and Politics I," *American Defense Policy*, Fifth Edition (Baltimore and London: Johns Hopkins University Press, 1983), p. 749. The first would exclude military leaders from such high policy making and "all roles that go beyond those traditionally defined as strictly military." The second would fuse all the elements of national policy and encourage high-level participation by military officers in the political, economic, and other as well as the military components of foreign policy.

26. Admiral William J. Crowe, Jr., who was serving as chairman when the Goldwater-Nichols Defense Reorganization Act became law, has observed that the increase in the chairman's authority has shifted the balance between the chairman and the secretary of defense for whom he works, and that as a result, a chairman can more easily frustrate the secretary. William J. Crowe, Jr., David Chanoff, *The Line of Fire* (New York: Simon and Schuster, 1993), p. 158. Unless and until the legislation is amended to correct this result—a result not intended by Congress—the particular experience and ability of each civilian secretary and the respective personalities of each secretary and chairman will be even more important than they have been in the past.

27. D. J. Atwood, Memorandum for Secretaries of the Military Departments, Chairman of the Joint Chiefs of Staff, August 20, 1990.

28. Sam Nunn, News Release, August 21, 1990.

29. News Services, "Bush: Reservists' Call-Up 'Essential to Completing Our Mission,'" *Washington Post*, August 23, 1990, p. A36.

30. John R. Galvin, *The Minute Men*, 2nd ed. (Washington, D.C.: Brassey's, 1989), p. 247.

Chapter II

1. Martin Gilbert, *Churchill: A Life* (New York: Henry Holt and Company, 1991), p. 551.

2. In his recent memoirs, former Secretary of Defense Robert S. McNamara has described what he believes to be one of the "major causes" of the "disaster" in Vietnam.

We failed to draw Congress and the American people into a full and frank discussion and debate of the pros and cons of a large-scale U.S. military involvement in Southeast Asia before we initiated the action.

[W]e had not prepared the public to understand the complex events we faced. . . . A nation's deepest strength lies not in its military prowess but, rather, in the unity of its people. We failed to maintain it."

Robert S. McNamara, *In Retrospect: The Tragedy and Lessons of Vietnam* (New York: Times Books, 1995), pp. 321–323.

3. Jim Hoagland, "Congress, Bush and the Generals," *Washington Post*, November 22, 1990, p. A31.

4. When I met in Panama during Operation Just Cause (early 1989) with Gen. Max Thurman, the commander in chief of the U.S. Southern Command, he had expressed only one concern: his frustration at being unable to seek a call-up of a handful of individuals from a reserve unit without having to take the entire unit.

5. It is useful to note Ambassador Paul Nitze's recollection of the advice he received in World War II from then Army Chief of Staff George C. Marshall on the implementation of the new Selective Service Act: "Marshall's point was that men should be selected or granted deferments on the fairest and most equitable basis possible, for if they weren't, there could be a serious public backlash against the administration, a loss of confidence in the government, and a crippling of the war effort. Paul H. Nitze, *From Hiroshima to Glasnost* (New York: Grove Weidenfeld, 1989), p. 12.

6. H. Norman Schwarzkopf, *op. cit.,* p. 323.

7. James Kitfield, *Prodigal Soldiers* (New York: Simon and Schuster, 1995), p. 349.

8. U.S. General Accounting Office, *Report to the Secretary of the Army* (GAO/NSIAD 91-263, National Guard Combat Brigades, September 1991), p. 8.

9. U.S. Department of Defense, *Conduct of the Persian Gulf War* (Washington, D.C.: Government Printing Office, April 1992), p. 36.

10. The postmobilization training plan called for small-unit training to commence immediately after call-up. Collective training would begin after individual soldier skills were determined to be

satisfactory. Robert H. Scales, Jr., *Certain Victory: The U.S. Army in the Gulf War* (Washington, D.C.: Brassey's, 1994), p. 53.

11. Schwarzkopf, *op. cit.*, p. 346.

12. *Ibid.*, p. 323.

13. Cited in Michael Howard, ed., *Soldiers and Governments* (London: Dyre & Spottiswoode, 1957), p. 14.

14. Russell F. Weigley, *Towards an American Army: Military Thought from Washington to Marshall* (Westport, Conn.: Greenwood Press, 1962), pp. 10–12.

15. George Wilson, "Pentagon's New Reliance on Reserves Tested," *Washington Post*, August 24, 1990, p. 1.

16. *Ibid.*

17. Quoted in Rick Maze, "Growing Reliance on Reserve Raises Concerns," *Army Times*, April 13, 1987, p. 8.

18. Stephen M. Duncan, Hearings before the Committee on Armed Services, United States Senate, One Hundredth Congress, First Session, October 16, 1987.

19. Joint Chiefs of Staff, *Publication 1-02*, December 1, 1989.

20. In the eyes of some, the new SORTS was the result of an intentional effort to downplay the combat-readiness connotations of the measuring system. Martin Binkin, William W. Kaufmann, *U.S. Army Guard & Reserve: Rhetoric, Realities, Risks* (Washington, D.C.: The Brookings Institution, 1989), p. 92.

21. Stephen M. Duncan, Hearings before the Subcommittee on the Department of Defense of the Committee on Appropriations, House of Representatives, One Hundred First Congress, First Session, April 6, 1989.

22. *Ibid.*

23. During 1989, National Guard and reserve officers trained for their wartime missions an average of sixty-one days and reserve enlisted personnel trained for an average of forty-two days. Testimony of Stephen M. Duncan, Hearings before the Readiness Subcommittee, House of Representatives, One Hundred First Congress, First Session, April 4, 1990.

24. A study concluded in 1988 identified sixty-seven army occupational specialty courses provided to reservists that took more than four months to complete. The navy identified eighty-nine enlisted

positions that were difficult to fill because of the length of the required training courses. General Accounting Office, *Reserve Components: Opportunities to Improve National Guard and Reserve Policies and Programs,* 1988, p. 54.

25. Dick Cheney, *Annual Report to the President and the Congress* (Washington, D.C.: U.S. Government Printing Office, 1990).

26. Air National Guardsmen had flown close air support missions with A-7 aircraft. Other Air Guard crews were flying airlift missions in C-141, C-130, and C-5 aircraft. Air Force Reserve crews had flown combat sorties aboard AC-130 gunships as well as aerial refueling, aeromedical evacuation, and other missions. Military police units from the Army National Guard and civil affairs units of the Army Reserve had also performed critical tasks. For a more detailed discussion of the contributions of the reserve components to Just Cause, see Stephen M. Duncan, Hearings before the Subcommittee on the Department of Defense of the Committee on Appropriations, United States Senate, One Hundred First Congress, Second Session, April 24, 1990.

Chapter III

1. G. V. Montgomery, "Pentagon Wrong Not to Include Guard, Reserve Combat Units in Call-Up," News Release, August 27, 1990.

2. G. V. Montgomery, Letter to Richard Cheney, August 28, 1990.

3. George Bush, Letter to G. V. Montgomery, August 28, 1990.

4. Les Aspin, quoted in Donna Cassata, "Lawmakers Want Reserve Combat Units Sent to Gulf," Associated Press, September 6, 1990.

5. *Ibid.*

6. Author's conversation with David Gribbin, September 5, 1990.

7. Colin Powell, Testimony to Senate Armed Services Committee 101st Congress, 2nd Session, 1990 Federal Information Systems Corporation, September 11, 1990.

8. Matt Yancy, "13 House Members Belong to Military Units," *Washington Post,* August 23, 1990, p. A23.

9. United States Constitution, Article I, Section 6, Clause 2.

10. *Reservists Committee to Stop the War v. Laird,* 323 F. Supp. 833, 837–839 (D.D.C. 1971), *aff'd mem.,* 495 F.2d 1075 (D.C. Cir.), *rev'd on other ground,* 418 U.S. 208, 214 n.4 (1974).

11. Douglas MacArthur, *Reminiscences* (New York: McGraw-Hill Book Company, 1964), p. 44.

12. William Manchester, *American Caesar* (Boston: Little, Brown and Company, 1978), p. 77.

13. *Ibid.*

14. Mirtha Maria Reyes Alonzo, "A Fighting Woman Heeds Different Call," *Newark Star-Ledger,* September 8, 1990, p. 1.

15. Stephen M. Duncan, Hearing before the Committees on Veterans Affairs, United States Senate and United States House of Representatives, One Hundred First Congress, Second Session, September 12. 1990.

16. The booklet "Ordered to Active Duty: What Now?" also included the names and addresses of organizations and relief societies that offered a variety of assistance to families. The National Guard and Family Coordinators within each state were also listed.

17. Raymond J. Celada, "National Emergency Declaration's Triggering Consequences," Congressional Research Service Memorandum, September 5, 1990.

18. Dick Cheney, Letter to Les Aspin, September 1990.

19. *Ibid.*

20. Stephen M. Duncan, *Aerospace Daily,* September 27, 1990, p. 511.

21. In an interview that appeared in the October 28, 1990, edition of the *Atlanta Journal & Constitution,* but which had been conducted the previous week, Schwarzkopf gave two reasons for his opposition to the use of the brigades:

> Right now, the authority is in place to call them up for six months and six months only. . . .
>
> You train them up for two months, then you get them over here. . . . It is probably another month before you get them up to the front where they can do you any good. Now three months have passed. . . . So you look at the back side of the thing and say, "It's probably going to take us another month to get them loaded up, back on the boats, muster them out of the service." So what does that give you? Two months in country.
>
> If you went out and talked to some of those guys in the 24th Mech, they'd tell you it took them a month before they felt com-

fortable that they really knew the terrain, knew the area, knew how to operate, were acclimated and that sort of thing. Given my choice of a unit, the one I want over here is not the one that I'm only going to have for two months. I want the unit that I can have in country as long as I can possibly keep them. . . .

Another thing you've got to remember—how do you think the 82nd [Airborne Division] would feel if they saw a unit come in country . . . months after they got here, and that unit stayed here two months and turned around and went home, and they (the 82nd) were still here. There is an equity thing here. And I don't think the National Guard wants the reputation of "last in, first out."

Joseph Albright, H. Norman Schwarzkopf, *Atlanta Journal & Constitution,* October 28, 1990, p. 12.

22. Former Army Chief of Staff Edward Meyer, who participated in meetings between military leaders and President Johnson during the Vietnam War, has described the importance of the tradition: "Once you start tampering with that tradition, you have a hell of a mess, like we did for a while in the Civil War. You just can't take it upon yourself to overrule the man who is fighting the battle." Mark Perry, *op. cit.,* p. 175.

23. Dick Cheney, Letter to G. V. Montgomery, October 9, 1990. Considering the intensity with which the issues involving the round-out brigades were being fought, the letter was remarkable for its brevity. No rationale was given by Cheney for his sudden support of a "prompt" legislative amendment. The passage of the amendment would not, of course, require the call-up of the brigades. It would eliminate the primary reason being advanced by Cheney's military advisors for their reluctance to recommend a call-up. Several weeks later, Cheney wrote again to Montgomery and described in general terms the basis of his support of the legislative amendment—"flexibility" and "the most effective use" of reserve units. Dick Cheney, Letter to G. V. Montgomery," November 29, 1990.

24. Les Aspin, Beverly Byron, G.V. Montgomery, "Anti-Reserve Bias Behind Combat Unit Absence, News Release, House Armed Services Committee, October 16, 1990.

25. *Ibid.*

26. *Ibid.*

27. Conference Report [to accompany H.R. 5803], *Making Appropriations for the Department of Defense,* Report 101-938, House of Representatives, One Hundred First Congress, Second Session, October 24, 1990.

28. John Keegan, *The Face of Battle* (New York: Penguin Books, 1978).

29. Eric Schmitt, "Pentagon Will Call Up Combat Reserved Units," *New York Times,* November 5, 1990, p. A10.

30. Associated Press, "Marines Order Call-Up of Reservists for Combat Roles," *Washington Times,* November 6, 1990, p. 12.

31. Caspar W. Weinberger, "The Uses of Military Power," Speech to the National Press Club, Washington, D.C., November 28, 1984.

32. Dick Cheney, Briefing by the Secretary of Defense and Chairman of the Joint Chiefs of Staff, Pentagon Briefing Room, *Reuter Transcript Report,* November 8, 1990.

33. *Ibid.*

34. Martin Gilbert, *op. cit.,* p. 758.

35. Colin Powell, *op. cit.,* pp. 471, 569.

36. Early in Cheney's tenure, a senior member of the Joint Staff informed me that military personnel perceived Cheney to be a "super action officer." I took that to mean that he was perceived as someone who tended to focus too much on the details of an issue he was interested in, at the expense of other important issues in which he was not interested. One of Cheney's senior aides who had worked closely with him for many years once described for me his own method of dealing with Cheney's impatience with meetings. "When I enter his office," he said, "I start a U-turn and time my message or question so that I have delivered it or received an answer just as I leave the office."

Chapter IV

1. Dick Cheney, Memorandum for the Secretaries of the Military Departments and Chairman of the Joint Chiefs of Staff, November 14, 1990.

2. Press conference by the president, White House Briefing Room, November 30, 1990.

3. Director, White House Office of National Drug Control Policy.

4. Dick Cheney, Memorandum for the Secretaries of the Military Departments and Chairman of the Joint Chiefs of Staff, December 1, 1990.

5. According to Defense Department figures, twenty percent of all active army personnel in dual-service marriages were married to members of the reserve components in 1992. B. J. Ramos, "Dual-Service Couples Find Gain, Sacrifice," *Army Times,* July 3, 1995, p. 28.

6. Dick Cheney, Prepared testimony to the Senate Armed Services Committee, One Hundred First Congress, Second Session, December 3, 1990.

7. Colin Powell, Prepared testimony to the Senate Armed Services Committee, One Hundred First Congress, Second Session, December 3, 1990.

8. See the discussion of the Base Force concept in Chapter VII.

9. Those pressures were substantial. For over forty years the reserve associations—led by the 102,000-member National Guard Association of the United States—have aggressively employed broad grass-roots organizations to lobby for matters considered to be important to guardsmen and reservists. One long-time observer concluded in 1992 that the reserve lobby "makes the gun lobby led by the National Rifle Association look like amateurs." Art Pine, "In Defense of 2nd Line Defenders," *Los Angeles Times,* March 13, 1992, p. 1. A November 1994 editorial in the flagship publication of the Reserve Officers Association candidly described how that association operates:

> Our process attempts to provide a clear representation of what ROA members are seeking and to work with members of Congress toward that end. . . . When one counts all of the drilling Reservists and their families and friends, there is a considerable constituency available to garner the necessary attention.

"The Voice of ROA," *The Officer,* November 1994, p. 8.

10. Douglas MacArthur, *op. cit.,* p. 426.

11. Department of Defense, *Total Force Policy Report to Congress,* De-

cember 31, 1990, p. 51. For a discussion of this study of the Total Force Policy, see Chapter VIII.

12. Robert H. Scales, Jr., *Certain Victory: The U.S. Army in the Gulf War* (Washington, D.C.: Brassey's, 1994), p. 53.

13. Stephen M. Duncan, Hearing before the Subcommittee on Manpower and Personnel, Armed Services Committee, United States Senate, One Hundred Second Congress, First Session, June 5, 1991.

14. *Ibid.*

15. U.S. General Accounting Office, *National Guard: Peacetime Training Did Not Adequately Prepare Combat Brigades for Gulf War* (GAO/NSIAD-91-263, September 1991), p. 13. Most of the brigade's maintenance work had previously been performed by centralized maintenance shops staffed by full-time technicians.

16. A validation decision was not made for either the 155th Infantry Brigade or the 256th Armor Brigade before a cease fire was reached in Desert Storm.

17. Colin Powell, Memorandum for the Secretary of Defense, January 8, 1991.

18. On January 12, 1991, the Senate gave its approval by a vote of 52 to 47. The vote in the House of Representatives was 250 to 183 in favor.

19. Colin Powell, Address to the (D.C.) Bar, Ramada Renaissance Techworld, January 10, 1991.

20. Bob Woodward, *The Commanders* (New York: Simon and Schuster, 1991), p. 367.

21. George Bush, "Ordering the Ready Reserve of the Armed Forces to Active Duty," Executive Order No. 12743, January 18, 1991.

22. Harry G. Summers, Jr., *On Strategy II: A Critical Analysis of the Gulf War* (New York: Dell, 1992), p. 45.

23. B. H. Liddell Hart, *Strategy,* second revised edition, (New York: Meridian, 1991), pp. 321–322.

24. Mark Perry, *op. cit.,* p. 152.

25. In his book chronicling the rebuilding and reenergizing of the armed forces after Vietnam, one author has noted that only three percent of the active duty forces in Desert Shield/Desert Storm were Vietnam veterans, but "they played the premier role in planning the operations and leading the forces into battle in the air, on land, and

at sea." Al Santoli, *Leading the Way: How Vietnam Veterans Rebuilt the U.S. Military* (New York: Ballantine Books, 1993), p. xvii.

26. James A. Baker, III, *The Politics of Diplomacy* (New York: G. P. Putnam's Sons, 1995), p. 409.

27. One reserve doctor from Wisconsin who volunteered to go to the Gulf was a veteran of World War II. And, contrary to the conventional wisdom that existed before the Gulf War, I did not have to deal with a single complaint by a reservist opposed to his activation. I did, however, have to face a room of Naval Reserve flag officers, most of whom were very outspoken in their unhappiness at *not* being activated after training for several years for just such an opportunity to serve in combat.

Chapter V

1. Norman Friedman, *Desert Victory* (Annapolis: Naval Institute Press, 1991), p. 120.

2. The extent of this danger has become evident only in recent years. While senior Pentagon officials were aware in 1990 that Iraq possessed at least a thousand tons of chemical agents and that Saddam Hussein had used such agents in the war against Iran, no one appreciated fully the steps that Iraq had taken to use them against the coalition forces. In August 1995, shortly after Hussein Kamel Hassan Majeed (the director of Iraq's weapons of mass destruction program) defected to Jordan, Iraqi officials admitted to the United Nations that in December 1990, Iraq had loaded three types of deadly nerve agents into roughly 200 bombs and missile warheads that were then distributed to air bases and a missile site. Iraq also admitted to having begun a crash program in August 1990—the month it invaded Kuwait—aimed at producing a nuclear weapon within a year. It was deterred from the use of the biological weapons by its fear of U.S. retaliation with nuclear weapons. Its own nuclear program was still at least three months from completion when the Gulf War ended. R. Jeffrey Smith, "Iraq Reveals Bid to Build an A-Bomb," *Washington Post,* August 24, 1995, pp. A1, A31; R. Jeffrey Smith, "U.N. Says Iraqis Prepared Germ Weapons in Gulf War," *Washington Post,* August 26, 1995, pp. A1, A19; "Baghdad's Dirty Secrets," *U.S. News & World Report,* September 11, 1995, p. 41.

3. Lawrence Freedman, Efraim Karsh, *The Gulf Conflict 1990–1991* (Princeton: Princeton University Press, 1993), p. 278.

4. *Ibid.*

5. U.S. Department of Defense, *Conduct of the Persian Gulf War* (Washington, D.C.: Government Printing Office, April 1992), p. 84.

6. *Ibid.,* p. 251.

7. *Ibid.,* p. 84.

8. The Iraqi Armed Forces General Command confidently claimed:

> Even without considering the state of morale, the difference in supply sources, and other considerations, all of which are in Iraq's favor—if the battle starts, the wicked U.S. administration would need a ratio of three to one to become technically able to launch an attack against the valiant and faithful God's forces. Iraqi News Agency, November 19, 1990.

9. Interview of Colonel Bob Efferson, September 29, 1995.

10. 926 TFG/706 TFS, *Operation Desert Shield/Storm After-Action Report*, August 17, 1991, p. 4.

11. Efferson interview.

12. Friedman, *op. cit.,* p. 192.

13. Wes Wright, "Scud Hunting with AFRES A-10-As," *Journal of Military Aviation*, September-October 1992, p. 23.

14. *After-Action Report, op. cit.,* p. 1; Efferson interview.

15. Chris Brown, David D. Livingstone, Memorandum for the Deputy Assistant Secretary of Defense for Reserve Affairs (Readiness, Training and Mobilization), July 24, 1992.

16. Stan Owen, "Marine Corps M1A1 Tanks in Operation Desert Storm," *Amphibious Warfare Review*, Summer/Fall 1992, p. 51.

17. Jeffrey R. Dacus, "Bravo Company Goes to War," *Armor*, September-October 1991, p. 9.

18. Undated memorandum of Company "B" (Rein.), 4th Tank Battalion, 4th Marine Division, FMF USMCR, Yakima, Washington.

19. Napoleon I: Letter to Barry E. O'Meara, St. Helena, September 29, 1817.

20. R. J. Englebrecht, "Fleet Hospital Five Open for Business in ME," *Dry Dock*, November 2, 1990, p. 1.

21. "Navy Medicine," *All Hands*, Special Issue, Number 892, 1991, p. 50.

22. 158th Field Artillery (MLRS), *After-Action Report*, 1991, p. 1.

23. U.S. Department of Defense, *Conduct of the Persian Gulf War*, p. 249.

24. *Ibid.*

25. Al Santoli, *op. cit.*, p. 215.

26. DoD, *op. cit.*, p. 243.

27. *Ibid.*, p. 245.

28. William H. McMichael, "Oklahoma's Finest," *Soldiers*, Vol. 46, No. 7, July 1991, p. 34.

29. National Guard Bureau, *Army National Guard After-Action Report* (2 August–28 February 1991), June 1991, p. 79.

30. John Keegan, "Victory in the Desert: From the War Room to the Battlefield," *Washington Post*, October 10, 1993, p. D-1.

31. DoD, *op. cit.*, p. 393.

32. *Armed Forces Journal International*, April 1991, p. 5.

33. U.S. Department of Defense, *Total Force Policy Report to the Congress* (Washington, D.C., December 1990), p. 29.

34. William G. Pagonis, Jeffrey L. Cruikshank, *Moving Mountains* (Boston: Harvard Business School Press, 1992), p. 6.

35. Donna Miles, "Sustaining the Force," *Soldiers*, May 1991, p. 22.

36. Pagonis, Cruikshank, *op. cit.*, p. 95.

37. *Ibid.*

38. Office of the Assistant Secretary of Defense for Reserve Affairs, *Reserve Components of the United States* (Washington, D.C., May 1990), p. 20.

39. Miles, *op. cit.*, p. 23.

40. Pagonis, Cruikshank, *op. cit.*, p. 9.

41. *Ibid.*

42. *Ibid.*, pp. 11–12.

43. DoD, *op. cit.*, p. 371.

44. Pagonis, Cruikshank, *op. cit.*, p. 101.

45. Rick Atkinson, *Crusade* (Boston: Houghton Mifflin, 1993), pp. 418–421; U.S. News & World Report, *op. cit.*, pp. 328–331.

46. *Ibid.*

47. Michael R. Gordon, Bernard E. Trainor, *The General's War* (Boston: Little, Brown and Company, 1995), p. x.

48. Rick Atkinson, "U.S. Victory Is Absolute," *Washington Post,* March 1, 1991, p. 1.

49. Colin Powell, *op. cit.,* p. 472.

50. George Bush, Address to Joint Session of Congress, March 6, 1991.

Chapter VI

1. Roger T. Kelley, "Introduction," *The All-Volunteer Force after a Decade* William Bowman, Roger Little, G. Thomas Sicilia, eds. (Washington, D.C.: Brassey's, 1986), p. 21.

2. William P. Snyder, *The All-Volunteer Force and American Society* (Charlottesville: University Press of Virginia, 1978), p. 3.

3. *Ibid.*

4. Title 38, U.S. Code, Section 2024(d).

5. *Fishgold v. Sullivan Drydock & Repair Corp.,* 328 U.S. 275, 284 (1946).

6. Title 38, U.S. Code, Section 2024(d).

7. In one of my first meetings in Brussels, Belgium, with the leaders of the reserve forces of the other members of NATO, I demonstrated a new video that we had just produced in which President Reagan appealed to the patriotism of American employers. The British representative demonstrated a new video that argued that the performance of British employees improved after they received reserve military training. A year later we had produced a video that incorporated some of the best British ideas. Meanwhile, our British colleagues had produced a new clip in which Prime Minister Thatcher and the leader of the opposition jointly appealed to the patriotism of British employers.

8. On March 8, 1995, Congressman G. V. Montgomery introduced a bill in the House of Representatives (H.R. 1168) to amend the IRS Code of 1986 to allow credit against income tax to employers of reservists and self-employed reservists. At the time it was introduced, circumstances had changed considerably since my earlier opposition to the idea. Nevertheless, upon hearing of the bill's introduction I remembered a comment made to me by one of Montgomery's senior aides in 1989. After I complained that Montgomery seemed to have no appreciation whatsoever for the fiscal conse-

quences of the reserve legislation he always supported, the aide replied: "You don't understand. Sonny is in the legislative branch and he doesn't worry about balanced budgets."

9. Stephen M. Duncan, Testimony to the Subcommittee on Manpower and Personnel, Armed Services Committee, United States Senate, One Hundred Second Congress, First Session, April 24, 1991.

10. Cheney's letter to the governors was also effective. It encouraged the governors to contact me if they needed additional information about any aspect of the problem. I received no inquiries and no complaints from activated reservists.

11. The survey was conducted by William M. Mercer, Inc.

12. *King v. St. Vincent's Hospital,* 498 U.S., 1081, 111A S.Ct. 940 (1991).

13. *St. Vincent's Hospital v. King,* 902 F.2d 1068 (11th Cir. 1990).

14. *Eidukonis v. Southeastern Pa. Transp. Authority,* 873 F.2d 633 (3rd Cir. 1989).

15. *Ibid.,* pp 695–696.

16. As recently as 1986, Congress had again stressed the importance of employer support of reservists. In a joint resolution, it had declared that "the National Guard and reserve forces of the United States are an integral part of the Total Force Policy of the United States for national defense." It further declared that "attracting and retaining sufficient numbers of qualified persons to serve in the Guard and reserve is a difficult challenge" and that, consequently, "the support of employers and supervisors in granting employees a leave of absence from their jobs to participate in military training without detriment to earned vacation time, promotions, and job benefits is essential to the maintenance of a strong Guard and reserve force." Act of May 2, 1986, Pub. L. No. 99-290, Section 1(a), 100 Stat. 413.

17. Title 38, U.S. Code, Section 4301.

18. The earlier and highly charged confrontation had begun when the governors objected to Pentagon plans to send National Guard units to Honduras for training. In response, Congress had passed the Montgomery Amendment (10 U.S.C. § 672[f]), which provides that when members of the National Guard of the United States are ordered to active duty outside the United States, the governor of a state

may not withhold consent to that duty because of objections to its location, purpose, type, or schedule. In passing the measure, Congress relied on the broad powers conferred upon it by the Army Clause of the Constitution (Article I, Section 8, Clause 12) to provide for the nation's defense and security. Challenging the constitutionality of the amendment, the governors had argued that the Militia Clauses of the Constitution (Article 1, Section 8, Clauses 15, 16) assigned to the states control over the peacetime training of the Guard. After working closely with the Pentagon in the preparation of the written briefs, Ken had personally presented the oral argument on March 27, 1990. On June 11, 1990, a unanimous Supreme Court affirmed our position. 496 U.S. 334, 110 S.Ct. 2418 (1990).

19. Stephen M. Duncan, Hearing before the Committee on Veterans Affairs, United States Senate, One Hundred Second Congress, First Session, May 23, 1991.

20. *King v. St. Vincent's Hospital,* 502 U.S. 215, 112 S.Ct. 570 (1991). The Court held that the terms of the VRRA were unambiguous, that their plain meaning demonstrated the intent of Congress to provide the benefits of the statute without conditions on length of service, and that consequently, no limitations should be implied by the court.

21. Jack Stokes Ballard, *The Shock of Peace: Military and Economic Demobilization after World War II* (Washington, D.C.: University Press of America, 1983), p. 74.

22. Pagonis, Cruikshank, *op. cit.,* p. 150.

23. *Ibid.,* pp. 157–158.

24. Relying upon the writings of Winston Churchill and Omar Bradley, one student of military service has described the similarity of the problems associated with the British demobilization in 1919 and the American demobilization in 1946 in the following fashion:

> Whereas only a few months earlier soldiers had accepted orders that would doom tens of thousands of them to injury or death, suddenly the British and American armies found their soldiers close to mutiny because of delays of a few weeks in demobilization. Generals who had been able to make their dispositions without reference to any particular concerns of equity

or abstract justice found themselves confronted with the necessity of dismantling armies posthaste. Although sound military practice and prudent foreign policy would have dictated
demobilization by unit, so as to retain an effective force, generals found themselves compelled to yield to the demand for
fairness, demobilizing those who had served longest first. The
result, of course, was the systematic stripping from all units of
their experienced cadres.

Eliot A. Cohen, *Citizens & Soldiers: The Dilemmas of Military Service*
(Ithaca: Cornell University Press, 1985), pp. 37–38.

25. Ballard, *op. cit.*, pp. 96–97, 101.

26. *Ibid.*, p. 90. In my own responses to members of Congress, I
explained the many steps that had already been taken to minimize
the hardships being incurred by activated reservists as well as the continuing military requirements that required a prudent pace of demobilization. I also expressed the view that the great majority of reservists understood and accepted the fact that their voluntary
decision to become and to remain a member of a reserve component carried with it the obligation "to serve when and where the nation needs them." See, e.g., Stephen M. Duncan, Hearing before the
Subcommittee on Manpower and Personnel, Armed Services Committee, United States Senate, One Hundred Second Congress, First
Session, June 11, 1991.

27. Michael R. Gordon, "Removing Troops and Equipment Isn't
Easy Either," *New York Times*, April 28, 1991, p. 14.

28. John M. Broder, Melissa Healy, "Hundreds More Reservists Will
Be Sent to Gulf," *Los Angeles Times*, March 1, 1991, p. A1.

29. The policy guidance addressed a range of administrative matters, such as pending disciplinary actions involving reservists, sepa-
ration physical examinations, accrued leave, enlistment termination
dates, and veterans benefits available to reservists upon their release
from active duty.

30. The Joint Staff recommended opposition to the resolution on
the ground that the arbitrary deadline of July 4 was not realistic and
the inability of the military services to meet it would place them in
the unavoidable position of failing to comply.

31. John McCain, Letter to Dick Cheney, April 23, 1991.

32. One student of American demobilization history asserts that "as a demobilization gets under way, it can hardly keep up with the impatience of Americans to be done with it." In other words, the faster the rate of discharges (or velocity), the more insistent the pressure. Ballard, *op. cit.*, p. 102.

33. Dick Cheney, Handwritten note to Stephen M. Duncan, May 20, 1991.

34. M.P.W. Stone, Memorandum to the Secretary of Defense, May 2, 1991.

35. In my testimony to the Senate Appropriations Committee on April 9, I noted that by the time that Desert Storm commenced on January 16, over 188,000 personnel and 375,000 short tons of equipment had been airlifted by the Air Reserve components to Saudi Arabia. The Joint Staff estimated that over 14,000 airlift missions would be required to redeploy the bulk of the force. Joe West, "Reserve Airlifters Among First In, Last Out of War Zone," *Air Force Times*, June 24, 1991, p. 6.

36. When asked about the issue in hearings, I speculated that if reserve physicians received the same homecoming celebrations and other forms of recognition that were expected for reservists who served in the combat arms, significant retention problems of a permanent nature would be unlikely. Few senior reservists make the sacrifices that are inherent in that service for the compensation they receive. Other, more powerful factors are at play, such as old-fashioned patriotism. I was very pleased, therefore, to be informed by the navy surgeon general at the conclusion of Desert Storm that one of his biggest administrative problems was dealing with the large number of applications by reserve doctors who wished to remain on active duty.

37. The preliminary results of the ongoing Rand study appear in David W. Grissmer, Sheila Natarzj Kirby, Man-bing Sze, David Adamson, *Insuring Mobilized Reservists Against Economic Losses: An Overview* (Santa Monica: Rand Institute, 1995).

38. Approximately fifty-five percent of the officers and forty-five percent of the enlisted personnel reported income losses. Approximately eighty percent of the officers and seventy percent of the en-

listed personnel incurred additional expenses, in many cases over $2,500. *Ibid.*, p. xiv.

39. Under the plan, a participating reservist will be entitled to a benefit of up to $5,000 per month for each month of active duty that exceeds thirty days, except that no reservist will be paid for more than twelve months of service served during any period of eighteen consecutive months.

40. George Bush, "National Desert Storm Reservists Day, 1991," Proclamation, May 21, 1991.

Summation

1. John Keegan, *The Face of Battle* (London: Penguin Books, 1978), pp. 302–303.

2. William J. Taylor, Jr., James Blackwell, "The Ground War in the Gulf," *Survival,* Vol. 33, No. 3 (May/June 1991), p. 245.

3. Rick Atkinson, *Crusade,* p. 495.

Part II: Chapter VII

1. Rowland Evans, Jr., Robert D. Novak, *Nixon in the White House* (New York: Random House, 1971), p. 105.

2. *Ibid.*, pp. 130–131.

3. Andrew J. Goodpaster, Lloyd H. Elliot, J. Allan Hovey, Jr., *Toward a Consensus on Military Service* (New York: Pergamon Press, 1982), p. 42.

4. *Ibid.*

5. Mark Perry, *op. cit.,* p. 226.

6. Thomas Barn, "Fragging: A Study," *Army,* April 1977, p. 46; Eugene Linden, "Fragging and Other Withdrawal Symptoms," *Saturday Review,* January 8, 1972, p. 12.

7. *Ibid.*

8. Goodpaster, Elliot, Hovey, *op. cit.,* p. 43.

9. William Bowman, Roger Little, G. Thomas Sicilia, *op. cit.,* p. 21.

10. *Ibid.*

11. Allan R. Millett, Peter Maslowski, *For the Common Defense* (London: The Free Press, 1984), p. 561.

12. In July 1969, the president had announced what was eventu-

ally referred to as the "Nixon doctrine." The specific intent of the doctrine was somewhat in doubt, but the basic message for American allies in the Western Pacific was apparently that while we could be depended on for military equipment in the future, they could not assume future assistance in the form of fighting manpower as we had contributed to Vietnam. See Bernard Brodie, *War & Politics* (New York: Macmillan, 1973), p. 357.

13. Millett, Maslowski, *op. cit.,* p. 562.

14. Richard Nixon, *U.S. Foreign Policy for the 1970's: A New Strategy for Peace,* Report to the Congress, February 1970 (Washington, D.C.: Government Printing Office, 1970), p. 129. According to the then Chief of Naval Operations, none of the members of the Joint Chiefs of Staff thought the nation had the capability in 1970 to fight even one and a half wars, but they were "under heavy political pressure not to let on." Elmo R. Zumwalt, Jr., *On Watch* (New York: Quadrangle/New York Times Book Company, 1976), p. 279.

15. Secretary of Defense Melvin B. Laird, Memorandum to the Secretaries of the Military Departments, August 21, 1970. This memorandum is reprinted in *Congressional Record,* September 9, 1970, p. 30968.

16. Department of Defense, *Annual Report to the Congress, Fiscal Year 1972,* p. 36.

17. Martin Binkin, William W. Kaufmann, *op. cit.,* p. 24.

18. Laird, *op. cit.*

19. *Ibid.*

20. *Ibid.*

21. Goodpaster, Elliot, Hovey, *op. cit.,* p. 43.

22. *America's Volunteers: A Report on the All-Volunteer Armed Forces* (Washington, D.C., December 1978), p. 366.

23. *Ibid.*

24. Secretary of Defense James R. Schlesinger, Memorandum, "Readiness of the Selected Reserve," August 23, 1973, pp. 1–2.

25. Binkin, Kaufmann, *op. cit.,* p. 25.

26. Arthur L. Moxon, "U.S. Reserve Forces: The Achilles' Heel of the All-Volunteer Force?" Bennie J. Wilson III, ed., *The Guard and Reserve in the Total Force* (Washington, D.C.: U.S. Government Printing Office, 1985), p. 99.

27. Richard V. L. Cooper, *Military Manpower and the All-Volunteer Force* (Santa Monica: Rand Institute, 1977), p. 152.

28. Department of Defense, *Annual Report Fiscal Year 1979* (Washington, D.C., 1978), p. 324; Department of Defense, *America's Volunteers,* p. 373.

29. Zumwalt, *op. cit.,* pp. 291, 304.

30. John F. Lehman, Jr., *Command of the Seas* (New York: Charles Scribner's Sons, 1988), p. 142.

31. National Defense Research Institute, *Assessing the Structure and Mix of Future Active and Reserve Forces: Final Report to the Secretary of Defense* (Santa Monica: Rand Institute, 1992), p. 35.

32. One study attributed the navy's reticence regarding the utility of the Naval Reserve to certain military and social characteristics of the navy, including the facts that navies have traditionally been national rather than local-based organizations (as opposed to the Anglo-American tradition of armies drawn from locally recruited militia); that navies require massive capital investment in ships and shore facilities, and acting on behalf of the central government at sea rather than on behalf of local interests do not have a tradition of "welling up from below"; and that massive and rapid mobilization is less important to navies than to armies or even air forces. James W. Browning II, Kenneth C. Carlon, Robert L. Goldich, Neal F. Herbert, Theodore R. Mosch, Gordon R. Perkins, Gerald W. Swartzbaugh, "The U.S. Reserve System: Attitudes, Perceptions, and Realities," Bennie J. Wilson III, ed., *op. cit.,* pp. 72–73.

33. Binkin, Kaufmann, *op. cit.,* p. 26.

34. *Ibid.,* p. 26.

35. One study has characterized the plan to add three divisions without increasing active duty manpower as "a return to Utopian thinking." See Rand Institute, *op. cit.,* p. 34.

36. Department of Defense, *Annual Report to the Congress, Fiscal Year 1975,* p. 96.

37. Lewis Sorley, *op. cit.,* pp. 361–366. James Schlesinger, secretary of defense during Abrams's service as Chief of Staff, apparently does not agree entirely with this characterization of Abrams's motive: "That would not really be like Abe. He had the view that the military must defer to the civilians, even to an extraordinary degree. I spec-

ulate that the military sought to fix the incentives so that the civilians would act appropriately."

38. See Chapter II.

39. Binkin, Kaufmann, *op. cit.*, p. 27. In the Defense Department Appropriation Authorization Act of 1975, Congress cut 18,000 military support positions in Europe but permitted the creation of an equal number of combat positions. In response, the army moved two additional combat brigades to Europe and moved certain support units back to the United States. In recent years, a growing and disturbing disparity has arisen between the spending for military "teeth" and "tail." "Teeth" (measured by strategic and general-purpose forces) have shrunk from about half of the defense budget in 1987 to less than forty percent. Harlan K. Ullman, *In Irons: U.S. Military Might in the New Century* (London: Gerald Duckworth & Co., Ltd. and RUSI), pp. 7, 157.

40. Binkin, Kaufmann, *op. cit.*, p. 27.

41. Defense Manpower Commission, *Defense Manpower: The Keystone of National Security* (Washington, D.C.: Government Printing Office, April 1976), p. 98.

42. Department of Defense, Reserve Forces Policy Board, *Annual Report, Fiscal Year 1981*, p. 1.

43. Edward J. Philbin, James L. Gould, "The Guard and Reserve: In Pursuit of Full Integration," Bennie J. Wilson III, ed., *op. cit.*, p. 50.

44. Caspar Weinberger, Memorandum to the Military Services, "Priorities for Equipment Procurement and Distribution," June 21, 1982.

45. *Ibid.*

46. Dennis S. Ippolito, "Defense Budgets and Spending Control: The Reagan Era and Beyond," William P. Snyder, James Brown, eds. *Defense Policy in the Reagan Administration*, (Washington, D.C.: National Defense University Press, 1988), p. 171.

47. Stephen M. Duncan, Hearing before the Subcommittee on Military Personnel and Compensation, Committee on Armed Services, House of Representatives, One Hundredth Congress, Second Session, March 10, 1988.

48. Stephen M. Duncan, Hearing before the Subcommittee on De-

fense, Senate Appropriations Committee, United States Senate, One Hundred Second Congress, Second Session, March 19, 1992.

49. James Kitfield, *Prodigal Soldiers* (New York: Simon and Schuster, 1995), pp. 198–200. By the army's own standards of measurement, six of ten stateside army divisions were not combat ready. Even one of the four frontline divisions in Europe was not combat ready.

50. *Ibid.*

51. David R. Segal, Nathan L. Hibler, "Manpower and Personnel Policy in the Reagan Years," William P. Snyder, James Brown, eds., *op. cit.*, p. 205.

52. Caspar W. Weinberger, *op. cit.*, pp. 52–56.

53. The senior manpower official in the Pentagon during the first Reagan administration has argued that "while some external factors beyond direct control of manpower policy affected manpower trends, the dominant influence on military manpower was the policies being pursued." Lawrence J. Korb, "Defense Manpower and the Reagan Record," Stephen J. Cimbala, ed., *The Reagan Defense Program: An Interim Assessment* (Wilmington: Scholarly Resources Inc., 1986), p. 65.

54. *Ibid.*, p. 83.

55. Segal, Hibler, *op. cit.*, p. 218.

56. Stephen M. Duncan, Hearing before the Subcommittee on Military Personnel and Compensation, Committee on Armed Services, House of Representatives, One Hundredth Congress, Second Session, March 10, 1988.

57. Bennie J. Wilson III, James R. Engelage, "Pretrained Individual Manpower: Albatross or Phoenix?" Bennie J. Wilson III, ed., *op. cit.*, p. 125.

58. Between fiscal years 1980 and 1987, for example, the number of active Guard/reserve personnel (AGRs) in the Army Reserve increased from 3,999 to 12,414 and the number in the Army National Guard increased from 3,218 to 25,237. By fiscal year 1986, the number of full-time support personnel in all the reserve components had reached 160,347. Reserve Forces Policy Board, *Fiscal Year 1986 Annual Report* (Department of Defense, Office of the Secretary of Defense, 1987), p. 20.

59. Lawrence J. Korb, Stephen J. Cimbola, eds., *op. cit.*, pp. 86–87.

60. Department of Defense, *Annual Report to the Congress, Fiscal Year 1990,* p. 226.

61. Office of the Assistant Secretary of Defense for Reserve Affairs, *Reserve Components of the United States Armed Forces* (Department of Defense, May 1990), pp. 28–29.

62. *Ibid.,* pp. 24–26.

63. Reserve Forces Policy Board, *Fiscal Year 1989 Report,* pp. 21–23.

64. Office of the Assistant Secretary of Defense for Reserve Affairs, *Reserve Components of the United States Armed Forces,* 1988, p. 14.

65. Vincent Davis, "The Reagan Defense Program: Decision Making, Decision Makers and Some of the Results," Stephan J. Cimbola, ed., *op. cit.,* p. 49.

66. Ronald Reagan, *National Security Strategy of the United States,* January 1987, pp. 30–31.

67. See Chapter II.

68. Reserve Forces Policy Board, *Fiscal Year 1986 Report,* p. 78.

69. John J. Pershing, *My Experiences in the World War,* Vol. I (New York: Frederick A. Stokes Company, 1931), p. 124.

70. Stephen M. Duncan, Hearing before the Subcommittee of Military Manpower and Personnel, Armed Services Committee, United States Senate, One Hundred First Congress, First Session, June 9, 1989.

71. These and certain other mobilization planning principles are discussed in some detail in Bennie J. Wilson III, James L. Gould, "Mobilizing Guard and Reserve Forces," Bennie J. Wilson III, ed., *op. cit.,* pp. 193–195.

72. During our work on mobilization procedures, a member of my staff suggested that we could hardly improve upon the procedures set forth in the mobilization order issued by Emperor Haile Selassie at the time of the Italian invasion of Ethiopia in 1935:

> Every one will now be mobilized and all boys old enough to carry a spear will be sent to Addis Ababa. Married men will take their wives to carry food and cook. Those without wives will take any woman without a husband. Women with small babies need not go. The blind, those who cannot walk, or for any reason cannot carry a spear are exempted. Anyone found at home after the receipt of this order will be hanged.

73. I fondly recall an encounter one day with the then secretary of the air force who was dealing with a retention problem among active force pilots, many of whom were leaving active service for civilian employment. He complained that I was "competing" with him and he implied that the competition was unfair because so many of the pilots leaving active service were joining the Air National Guard or Air Force Reserve. I found it necessary to remind him that the Air Guard and Air Reserve were part of the "total" air force.

74. Stephen M. Duncan, Hearing before the Subcommittee of Military Manpower and Personnel, Armed Services Committee, United States Senate, June 9, 1989.

75. Senator John Glenn, Hearing of the Subcommittee of Military Manpower and Personnel, Armed Services Committee, United States Senate, June 9, 1989.

76. Stephen M. Duncan, Hearing before the Subcommittee of Military Manpower and Personnel, Armed Services Committee, United States Senate, One Hundred First Congress, First Session, June 9, 1989.

Chapter VIII

1. Hearings before the Subcommittee on Manpower and Personnel, Committee on Armed Services, United States Senate, One Hundred First Congress, First Session, June 9, 1989.

2. Michael R. Beschloss, Strobe Talbott, *At the Highest Levels* (Boston: Little, Brown and Company, 1993), p. 106.

3. *Ibid.*, p. 66.

4. *Ibid.*, p. 70.

5. I flew to Boston that day to address a conference sponsored jointly by the Army War College, the National Defense University, and the International Security Studies Program of the Fletcher School of Law and Diplomacy, Tufts University. The theme of the conference was "The United States Army: Challenges and Missions in the 1990s." As I arrived I was informed of the opening of the wall. A few moments later, the remarks of the speaker who preceded me, Gen. Gordon Sullivan, then the army's Vice Chief of Staff and later its chief, were interrupted as he was informed of the news. The historical significance of the event didn't interfere with Sullivan's wry

New England humor. He immediately remarked, "I'm supposed to talk about the future of the army and I've just been informed that the Berlin Wall has been opened. I can't begin to tell you what I don't know about the future of the army."

6. In her memoirs, the former prime minister remembered telling the president that defense spending was like house insurance. "You did not stop paying the premiums because your street was free from burglaries for a time." Conceding that she was, perhaps, insensitive to the president's difficulties with a Democrat Congress, she expressed her view that "the U.S. defense budget should be driven, not by Mr. Gorbachev and his initiatives, but by the United States defense interests." Margaret Thatcher, *The Downing Street Years* (New York: HarperCollins, 1993), p. 794.

7. At a senior staff meeting conducted in February 1988 by then Secretary of Defense Frank Carlucci, the subject had been how to make approximately $30 billion in defense cuts from a baseline budget of $330 billion. I recall thinking at the time that the size of the reduction was of historic proportions and would surely satisfy everyone in Congress. I was a new assistant secretary of defense. I had much to learn.

8. The defense budget had actually been shrinking each year since 1985. The reductions requested for fiscal year 1991 would put defense spending in 1995 at the lowest level since before World War II, measured either as a share of the GNP or as a portion of total federal spending.

9. Office of the assistant secretary of defense (Public Affairs), News Release, No. 29-90, January 29, 1990, p. 1.

10. The DPRB and its immediate predecessor, the Defense Resources Board, as it was called during the Pentagon tenure of Secretaries Weinberger and Frank Carlucci, was in many ways a de facto executive committee for the Department of Defense. Most major budget and defense policy issues were deliberated in DPRB meetings. The formal membership of the DPRB was smaller than the DRB and included the secretary of defense, the deputy secretary, the under secretaries for policy and acquisition, the assistant secretary for program analysis and evaluation, the service secretaries, and the department's comptroller. The military chiefs of each service attended

as advisors, as did certain of the assistant secretaries of defense whose areas of responsibility were the subject of particular meetings. Since manpower and related issues were at least indirectly a part most subjects discussed, I attended most meetings.

11. In fact, changes in the planning assumptions upon which the military strategy was based were being considered by the Joint Staff as early as 1987. Lorna S. Jaffe, *The Development of the Base Force, 1989–1992* (Washington D.C.: Joint History Office, Office of the Chairman of the Joint Chiefs of Staff, July 1993), p. 2. The efforts of the Joint Staff and other efforts within the department to adapt to the changes in the world were spurred by a series of floor speeches by Sen. Sam Nunn, the chairman of the Senate Armed Services Committee. Over a several-week period that commenced on March 22, the senator criticized what he characterized as the "blanks" in the defense budget proposed by the president. He also expressed his own views on a changed force structure.

12. During my first five years of service in the Pentagon I testified in approximately sixty congressional hearings. Not once did I testify before a committee controlled by my own party. It was with some amusement, therefore, that I examined the members of Congress— most of whom were Democrats—who appeared before the study group.

13. Each fiscal year cycle in the PPBS began with the preparation of the Defense Planning Guidance (DPG), a broad policy document that described the department's strategic plan for the development and use of future forces, and the issuance of the administration's "fiscal guidance" by the secretary of defense to each military department. Each military department would then prepare a program objective memorandum (POM) in response. The programs proposed in each POM would be received by the office of the secretary of defense and debated in meetings of the DRB/DPRB to ensure that they were consistent with the secretary's guidance. Program decisions would then be made by the deputy secretary and announced in program decision memoranda (PDMs). The preparation of the budget would then commence under the direction of the department's comptroller.

14. I was never certain whether the ideas were simply overlooked

by those in a position to object, or whether the likely opponents of the ideas elected to not challenge them for the time being. After a hearing at which I explained the ideas, a senior congressional staffer asked me with some amazement how I ever obtained approval of the statement.

15. Stephen M. Duncan, Hearing before the Committee on Armed Services, United States Senate, One Hundred First Congress, Second Session, May 10, 1990. Senator Sam Nunn later referred to this principle with approval during a floor speech in which he laid out his own approach to force planning.

16. The delay in the issuance of the DPG was the result of disagreement between Cheney and Wolfowitz on the one hand and Gen. Colin Powell on the other on the most appropriate response to the rapidly changing strategic circumstances. Generally speaking, Cheney was skeptical of the optimistic gloss that Powell was placing on developments in the Soviet Union.

17. Sen. Sam Nunn, "Defense Budget Blanks," Senate Floor Speeches, March 29, 1990.

18. George Bush, *National Security Strategy of the United States,* March 1990, p. 27.

19. R. Jeffrey Smith, "Powell Says Defense Needs Massive Review," *Washington Post,* May 7, 1990, pp. A1, A8. The interview was apparently part of a somewhat presumptuous effort by Powell to communicate a "mark-on-the-wall" strategic concept that had still not been endorsed by Cheney. Lorna S. Jaffe, *op. cit.,* pp. 28–30, 32–33.

20. The term is one used by Colin Powell to describe solutions based on overthinking that does not take into account the realities of the political process. Bob Woodward, "Who Needs It," *Washington Post Magazine,* September 24, 1995, p. 27.

21. See the discussion of the legislation in Chapter I, Note 26. A former secretary of the navy has argued that "civilian control" of the armed forces "has been eliminated by years of well-meaning reform legislation, culminating in the Goldwater-Nichols Act, drafted almost entirely by military staff officers from the Joint Chiefs of Staff and the [congressional] committee staffs." In his view, the Joint Staff has become the personal preserve of the chairman, becoming in effect a general staff like that which existed in Germany in World Wars I

and II. He further contends—more correctly in my view—that presidents and secretaries of defense should always have differing military service perspectives represented in important policy and crises meetings "so that they, the civilians, hear real differences and have real options to choose from." John Lehman, "An Exchange on Civil-Military Relations," *The National Interest,* Summer 1994, pp. 23–25; John Lehman, "Is the Joint Staff a General Staff," *Armed Forces Journal International,* August 1995, p. 16. The current chairman of the Joint Chiefs of Staff predictably disagrees that the Joint Staff operates like a general staff. Barbara Starr, "JCOS Chairman Urges Better Joint Training," *Jane's Defense Weekly,* September 9, 1995, p. 6. Colin Powell argues that the Joint Staff is the finest military staff in the world. Colin Powell, *op. cit.,* p. 445. That is undoubtedly true for operational matters. In my opinion, it is not true for personnel and resource matters.

22. Powell's former public affairs officer has applied this term to him. David Roth, *Sacred Honor: A Biography of Colin Powell* (Grand Rapids: Zondervan Publishing House, 1993), pp. 90ff. And in his own memoirs Powell relates a story about a meeting with Cheney shortly after the two had talked to President Bush about an appropriate response to Iraq's invasion of Kuwait. According to Powell, Cheney had to remind him to "stick to military matters." Colin Powell, *op cit.,* pp. 465–466. Similarly, Gen. Lee Butler, a former commander in chief of the Strategic Air Command and in 1990 Powell's Joint Staff representative on the Total Force Policy Study Group, has euphemistically described Powell as "the master of the Washington bureaucracy." General George Lee Butler, "Disestablishing SAC," *Air Power History,* Fall 1993, p. 10.

23. The "Base Force" was later defined simply as the mix of forces necessary to execute the (new) national military strategy. See *National Military Strategy of the United States,* January 1992, p. 16.

24. In order to ensure its favorable reception by Atwood, I had previously obtained the support of Dr. David Chu, the assistant secretary of defense for program analysis and evaluation. David's views on appropriate agenda items for the DPRB and his analytical skills had been respected for many years, and deservedly so.

25. In his June 15, 1988, testimony before a joint session of the

Senate and House Armed Services Committees, then Secretary of Defense Frank Carlucci had declared that he was "absolutely opposed to the assignment of a law enforcement mission to the Department of Defense." He further declared that nothing should "stand in the way of our readiness of our preparedness to perform" what he called the "primary role" of the Department of Defense—the protection and defense of the country from armed aggression.

26. Peter Reuter, Gordon Crawford, Jonathan Cave, *Sealing the Borders: The Effects of Increased Military Participation in Drug Interdiction* (Santa Monica: Rand Institute, 1988).

27. The study also noted that as a matter of historical doctrine, "there is considerable uneasiness about the use of the military for civilian police functions. . . ." *Ibid.,* p. xi.

28. The drug strategy established policies to unite federal counterdrug efforts with those of state, local and private entities. It committed new resources for drug enforcement, treatment, prevention efforts, and the support of foreign allies.

29. Dick Cheney, *Department of Defense Guidance for Implementation of the President's National Drug Control Strategy,* September 18, 1989, p. 5.

30. One activity involved a concept referred to as "barrier operations." The idea was to establish a series of radar "barriers"—i.e., lines of ships and aircraft with staggered radar coverage areas—through which drug traffickers would have to travel. Unfortunately, the barrier operations were scheduled to commence just as a navy aircraft carrier task force was leaving Norfolk for brief training in the Caribbean prior to its departure to the Mediterranean for a several-month deployment. An American news reporter mistakenly concluded that a physical naval blockade was about to be set just off the South American coast. Her subsequent article set off instant cries in the media of some South American countries about a pending Yankee blockade. It took us a few days to convince our South American allies in the "drug war" that no such blockade was even being contemplated.

31. In his memoir of Desert Storm, Gen. H. Norman Schwarzkopf described the interior of the tank and noted that he had never set foot there in ten years as a general. He also described what he char-

acterized as the "strict protocol" that permitted the Joint Chiefs only to speak when they were in session. H. Norman Schwarzkopf, *op. cit.,* p. 268. While mindful of the tank protocol for uniformed personnel, I never felt constrained about speaking out there on subjects for which I was responsible.

32. Colin Powell states that the Base Force became the administration's position on August 1, 1990, the day that Cheney, Wolfowitz, and Powell gave their final briefing to the president and "won his approval." Colin Powell, *op. cit.,* p. 458.

33. Melissa Healy, Douglas Jehl, "Debate in Congress Takes a New Tone on Defense Budget," *Los Angeles Times,* August 6, 1990, p. 1.

34. Two students of these events, including President Bill Clinton's deputy secretary of state, have concluded that in some respects, the CFE Treaty was "the most impressive accomplishment in the history of arms control," and that "to an extent unimaginable a few years earlier, it reduced the danger that a surprise attack would be launched against Western Europe." Beschloss, Talbott, *op. cit.,* p. 288.

35. The heat of Soviet rhetoric regarding the Baltics increased in late November and December. On January 7, 1991, it was announced that Moscow was dispatching elite paratroops to the region to enforce conscription and related laws. On January 11, some of the troops shot protestors in Vilnius, Lithuania. Two days later, many additional Lithuanians were killed or wounded.

36. See the discussion of this development in Chapter III.

37. One of my favorite recollections of this period involved a discussion with a vice admiral who asked me what I thought of the navy's concept of establishing a "nesting" program for frigates. The idea was to use eight frigates as training platforms for thirty-two Naval Reserve crews who could then man thirty-two Knox class (1052) frigates taken out of mothballs in the event of a major crisis. Before I could answer, the admiral proudly observed that because of my constant harking for greater innovation in the use of reserve forces, the navy was formally referring to the concept as the "Innovative Naval Reserve Frigate Training Program." I replied that while I was encouraged by the proposal, it should be remembered in the future that calling a program "innovative" did not make it so.

38. Christopher Jehn, Stephen M. Duncan, *Total Force Policy Report*

to the Congress, (Washington, D.C.: Department of Defense, December 1990).

39. Richard H. Kohn, "Out of Control: The Crisis in Civil-Military Relations," *The National Interest,* Spring 1994, p. 10.

40. Lorna S. Jaffe, *op. cit.,* p. 50.

Chapter IX

1. Paul H. Nitze, "Grand Strategy Then and Now: NSC-68 and Its Lessons for the Future," *Strategic Review,* Winter 1994, p. 17.

2. David C. Hendrickson, "The Recovery of Internationalism," *Foreign Affairs,* September/October 1994, p. 26.

3. Peter McGrath, "The Lonely Superpower," *Newsweek,* October 7, 1991, p. 36.

4. Analyses of the several views appear regularly in the literature of American foreign policy. See, for example, Henry Kissinger, *Diplomacy* (New York: Simon and Schuster, 1994), p. 18; Richard N. Haass, "Paradigm Lost," *Foreign Affairs,* January/February 1995, pp. 45–50.

5. The term "democratic internationalism" appears in a 1994 report of Rand. Based on a series of workshops in 1992 and 1993 involving a large number of Rand analysts, the report describes four "pure types" of strategic world views ranging from the European *realpolitik,* balance of power approach to the neo-isolationism of "America-firsters." Somewhere in between, the report asserts, lie (1) the school of "multilateral security," which emphasizes Western interdependence, consultative mechanisms, and arrangements for collective security, rather than unilateral U.S. action, and (2) democratic internationalism. *Rand Research Review,* Vol. XVIII, No. 1, Summer 1994, pp. 1–2.

6. Henry Kissinger, *op. cit.,* pp. 18, 832.

7. *Ibid.;* Richard N. Haass, *op. cit.,* p. 49.

8. *Rand Research Review,* p. 1.

9. William J. Taylor, "Will North Korea Get the Message in Time?" *Washington Post,* May 22, 1994, p. C7.

10. *Ibid.*

11. *Ibid.;* Richard N. Haass, *op. cit.,* p. 48.

12. Henry Kissinger, *op. cit.,* pp. 809–811.

13. Eugene V. Rostow, *Toward Managed Peace* (New Haven: Yale University Press, 1993), p. 6.

14. In 1994, pollster Daniel Yankelovich asserted that among "settled" opinions is that Americans believe the United States has "strong leadership responsibilities." But they also want U.S. economic interests to have priority over military and human rights interests. They are fearful of quagmires, but they insist that the United States ought to "hang tough in the pursuit of American interests." Ann Devroy, Daniel Williams, "GOP Attacks Clinton, Claims Incompetence in Foreign Relations," *Washington Post,* July 28, 1994, p. A23. In a January 1996 nationwide survey by the Program on International Policy Attitudes at the University of Maryland, seventy-one percent of those interviewed believed that the United States plays the role of world policeman too frequently. Tim Zimmermann, "Yankees, Come Here," *U.S. News & World Report,* February 19, 1996, p. 63.

15. In a bipartisan national poll conducted in June 1995, sixty-nine percent of the respondents said that the United Nations should take the lead in facing down aggression on the world scene. Only twenty-eight percent said that the United States should take the lead. Patrick Pexton, "Public Wants More Cuts to Defense, Poll Finds," *Army Times,* August 14, 1995, p. 16.

16. Frank Carlucci, the only person to have served both as secretary of defense and national security advisor to the president, believes that leadership—which he defines as the "ability to rise above domestic interests"—is the first of five fundamental elements of a successful foreign policy (the other elements include consistency, the maintenance of foreign aid and other foreign policy tools, a strong defense, and a focus on key international relationships), that "leaders have to explain what is at stake" on difficult foreign policy issues, and that only the president can shape public opinion on matters of importance to the nation. Frank Carlucci, Address, American Bar Association Standing Committee on Law and National Security, Washington, D.C., September 26, 1995.

17. Kenneth J. Cooper, "A Firm House Tells Clinton to Lift Bosnia Arms Embargo Unilaterally," *Washington Post,* June 10, 1994, p. A24.

18. John M. Boshko, "In the Foreign Service, Complaints Grow about Clinton's Team," *Washington Post,* June 20, 1994, p. A13.

19. Harlan K. Ullman, *op. cit.,* p. 105. The absence of a strategic framework was reminiscent of the circumstances (the Baldwin government's failure to respond to Hitler's militarization of the

Rhineland) that compelled Churchill's famous remarks in 1936 that "the government simply cannot make up their minds, or they cannot get the prime minister to make up his mind. So they go on in strange paradox, decided only to be undecided, resolved to be irresolute, adamant for drift, solid for fluidity, all-powerful to be impotent."

20. R. Jeffrey Smith, "U.S. Considers Ditching Big-Stick Foreign Policy," *Washington Post,* May 31, 1994, p. A18.

21. Richard N. Haass, *op. cit.,* p. 45.

22. In the summer of 1995, Democrat and Republican pollsters agreed that the public simply did not understand the rationale for the level of defense spending favored by both parties. Patrick Pexton, *op. cit.*

23. John F. Harris, "Clinton Warns Hill on Bosnia," *Washington Post,* October 7, 1995, p. A22.

24. Chas. Freeman, "The End of Taiwan?" *New York Times,* February 15, 1996, p. 21.

25. Helen Dewar and Guy Gugliotta, "Senate Backs Troops to Bosnia; House Retreats on Fund Cutoff," *Washington Post,* December 14, 1995, p. A39.

26. *Wall Street Journal,* April 23, 1996, p. A22; *Wall Street Journal,* March 7, 1996, p. A20.

27. John B. Judis, *Grand Illusion* (New York: Farrar, Straus & Giroux, 1992), p. 303.

28. George Bush, Address, U.S. Military Academy, West Point, N.Y., January 5, 1993.

29. Richard Nixon, *Beyond Peace* (New York: Random House, 1994), p. 243.

30. To critics, the argument that the United States is "bound to lead" places burdens upon the American people, diverts resources from domestic claims, and takes American democracy away from its original foreign policy principles. Paul Kennedy, *Preparing for the Twenty-first Century* (New York: Random House, 1993), p. 293.

31. Dr. Arnold Kanter, who served as under secretary of state for political affairs from 1991 to 1993, argues that "it is far from self-evident that most Americans have a broad rather than a narrow, even a selfish, view of our role in the world. Nor is it apparent that there

is political support in this country for exercising international leadership." *Rand Research Review,* pp. 3, 5.

32. Eugene V. Rostow, *op. cit.,* pp. 18–19. Even senior policy makers struggle to define the national interest. Shortly after President Clinton deployed the U.S. armed forces to Haiti in the face of widespread public and congressional opposition, his secretary of defense argued that the military involvement was in the national interest, but just not in the "supreme national interest." "Perry Delineates Haiti's Place in National Interest," *Boston Globe,* September 22, 1994, p. 11.

33. Caspar Weinberger, Address, National Press Club, Washington, D.C., November 28, 1984.

34. Comments to the author, September 27, 1994.

35. Frank Carlucci, Address, American Bar Association Standing Committee on Law and National Security, Washington, D.C., September 26, 1995.

36. George Bush, Address, U.S. Military Academy, West Point, N.Y., January 5, 1993.

37. Thomas E. Ricks, Jeffrey H. Birnbaum, "Clinton Aides Hope D-Day Trip Will Establish a Beachhead with His Own Uneasy Military," *Wall Street Journal,* June 1, 1994, p. 16.

38. Harry G. Summers, Jr., *The New World Strategy* (New York: Simon and Schuster, 1995), p. 172.

39. Jim Wolffe, "Gore: U.S. Committed Overseas," *Army Times,* May 15, 1995, p. 2.

40. William Perry, "Use of Force Must Be Weighed with Great Wisdom," *Army Times,* May 15, 1995, p. 33. The irresistible urge of the administration to use military forces for humanitarian purposes was explained by Clinton's national security advisor on June 12, 1996. In a commencement address to the National Defense University, Anthony Lake observed that: "More than any institution in the world, when America's military is asked to do something it delivers. It is hard to convey how much it means to policy makers to have an instrument like that at our disposal . . . [S]ometimes a humanitarian crisis . . . may swamp the ability of relief organizations to respond. Sometimes only our military has the capability to kick-start longer-term disaster response."

41. Kay Halle, *The Irrepressible Churchill* (London: Robson Books, 1985), p. 226.

42. B. H. Liddell Hart, "The First Modern Man of War," *A Sense of History* (New York: American Heritage Press, Inc. 1985), pp. 326, 336. Interestingly, one congressional leader who had great influence over military affairs at the time left an impression in 1994 that he would never have the will to recommend the use of military force in support of policy. See John B. Judis, "The Dellums Dilemma," *New Republic*, June 4, 1994, p. 23.

43. Richard Nixon, *In the Arena* (New York: Simon and Schuster, 1990), pp. 306, 313–314.

44. *Ibid.*

45. Rick Atkinson, "Warriors Without a War," *Washington Post*, April 14, 1996, p. A22.

46. In an effort to justify immediate use of military force in Haiti and to avoid a congressional vote on the matter, President Clinton even used graphic photographs of alleged atrocities against civilians. Ann Devroy, "White House Steps Up Invasion Talk," *Washington Post*, September 15, 1994, p. A1.

47. Frederick Tilberg, *Antietam* (Washington, D.C.: Government Printing Office, 1960), Appendix.

48. *Aviation Week & Space Technology*, March 6, 1995, p. 17.

49. *Ibid.*

50. Henry Kissinger, *op. cit.*, pp. 23, 805. See also, Seyom Brown, "Is Military Force Losing Its Utility I," *American Defense Policy*, 5th ed., John F. Reichart and Steven R. Sturm, eds. (Baltimore: Johns Hopkins University Press, 1982), p. 25; Laurence Martin, "Is Military Force Losing Its Utility II," *ibid.*

51. Harlan K. Ullman, *op. cit.*, p. 50.

52. Americans continue to support a higher level of defense spending than in other countries, but the number of people who believe that defense expenditures are excessive has risen steeply since the end of the Cold War. In 1981, only fifteen percent of the respondents in a national poll said that the government was "spending too much" on national defense. In a similar poll taken in 1995, forty-two percent expressed that view. Patrick Pexton, *op. cit.*

53. Arthur Schlesinger, Jr., "The Measure of Diplomacy: What Makes a Strategy Grand?" *Foreign Affairs*, July/August 1994, p. 146.

54. Donald Kagan, *On the Origins of War and the Preservation of Peace* (New York: Doubleday, 1995), p. 572. This aversion is widely recognized. It was even an important subject of the confirmation hearing (for a second two-year term) of the chairman of the Joint Chiefs of Staff before the Senate Armed Services Committee in September 1995. Rejecting the myth that the U.S. can consistently fight wars without suffering or causing casualties, Gen. John Shalikashvili expressed particular concern that fear of casualties and being second-guessed about decisive action may breed timidity in young military leaders. William Matthews, "Shali Scorns Myth That Wars Can Be Casualty Free," *Army Times,* October 2, 1995, p. 10. In a paper presented at the Pentagon in the summer of 1995, a defense consultant also observed that "it has become intolerable to risk lives." He then proposed three possible solutions to what he called "timidity" about shedding American blood on battlefields: the use of foreign mercenaries, the use of robotic weapons, and the establishment of a foreign legion. Gilbert A. Lewthwaite, "Robotic Weaponry in Works," *Baltimore Sun,* August 28, 1995, p. 1.

55. David Gompert, "How to Defeat Serbia," *Foreign Affairs,* July/August 1994, p. 42.

56. Jim Hoagland, "A Too-Perfect Victory," *Washington Post,* July 7, 1994, p. A19. Many Europeans believe that President Clinton's efforts to oust the military leaders of Haiti corroborated this conclusion. What was characterized as chronic indecisiveness and prolonged hand-wringing about the use of military force there led the French general who formerly headed U.N. forces in Bosnia to observe that this syndrome may erode American will to intervene abroad in the future if U.S. political and military leaders refuse to engage in anything but "zero-dead wars." William Drozdiak, "For Europe, Haiti Confirms U.S. Hesitation," *Washington Post,* September 17, 1994, p. A12. The problem is made more complex by evidence that potential third world adversaries are stocking up and even manufacturing the kinds of sophisticated weapons used by the U.S. in Desert Storm. The consequence, according to some experts, is that Americans are likely to suffer higher casualties in future armed conflicts. Art Pine, "Potential U.S. Enemies Amass High-Tech Weapons," *Los Angeles Times* (Washington, D.C., edition), September 6, 1994, p. 4.

57. Phil Patton, "Robots with the Right Stuff," *Wired*, March 1996, p. 215.

58. This new concept of war would, in the mind of its proponent, "inject unheroic realism into military endeavor precisely to overcome excessive timidity in employing military means." It would require the acceptance and even the "desirability of partial results when doing more would be too costly in U.S. lives, and doing nothing is too damaging to world order and U.S. self-respect." Edward N. Luttwak, "Toward Post-Heroic Warfare," *Foreign Affairs*, May/June 1995, p. 122.

59. Keay Davidson, "In-House Analyst Urges Pentagon to Stand Guard on Internet," *Washington Times*, February 28, 1996, p. 6.

60. Edward N. Luttwak, "Where Are the Great Powers?—At Home with the Kids," *Foreign Affairs*, July/August 1994, p. 23. One recent illustration of this point occurred in the summer of 1995. After having deployed troops to Bosnia in 1992 in response to public outrage at scenes they were witnessing on television, British political leaders were becoming deeply suspicious of the usefulness of military power in the Balkan conflict. David Howell, who headed the House of Commons Foreign Affairs Committee, was quoted as saying: "There's no will here. You can get things stirred up for forty-eight hours, but there's no sustained will to get British troops into the war with the Bosnian Serbs. . . . It would be splendid and popular to announce that we're going to go roaring into Gorazde. There would be a cheer for about ten minutes. Thereafter, as the first helicopter is picked off and the first soldier is killed, the politicians know that what sounds popular today might not be popular tomorrow. Outrage is not will." Fred Barbash, "Britain Sees Talks as Key for Bosnia," *Washington Post*, July 20, 1995, p. A22.

61. In their 1968 book, Will and Ariel Durant asserted that in the 3,421 years of recorded history, only 268 were free of war. Will and Ariel Durant, *The Lessons of History* (New York: Simon and Schuster, 1968), p. 81. Since the publication of their book, no year has been.

62. Paul Kennedy, *The Rise and Fall of the Great Powers* (New York: Random House, 1987), p. 536.

63. Don Kagan, *op. cit.*, p. 567. In a March 16, 1995, address to the German Foundation of World Population in Hamburg, former West German chancellor Helmut Schmidt predicted that the twenty-first

century will be plagued with wars as worldwide overpopulation causes massive population shifts.

64. Eugene V. Rostow, *op. cit.*, p. 22; Don Kagan, *op. cit.*, p. 570.

65. Theodore Roosevelt, *An Autobiography* (New York: Macmillan, 1914), p. 209.

66. Samuel P. Huntington, "The Clash of Civilizations?" *Foreign Affairs*, Summer 1993, p. 22.

67. Daniel Williams, "Christopher Lists Six Goals of Clinton's Foreign Policy," *Washington Post*, November 5, 1993, p. A29.

68. Julia Preston, "Boutros-Ghali: 'Ethnic Conflict' Imperils Security," *Washington Post*, November 9, 1993, p. A13.

69. Anthony Lake, "Confronting Backlash States," *Foreign Affairs*, March/April 1994, p. 45.

70. Art Pine, "U.S. Preparing Public for a Korea Crisis," *Philadelphia Inquirer*, May 3, 1994, p. 2.

71. Harlan K. Ullman, *op. cit.*, pp. 50–53.

72. Margaret Thatcher, "Why America Must Remain Number One," *National Review*, July 31, 1995, pp. 25–26.

73. Richard N. Haass, *op. cit.*, p. 44.

74. Melissa Healy, "Cheney Would Reduce Reserve Combat Role," *Los Angeles Times*, March 14, 1991, p. 1.

75. Barton Gellman, "Cheney Says Guard Units May Need Reorganizing," *Washington Post*, March 15, 1991, p. 34.

76. Dick Cheney, Address to the Magazine Publishers' Association, Willard Hotel, Washington, D.C., July 16, 1991.

77. Edwin H. Burba, Jr., Letter to Dick Cheney, July 10, 1991.

78. John Greiner, "Governors Want Current Level of Guards to Remain," *Daily Oklahoman*, August 22, 1991, p. 17.

79. Robert Unger, "Army Guard Digs In for Battle As Cuts in Federal Budget Loom," *Kansas City Star*, September 23, 1991, p. 1.

80. Colin Powell, Letter to Chairman, Committee on Armed Services, United States Senate, September 24, 1991, Enclosure, p. 20.

81. *Ibid.*

82. Les Aspin, Memorandum to National Guard and Reserve Supporters, November 20, 1991.

83. John Lancaster, "White House Outlines Vision of New Military," *Washington Post*, January 30, 1992, p. A10.

84. National Guard Association of the United States and Adjutants General Association of the United States, *An Alternative Force Structure Proposal,* February, 1992.

85. Les Aspin, Chairman, House Armed Services Committee, *An Approach to Sizing American Conventional Forces for the Post-Soviet Era, Four Illustrative Options,* February 25, 1992.

86. James C. Hyde, "HASC Staff Is Reorganized, Ready for FY 93 Defense Showdown," *Armed Forces Journal International,* February 1992, pp. 7–8.

87. Rand, *Assessing the Structure and Mix of Future Active and Reserve Forces: Final Report to the Secretary of Defense,* 1992, p. 177.

88. Larry Grossman, "Base Force," *Government Executive,* May 1992, p. 11.

89. Office of the Assistant Secretary of Defense (Public Affairs), *News Release,* March 26, 1992.

90. We did not always reach agreement on these matters. Even as the reductions were being announced I was challenging the navy's decision to deactivate two active and four reserve aviation patrol (VP) squadrons and to reduce the Naval Reserve's surface mine countermeasures capability. In light of the reduced submarine threat and the cost savings presented by reserve units, the moves made no sense to me. The sheer pace of events was, of course, making such decisions a struggle for all.

91. Secretary of Defense Dick Cheney, News Briefing, March 26, 1992.

92. *Ibid.*

93. *Ibid.*

94. *Ibid.*

95. David Evans, "Plan to Cut Guard Riles Congress," *Chicago Tribune,* March 27, 1992, p. 1.

96. *ROA News,* April 30, 1992.

97. *Ibid.*

98. "The Reserve-Cut Furor," *Boston Globe,* March 28, 1992, p. 18.

99. *Report of the Commission on Roles and Missions of the Armed Forces,* May 24, 1995, pp. 2–24. Secretary of Defense William Perry refused to confront this issue. According to one account, after learning that Perry's office was preparing to order the army to make the cuts rec-

ommended by the commission, the executive director of the National Guard Association hand-delivered a letter to Perry on August 14, 1995, warning that elimination of the Guard divisions could have political consequences: "Since significant elements of the eight National Guard divisions are located in twenty-five states which control 363 electoral votes, the precipitous restructuring . . . could very well affect the 1996 elections." Only eleven days later Perry sent a letter to Congress urging that the commission's recommendations be studied further. Katherine McIntire Peters, "Guard's Combat Divisions in Crosshairs," *Army Times,* September 25, 1995; William Matthews, "Perry Punts on Roles and Missions Report: More Study!" *Navy Times,* September 11, 1995, p. 25.

100. See the discussion of the congressional reaction to this proposal in Chapter X.

101. Stephen M. Duncan, Hearing before the Subcommittee on Manpower Personnel and Compensation, House Armed Services Committee, One Hundred Second Congress, Second Session, May 1, 1992. By 1996, my prediction was already becoming true and the overuse of reservists was affecting recruiting as well. At a March 21, 1996, hearing of the Senate Armed Services Committee's Subcommittee on Readiness, the chief of the Army Reserve candidly admitted that the use of reservists in operations in "the Rwandas and Haitis of the world" was adversely affecting recruiting. A Defense Department report requested by Congress and completed in April 1996 also concluded that negative perceptions of the military's humanitarian and peacekeeping roles in foreign countries was making today's youth less likely to consider military service than their predecessors.

102. As a result of President Bush's defeat less than five months later, the meeting never took place. Volkogonov resigned as Yeltsin's military advisor in December 1993, when he was elected a member of Parliament for Russia's Choice, the political party led by former prime minister Yegor T. Gaidar.

103. George Bush, Remarks to the 114th General Conference of the National Guard Association of the United States, Salt Lake City, Utah, September 15, 1992.

104. *Ibid.*

105. Bill Clinton, Address to the National Guard Association Convention, Salt Lake City, Utah, September 15, 1992.

106. *Ibid.*

107. William Mathews, "Remaining 'Relevant' Is Premise to New Guard Role," *Army Times,* February 19, 1996, p. 14. In November 1995, the executive director of the National Guard Association had denounced proposals to convert combat units as an "emasculation of the combat role" of the Army Guard and had further asserted that it "would be a monumental military blunder." William Matthews, "As Budget Shrinks, Change in Role Needed If Guard Is to Maintain Funding," *Army Times,* February 12, 1996, p. 22. Such hyperbole contrasted sharply with two March 1996 reports of the Government Accounting Office that concluded that the Army Guard's combat forces "far exceeded projected requirements for two major regional conflicts and that the army had a critical shortage of 60,000 support personnel. *Army National Guard: Validate Requirements for Combat Forces and Size Those Forces Accordingly* (GAO/NSIAD-96-63, March 14, 1996); *DoD Reserve Components: Issues Pertaining to Readiness* (GAO/T-NSIAD-96-130, March 21, 1996).

108. George Bush, Statement, White House, October 23, 1992.

109. "There is a need for a fairly major restructuring in the Reserves and National Guard, which is a very tough political problem. We attempted to make some changes there while I was Secretary, and we ran into a brick wall—the combination of the Guard and Reserve lobbies and the Congress." Brendan M. Greeley, Jr., Fred L. Schultz, "About Fighting and Winning Wars: An Interview with Dick Cheney," U.S. Naval Institute *Proceedings,* May 1996, p. 34. "When we tried to cut [the number of guardsmen and reservists] back to sensible levels, however, we had our heads handed to us by the National Guard and Reserve associations and their congressional supporters. We were threatening part-time jobs, armories, money going into communities." Colin Powell, *op. cit.,* p. 550.

110. The results of the election had no apparent effect on some of the Pentagon bureaucrats. Ignoring the successful use of reservists in Desert Storm and the hard lessons learned over the previous two decades, some officials in the office of the under secretary of defense for policy continued to argue that Rand's recommenda-

tion of the early use of reservists was unwarranted; that public support for a particular military operation could be ensured only by rapid, decisive success (presumably by active forces only), and not widespread involvement; and that the risk of a negative effect on public support of large reserve casualties outweighed the advantages of their use.

Chapter X

1. Since the end of the Cold War, the defense budget has been cut by approximately thirty-five percent. The budget for fiscal year 1997 was $243.4 billion, only 3.4 percent of the gross domestic product. By comparison, in 1994 Americans bet $482 billion in legal gambling. Harry Summers, "Thou Shalt Fund Defense Spending," *Army Times,* April 15, 1996, p. 62.

2. Eighteen months after President Clinton assumed office, the Pentagon released the findings of a year-long study by the Defense Science Board's Task Force on readiness. The task force had been appointed by Les Aspin, the administration's first secretary of defense. The group concluded that "we found it difficult to evaluate the adequacy of the readiness of certain forces when no specific national security policy had been provided. The effect of this void is the inability to answer the question: '[Ready] to do what?'" *Armed Forces Journal International,* September 1994, p. 68.

3. In a report accompanying its version of the 1995 Defense Authorization Bill, the Senate Armed Services Committee wisely voted to require the secretary of defense to prepare a report that identifies specific positions that might be opened to reservists. William Matthews, "More Opportunities? Senate Says Reservists Could Be Used Better," *Air Force Times,* July 4, 1994, p. 22.

4. A navy policy instruction (OPNAVINST 100.21A) adopted in 1992 defines "peacetime support" as "that work performed by the Naval Reserve as tasked by Navy Component Commanders, which enhances the readiness and proficiency of the Total Force." In fiscal years 1994 and 1995, naval reservists provided 1.3 and 1.7 million mandays, respectively, of contributory support to active naval forces around the globe.

5. From 1988 to 1993, for example, the commander in chief of the

Southern Command used reserve forces extensively in Latin America to provide medical care, build roads and schools, dig wells, and engage in other "nation-building" tasks. The reserve force presence was even credited with part of the "quiet revolution" success associated with the demise of several dictatorships and the establishment of new democracies over a period of two decades.

6. A "contingency operation" is defined at Title 10, Section 101 (a)(13) of the U.S. Code as "a military operation that (A) is designated by the Secretary of Defense as an operation in which members of the armed forces are or may become involved in military actions, operations, or hostilities against an enemy of the United States or against an opposing military force; or (B) results in the call or order to, or retention on, active duty of members of the uniformed services under section 672(a), 673, 673b, 673c, 688, 3500, or 8500 of Title 10 U.S.C., or any other provision of law or during a national emergency declared by the President or Congress."

7. See the discussion in Chapter IX. My proposal was submitted to Congress, but because it was an election year, it was not fully considered.

8. William Matthews, "Call-Up Power Remains with the President," *Army Times*, August 22, 1994, p. 22. A compromise amendment relating to one part of the proposal was adopted. The president is now authorized to involuntarily activate reservists for as long as 270 days, but no extension of that period is permitted.

9. In a June 23, 1992, floor speech, Sen. Sam Nunn, then chairman of the Senate Armed Services Committee, proposed using the armed forces to address problems of "drugs, poverty, urban decay, unemployment, and racism." He later proposed "authorizing," but not ordering, the Defense Department to coordinate the training of specialized military units to meet the needs of U.S. cities. The proposal was endorsed by several members of Congress. "New Military Mission," *The Virginian-Pilot*, June 29, 1992, p. 6.

10. Les Aspin, *The Bottom-Up Review* (Washington, D.C.: Brassey's 1994), p. 13-0.

11. In a public opinion poll conducted in June 1995 by the American Talk Issues Foundation, a bipartisan polling group headquartered in Washington, D.C., nearly two-thirds—sixty-six percent—of

the poll's respondents said that American troops should take part in military operations only under U.S. command. Patrick Pexton, *loc. cit.*

12. In a 1996 speech delivered at the New Atlantic Initiative's Congress of Prague, former British prime minister Margaret Thatcher referred to "today's multilateralists, who retain a naive conviction that international institutions, rather than alliances of powerful nation states, can preserve the peace." *Wall Street Journal,* May 14, 1996, p. A20.

13. David C. Hendrickson, *op. cit.,* pp. 26–27.

14. *Ibid.*

15. Thomas W. Lippman, "Christopher Puts Environment at Top of Diplomatic Agenda," *Washington Post,* April 15, 1996, p. A10.

16. William Matthews, "Developing Countries Is a New Job for Military, Perry Says," *Army Times,* April 22, 1996, p. 17.

17. John Yemma, "Perry, at Harvard, Issues a Plan for 'Preventive Defense' Strategy," *Boston Globe,* May 14, 1996, p. 4.

18. The proposal received prompt objections from military leaders. Katherin McIntire Peters, "Reimer Is Leery of Policy Role," *Army Times,* May 15, 1995, p. 17. It was also rejected by Congress.

19. In the spring of 1996, former Vietnam P.O.W. Sen. John McCain of Arizona declared that "the administration's foreign policy is based on international social work, not on defending United States' interests." "Social Policy," *Washington Times,* March 21, 1996, p. 10. Former secretary of state Henry Kissinger characterized the administration's "special approach to world affairs" as one that involved an emotional commitment to "soft issues" (the environment, nonproliferation, human rights), that avoided a strategic approach or structural concept of equilibrium, and that relied instead on changing other countries' domestic practices. Henry Kissinger, "Moscow and Beijing: A Declaration of Independence," *Washington Post,* May 14, 1996, p. A15.

20. Department of the Army, *U.S. Army Field Manual* 100-5: Fighting Future Wars (Washington, D.C.: Brassey's, 1994), p. 13-0.

21. *Ibid.,* pp. 2-0, 13-4-13-7.

22. *Report of the Commission on Roles and Missions of the Armed Forces,* May 24, 1995, pp. 2-15–2-19. In his response to Congress on the commission's report, Secretary of Defense William Perry agreed that

whenever possible, "operations other than war" should be given to reservists. William Matthews, "DoD Roles Review Rolls On," *Defense News,* August 28–September 3, 1995, p. 4.

23. Steve Komarow, "Shalikashvili Reshaping Strategy," *USA Today,* May 13, 1996, p. 1/13.

24. Plans were made to transform the U.S. naval base at Guantanamo Bay, Cuba, into a tent city for as many as 40,000 Cuban and Haitian refugees—2 1/2 times the number already there. The logistical challenge of housing the refugees, treating the sick, maintaining order, and handling the paper flow was one for which certain reservists, especially combat service support elements within the army, were clearly qualified. Unfortunately, the handling of refugees from a poor island ninety miles off the Florida coast had very little to do with American security interests; talk of calling up reservists took place while senior national security officials were on vacation; and even members of the administration called the policy haphazard, lacking a thought-out set of options, and driven primarily by immediate political considerations that apparently included the president's hopes of electoral gains in Florida. John F. Harris, "At Guantanamo, Military Mission Is in Retreat," *Washington Post,* August 24, 1994, p. A21; Ann Devroy, "U.S. to Double Refugee Capacity at Guantanamo," *Washington Post,* August 25, 1994, pp. A1, A24; Daniel Williams, "U.S. Policy in Cuba Awash in Contradictions," *Washington Post,* August 25, 1994, pp. A1, A25.

25. The battalion included Army National Guard volunteers (seventy-two percent), Army Reserve volunteers (eight percent), and regular soldiers (twenty percent). Several problems were encountered. Approximately half the enlisted soldiers had less than a week's notice for the mission because of administrative problems recruiting guardsmen and informing them of their selection. Because of the last-minute rush, many who were selected late in the process did not immediately meet the army's fitness standards. Because the unit was a newly created composite unit, substantial predeployment training was required. And the army spent an additional $18 million above its normal operating budget for the mission. Katherine McIntire Peters, "Smaller Army, More Opportunities," *1995 Handbook for the Guard & Reserve,* September 11, 1995, p. 47.

26. Eric Schmitt, "Military Planning an Expanded Role for the Reserves," *New York Times,* November 25, 1994, p. 1; William Matthews, "Larger Reserve Role Means Longer Drills, Overseas Rotations," *Army Times,* October 24, 1994, p. 26; Robert A. Erlandson, "Md. Guard Swoops Home; Air Fighter Group Saw Action in U.S. Bosnia Mission," *Baltimore Sun,* September 15, 1994, p. B1.

27. William Matthews, "Pentagon Insists on Call-Up Authority," *Army Times,* July 18, 1994, p. 26.

28. Some National Guard officials, for example, have observed that global humanitarian missions present opportunities for the Guard to "fend off more draw-down-related cuts." William Matthews, "Ready-to-Go Units Aim for Greater Role," *Army Times,* August 16, 1993, p. 26.

29. "The National Guard as Political Football," *Washington Times,* October 17, 1993, p. 20. That effort was characterized as "a veiled attempt at the piecemeal expansion of mayoral powers . . . by playing to very real public fears." Many big city mayors ridiculed the idea. B. Drummond Ayers, Jr., "Idea of Using National Guard to Help Police Draws Disdain," *New York Times,* October 27, 1993, p. 21.

30. *Army Times,* October 24, 1993, p. 24.

31. *Army Times,* June 28, 1993, p. 22; *Army Times,* August 16, 1993, p. 31.

32. William Matthews, "Reserves Get Larger Role in Battle on Domestic Ills," *Army Times,* July 25, 1994, p. 22. By 1996, not much had changed. In its fiscal year 1997 budget request for the Defense Department, and at a time when badly needed modernization programs had been cancelled because of a lack of funding, the administration requested $3.5 million for its Homeless Support Initiative

33. Deborah R. Lee, Remarks to the National Guard Association of the United States, Boston, Massachusetts, September 2, 1994.

34. Jennifer Packer, "Pentagon to Turn to Reserves," *Dallas Morning News,* October 26, 1994, p. 21.

35. William Matthews, "Pentagon Insists on Call-Up Authority," *loc. cit.*

36. The National Defense Authorization Act for fiscal year 1996 terminated funding for the Office of Civil-Military Programs within the office of the assistant secretary of defense for reserve affairs. 10

U.S. Code, Section 2012. The primary congressional sponsor of the legislation argued that the idea of military support of civil programs was based on the incorrect premise that reserve units would have less to do in the post–Cold War period. Rowan Scarborough, "Republicans Take Social Work out of Pentagon's Funding Bill," *Washington Times,* February 5, 1996, p. 4.

37. General John Shalikashvili, the chairman of the Joint Chiefs of Staff, is reported to have said to the *New York Times* that "my feeling is that [National Security Advisor Anthony Lake] must always be conscious when it comes to making military decisions on the use of military power that the president has not served and that he has not served." Charles Peters, "Tilting at Windmills," *Washington Monthly,* September 1995, p. 4. Even Les Aspin, President Clinton's first secretary of defense, and the person responsible for bringing several young congressional staffers with no military experience into the Pentagon, is also reported to have observed that "many Washington power brokers have no experience of what the military's all about. . . . [A]lmost anywhere you look here there's a diminishing pool of people with military experience." *Ibid.*

38. In what was described as the most tangible sign yet that reservists were reaching their limits, increasing numbers of reserve units were turning down requests of the active forces for voluntary assistance. Andrew Compart, "Harried Units Turn Down New Missions," *Army Times,* July 18, 1994, p. 26.

39. William Matthews, "Call-Up Plan Hits Snag in Senate," *Army Times,* June 27, 1994, p. 20.

40. William Matthews, "Call-Up Proposal Lives On: But Reserve, Guard Are Wary of More Work," *Air Force Times,* July 18, 1994, p. 22.

41. Many in Congress and elsewhere were urging that if the administration wished to undertake humanitarian and other nonmilitary operations, it should agree to the establishment of a separate account, outside of the defense budget, specifically for the funding of such operations. Thomas W. Lippman, "U.S. Costs Mounting in Rwanda, Caribbean," *Washington Post,* August 27, 1994, p. A10.

42. Thomas W. Lippman, "Money Shortage Forces Navy to Curtail Training of Reserve Forces," *Washington Post,* September 23, 1994, p. A16.

43. Bradley Graham, "Pentagon Study Finds Areas of 'Unreadiness,'" *Washington Post,* July 23, 1994, p. 11. Seven days after the November 1994 elections shifted control of both houses of Congress from the Democratic party to the Republican party, the secretary of defense acknowledged that three stateside army divisions were unready to perform all of their wartime missions. This was the first time in twelve years that the army had as many as three divisions rated C-3. Sean D. Naylor, "Ready to Go? 4 Divisions Fail the Test," *Army Times,* November 28, 1994, p. 3. The following month the army's European commander in chief disclosed that the readiness of his two major combat divisions had eroded during the previous two years as training funds were diverted to pay urgent quality-of-life expenses. Rick Atkinson, "U.S. Troops in Europe Slip in Readiness," *Washington Post,* December 8, 1994, p. A40.

44. R. Jeffrey Smith, "U.S. Mission to Rwanda Criticized," *Washington Post,* September 5, 1994, p. A1, A16.

45. "Shalikashvili: Focus Remains on Warfighting, Not Peacekeeping," *Defense Daily,* September 2, 1994, p. 354; Bradley Graham, "Pentagon Officials Worry Aid Missions Will Sap Military Strength," *Washington Post,* July 29, 1994, pp. A29.

46. Bradley Graham, "Aid Missions May Force Defense Cuts, Perry Says," *Washington Post,* August 5, 1994, p. A27.

47. The under secretary of defense for policy was asked by the Senate Armed Services Committee prior to his confirmation if he was concerned that the U.S. participation in United Nations peacekeeping operations and operations other than war risks "dissipating our military power in areas where we have vital interests." He replied that he was "conscious" of the problem. "Pentagon Policy Chief-to-Be Says Military Has No Readiness Problem," *Inside the Army,* August 15, 1994, p. 20.

48. William Matthews, "Call-Up More Likely," *Army Times,* June 6, 1994, p. 20.

49. Robert Burns, "Military Cuts Taking Toll on Troop Morale," *Pacific Stars & Stripes,* October 4, 1995, p. 1. Some of the burnout was evident as early as 1994. Only a week after arriving home in June 1994 from a standard six-month deployment to the Mediterranean, the 24th Marine Expeditionary Unit was ordered to pack for Haiti.

When it returned home again, morale and training problems were evident. Sam Walker, "A Few Good Men Are Being Stretched Too Thin," *Christian Science Monitor,* August 19, 1994, p. 1.

50. At a May 1, 1996, hearing of the Senate Appropriations Committee's defense subcommittee, the chief of the Army Reserve expressed concern that the 270-day deployments of reservists then being used by the army might prompt the citizen-soldiers to leave the service. Other factors that were affecting the retention and recruitment of reservists included the facts that the number of recruit-age people was decreasing, that the end of the active drawdown was pushing fewer experienced army personnel into the reserve components, and that the economy was improving. William Matthews, "Nine-Month Call-Up Too Long for Troops," *Army Times,* May 13, 1996, p. 24. See also, Katherine McIntire Peters, "Price of Peace for Reservists: A Stable Life Back at Home," *Army Times,* January 1, 1996, p. 28.

51. Sam Walker, "A Few Good Men Are Being Stretched Too Thin," *loc. cit.*

52. *Ibid.*

53. Lewis Sorley, *op. cit.,* p. 364.

54. In a March 1996 interview, the chief of the National Guard Bureau asserted that "there is still tremendous . . . untapped potential" for the use of the National Guard, especially the Army National Guard, for "humanitarian assistance, nation building and peace-keeping operations." William Matthews, "Lt. Gen. Edward Baca, Chief National Guard Bureau," *Army Times,* April 8, 1996, p. 22.

55. Harry G. Summers, Jr., *The New World Strategy* (New York: Simon and Schuster, 1995), p. 192.

56. Brendan M. Greeley, Jr., Fred L. Schultz, "About Fighting and Winning Wars: An Interview with Dick Cheney," U.S. Naval Institute *Proceedings,* May 1996, p. 40.

57. In an April 24, 1996, hearing before the House Appropriations National Security subcommittee, the Army Vice Chief of Staff candidly stated that "forces deployed in peace operations are not doing the same sorts of things that they would be doing in war." Bernard Adelsberger, "Griffith: 'Endeavor Hampers Two-War Strategy,'" *Army Times,* May 6, 1996, p. 3.

58. In October 1995, almost three years after his election, President Clinton appealed broadly for an activist foreign policy and warned of dire consequences if Congress blocked his early pledge to European allies to send up to 25,000 U.S. troops to Bosnia to help police a peace settlement there. John F. Harris, *op. cit.* The secretary of defense conceded, however, that not enough had been done to prepare the public for the U.S. role. Steve Komarow, Susan Page, "U.S. Set for 'Risky' Duty in Bosnia," *USA Today,* October 3, 1995, p. 1. For several months, and despite his rhetoric, Clinton continued to steer clear of direct public involvement in the Bosnian peace process, leaving the impression that he was still wary of identifying himself too closely with its still-uncertain outcome. Michael Dobbs, "Bosnia Cease-Fire Agreement Reached," *Washington Post,* October 6, 1995, pp. A1, A28. His conduct seemed to confirm the admissions of some White House aides that the president's recent efforts in Bosnia were due in significant part to domestic political considerations, namely his reelection effort.

59. Karen Elliott House, "The Wrong Mission," *Wall Street Journal,* September 8, 1994, p. A18.

60. Deborah R. Lee, Remarks to the National Guard Association of the United States, September 2, 1994.

61. Eliot A. Cohen, "A Revolution in Warfare," *Foreign Affairs,* March/April 1996, p. 49.

62. In an April 1995 interview, the then Chief of Naval Operations addressed the question of readiness for operations other than war in this fashion: "There are many variables in operations other than war. . . . Therefore, I'd prefer to look at readiness for war fighting, and then look at operations other than war as lesser included operations when possible." Fred Rainbow, John Miller, "An Interview with Admiral Boorda . . . We're Tinkering with Success Here," U.S. Naval Institute *Proceedings,* April 1995, p. 31. In July 1995, retired Army Chief of Staff Gen. John Wickham cautioned against relying too heavily on reservists to relieve active troops. Describing reservists as a "national asset," he nevertheless expressed concern that too high a peacetime operational tempo for reservists would lead to low morale and retention problems. His views were endorsed by former Secretary of the Air Force Edward C. Aldridge, Jr. Neff Hudson, "Panel Ze-

roes In on Reducing Personnel Tempo," *Army Times,* July 10, 1995, p. 11.

63. In a 1995 Pentagon survey of 686 employers, sixty-seven percent of the employers who had reservists in key positions said that they could not tolerate an absence of more than thirty days. A. C. Gerry, "RFPB Update on Reserve Component Issues," *The Officer,* April 1996, p. 21.

64. A U.S. Army colonel who commanded a battalion in Desert Storm described this problem quite clearly while commanding a brigade in Bosnia in 1996:

> Somebody asked me how I'll feel about Bosnia after I'm out of here. And the answer is that I can't imagine ever being out of Bosnia.
>
> I'll admit that the army was fun for me every day until we started this stuff . . . it was exhilarating. This is not exhilarating. . . . It's sort of like washing dishes: Just when you think you've got the last dish done, you've got to eat again and make more dirty dishes.

Rick Atkinson, "Warriors Without a War," *Washington Post,* April 14, 1996, p. A22.

65. Admiral William A. Owens, a former vice chairman of the Joint Chiefs of Staff who spent a career in nuclear submarines is, perhaps, the person most closely identified with the argument that U.S. defense and foreign policy strategies must be changed substantially to reflect our growing comparative advantage in several technologies and our ability to tie them together. He also rejects an approach to force planning that simply divides defense budgets between immediate needs and the need to cope with a more dangerous future world. He asserts that as a result of the end of the Cold War, we must apply more of our resources to the shaping of the future. William A. Owens, *High Seas: The Naval Passage to an Uncharted World* (Annapolis: Naval Institute Press, 1995), pp. 174–176.

66. Harry G. Summers, Jr., *op. cit.,* pp. 233–234.

67. Eliot A. Cohen, *op. cit.,* p. 47. On February 22, 1996, President Jacques Chirac of France appeared on national television to an-

nounce that France's 198-year-old tradition of conscription would be abolished in favor of smaller, volunteer armed forces. Although conscripts constituted sixty percent of France's 409,000-man army at the time of the announcement and the draft had long been considered to be an essential part of French citizenship, Chirac was frustrated by France's dependence upon American logistics and intelligence assets in Desert Storm and determined to create a volunteer army that can project power far beyond French borders. William Drozdiak, "Chirac Lays Out Radical Plan to Reorganize French Military," *Washington Post,* February 23, 1996, p. A1.

68. In a legal move that outraged several members of Congress and veterans, attorneys for President Bill Clinton argued in 1995 and 1996 that even though he had evaded military service and opportunities to serve in either a Naval Reserve unit or an Army ROTC program, as commander in chief of the armed forces he was protected from a sexual harassment lawsuit by the same provisions of the Soldiers and Sailors Civil Relief Act of 1940 that were designed to protect servicemen in World War II. Brian Blomquist, "Clinton's Military Claim Derided," *Washington Times,* May 23, 1996, p. 1.

69. This view is expressed and defended in Mackubin Thomas Owens, "Civilian Control: A National Crisis?" *Joint Force Quarterly,* Autumn/Winter 1994–95, p. 80.

70. Professor Cohen believes that the availability of vast quantities of centralized information, the predominance of warfare for limited objectives, and the obscurity of military power may also make civil-military relations more awkward: "Politicians will seek to use means they can readily see, . . . but do not understand; generals will themselves be handling forces they do not fully comprehend and will be divided on the utility of various forms of military power." Eliot A. Cohen, *op. cit.,* pp. 53–54.

71. Brendan M. Greeley, Jr., Fred L. Schultz, "About Fighting and Winning Wars: An Interview with Dick Cheney," p. 34.

72. Colin Powell has described the post–Cold War transition period strategy provided by the Clinton administration's "bottom-up review" as "the Bush [two regional war] strategy, but with Clinton campaign cuts." He has also questioned whether the administration's "cuts in personnel and budget have taken us below the levels re-

quired to support the strategy." Colin Powell, *op. cit.*, pp. 579–580.
The Commission on Roles and Missions recommended that a national strategy review be made every four years. This factor and the
reluctance to conduct such a review during the election year of 1996
suggests that the next review is likely to take place in the spring of
1997.

73. Harlan K. Ullman, *op. cit.*, p. 95.

74. Stephen M. Duncan, Hearings before the Committee on
Armed Services, United States Senate, One Hundred First Congress,
Second Session, April 18, 1990.

75. This general concept is discussed in greater detail in David S.
Alberts, "Mission Capability Packages," *Institute for National Strategic
Studies (National Defense University) Strategic Forum,* No. 14, January
1995. Very similar approaches to force planning have also been recommended by Rand, whose *strategy-to-tasks* framework was designed
to evaluate the procurement of weapons systems that would support
theater or campaign operational objectives, and by two military
planners whose *strategy-capabilities evaluation methodology* was designed
to aid the debate on military roles and missions. See David F. Todd,
Ralph M. Hitchen, "Cutting Defense: Method Instead of Madness,"
Joint Forces Quarterly, Summer 1994, p. 91.

76. This general definition of planning principles was used in the
recent past by one of the deans of the American foreign policy establishment, albeit in connection with the conduct of foreign policy, not the design of military force structure/mix. See George F. Ken-
nan, "On American Principles," *Foreign Affairs,* March/April 1995,
pp. 116–121.

77. Frederic J. Brown, *The U.S. Army in Transition II* (Washington,
D.C.: Brassey's, 1993), p. 53.

78. Interest group politics are not restricted to the reserve components. One observer has noted that political maneuvering is engaged in routinely within the Pentagon: "Much of the action occurs
behind the scenes through negotiation, intrigue, deal-making, and
the occasional artful dodge—a complex game that [is played] with
single-mindedness and considerable skill." A. J. Bacevich, "Civilian
Control: A Useful Fiction?" *Joint Forces Quarterly,* Autumn/Winter
1994–95, p. 77.

79. A policy of integration needs champions. It has been rightly observed that no serious policy can be sustained without the support of those who must implement it. It was Churchill's practice, especially after his experience in the World War I Dardanelles campaign, not to entrust the execution of any measure to men who doubted its worth. John Wheeler-Bennett, ed., *Action This Day: Work with Churchill* (New York: St. Martin's Press, 1969), p. 27; Robert Eden, "History as Postwar Statecraft in Churchill's War Memoirs," a paper prepared for the Conference on Winston Churchill in the Postwar Years, The Woodrow Wilson International Center for Scholars, Washington, D.C., April 12, 1996, p. 4. Unfortunately, recent data indicate that disincentives limit some efforts to integrate active and reserve components. Active army majors and captains assigned to that service's reserve components in 1995 were selected for promotion at rates considerably below those of their peers in regular army units. Jim Tice, "From Active to Reserve," *Army Times,* May 27, 1996, p. 6.

80. See, for example, the August 1995 policy statement of the new commandant of the Marine Corps:

There is only one Marine Corps—a Total Force Marine Corps. The days of two Marine Corps are gone . . . forever. Our [A]ctive and [R]eserve will be broadly and seamlessly integrated, and indivisible as a balanced warfighting force. The full acceptance of this reality is critical to our future.

General Charles C. Krulak, *The 31st Commandant's Planning Guidance,* August 1995, p. A-7. The policy statement was not a group of idle words. In a marinewide message on September 5, 1995, General Krulak ordered that on November 10, 1995—the Corps's 220th birthday—operational units of reservists would no longer be labeled or designated as "Selected Marine Corps Reserve."

81. Shortly after American troops landed in Panama in Operation Just Cause, I visited Gen. Max Thurman, the commander in chief of the Southern Command to inquire about his needs. He immediately replied that access to individual reservists with special skills was his highest priority.

82. The Individual Ready Reserve is a manpower pool of pre-

trained individuals who have already served in active component units or in the Selected Reserve. Members of the IRR are liable for call-ups for involuntary active duty and the fulfillment of mobilization obligations.

83. Frederic J. Brown, *op. cit.*, p. 45.

84. Approximately 22,000 naval reservists (fifteen percent of the entire force) were activated, half of which were medical personnel.

85. On October 2, 1995, "Mr. National Guard," Rep. G. V. Montgomery, announced that after fifteen terms of vigorous leadership in the House of Representatives, he would not run for reelection in 1996. Shortly thereafter, Sen. Sam Nunn also announced his retirement at the end of his present term.

86. A leading military sociologist has concluded that in general terms, military/family conflict in the active forces is likely to be more severe at junior levels than at senior levels because coping processes reduce family conflict as a career member advances through the system. In the reserves, however, time demands for training in excess of the statutorily required thirty-nine days are minimal for junior personnel, but become increasingly pronounced for career reservists. Charles Moskos, "Reserve Forces: A Comparative Perspective," Paper presented at the Royal Military Academy, Sandhurst, England, June 5, 1994.

87. In a 1996 report, the U.S. General Accounting Office corroborated the high stress placed on soldiers with certain military specialties as a result of the Clinton administration's extensive use of the armed forces for peacekeeping and related operations. The report also suggested that there were other contributing factors, including competition for deployments among unit commanders to underscore the value of their units during the budgetary drawdown, a "can-do" culture in the armed forces, and demands by other governmental departments and agencies for the use of military personnel and assets. *Military Readiness: A Clear Policy Is Needed to Guide Management of Frequently Deployed Units* (GAO/NSIAD-96-105, April 1996), pp. 5–11.

88. In a June 1995 survey conducted by the Americans Talk Issues Foundation, some sixty-six percent of the poll's respondents said that American troops generally should take part in military operations only under U.S. command. Patrick Pexton, *loc. cit.*

89. In addition to civilian support staff, the full-time support personnel include Active-Guard/Reserve (AGR) and Training and Readiness (TAR) personnel (National Guard or reserve members of the Selected Reserve who are ordered to active duty with their consent to serve as full-time auxiliaries with a reserve unit), military technicians (federal civilian employees who provide full-time support while maintaining their status as drilling reservists in the same unit), and active force advisors. In 1994 the level of full-time support personnel in the Air National Guard and Air Force Reserve, which have had the highest readiness of the reserve components in recent years, was 26 percent (of total strength) and 14 percent respectively. Full-time support in the Army Reserve, which has had the greatest readiness problems in recent years, was 8.7 percent.

90. As many as ninety percent of air force reservists are recruited from the active component. They leave active duty trained, qualified, and experienced in their military specialties—all at great costs savings to the Air Force Reserve. Major Gen. John J. Closner III, USAF, Prepared statement for the Subcommittee on Force Requirements and Personnel, Senate Armed Services Committee, May 1994, p. 9.

91. The Clinton administration's "bottom-up review" concluded that the total end strength of the army's reserve components should be reduced to 575,000 by the end of fiscal year 1999. The secretary of defense delegated to the army the authority to determine the split between the Army National Guard and the Army Reserve. This necessarily included the determination of combat, combat support, and combat service support responsibilities. Major Gen. Roger W. Sandler AUS (Ret.) (Executive Director, Reserve Officers Association of the United States), Prepared statement for the Subcommittee on Force Requirements and Personnel, Senate Armed Services Committee, May 10, 1994, p. 10.

92. On October 1, 1996, the Reserve Officer Personnel Management Act (ROPMA) became effective (I championed this legislation during my service in the Pentagon and managed to convince the House of Representatives to conduct a hearing on it. Because of its complexity, however, it was not passed by Congress until 1995). The previous law governing promotions required that "fully qualified" criteria be used for promotion of officers to o-3, o-4, and o-5 ("fully qualified" meant that an officer had been screened to ensure that

he qualified "physically, professionally, and morally, and [had] demonstrated integrity and [was] capable of performing the duties expected of an officer" in the next higher grade). Under ROPMA, all officers will now be considered for promotion under "best qualified" criteria (under the "best qualified" standards, a limited number of promotions will be made of officers who meet the "fully qualified" standards and who compare favorably in competition with their peers).

Epilogue

1. Mason Locke Weems, an early biographer of George Washington who was known for his emphasis on public virtue and civic duty, and who is said to have dealt with symbols rather than narrative logic, concluded his telling of the Cincinnatus story in this fashion:

> Soon as this great work was done, [Cincinnatus] took an affectionate leave of his gallant army and returned to cultivate his four acres with the same hands which had so gloriously defended the liberties of his country.

Garry Wills, *Cincinnatus: George Washington and the Enlightenment* (Garden City, New York: Doubleday & Company, Inc., 1984), p. 36.

2. *Ibid.*, p. 13.

3. Samuel P. Huntington, *The Soldier and the State* (New York: Vintage Books, 1957), p. viii.

4. *Ibid.*, p. 466.

5. Thomas E. Ricks, "'New' Marines Illustrate Growing Gap Between Military and Society," *Wall Street Journal*, July 27, 1995, p. A1.

Index